MORAL THEORY AND MORAL JUDGMENTS IN MEDICAL ETHICS

PHILOSOPHY AND MEDICINE

Editors:

H. TRISTRAM ENGELHARDT, JR.

*Center for Ethics, Medicine, and Public Issues,
Baylor College of Medicine, Houston, Texas, U.S.A.*

STUART F. SPICKER

*School of Medicine, University of Connecticut Health Center,
Farmington, Connecticut, U.S.A.*

VOLUME 32

MORAL THEORY AND MORAL JUDGMENTS IN MEDICAL ETHICS

Edited by

BARUCH A. BRODY

Center for Ethics, Medicine, and Public Issues, Houston, Texas, U.S.A.

KLUWER ACADEMIC PUBLISHERS

DORDRECHT / BOSTON / LONDON

Library of Congress Cataloging-in-Publication Data

Moral theory and moral judgments in medical ethics.

(Philosophy and medicine ; 32)
Includes index.
1. Medical ethics. 2. Bioethics. 3. Judgment
(Ethics) I. Brody, Baruch A. II. Baylor College of
Medicine. III. Institute of Religion (Houston, Tex.)
IV. Rice University. V. Series: Philosophy and
medicine ; v. 32. [DNLM: 1. Ethics, Medical.
2. Judgment. 3. Morals. W3 PH609 v.32 / W50 M8277]
R724.M824 1988   174'.2   88-4684
ISBN 1-55608-060-3 (U.S.)

Published by Kluwer Academic Publishers,
P.O. Box 17, 3300 AA Dordrecht, The Netherlands

Kluwer Academic Publishers incorporates the publishing programmes of
D. Reidel, Martinus Nijhoff, Dr. W. Junk, and MTP Press.

Sold and distributed in the U.S.A. and Canada
by Kluwer Academic Publishers,
101 Philip Drive, Norwell, MA 02061, U.S.A.

In all other countries, sold and distributed
by Kluwer Academic Publishers,
P.O. Box 322, 3300 AH Dordrecht, The Netherlands

TABLE OF CONTENTS

SECTION IV / CHRISTIAN CASUISTRY

SECTION V / FROM THEORY TO PRAXIS

BARUCH A. BRODY

INTRODUCTION – MORAL THEORY AND MORAL JUDGMENTS IN BIOMEDICAL ETHICS

THE NEED FOR MORAL THEORY

Bioethicists regularly make moral judgments about the appropriateness or inappropriateness of particular actions. They may judge that it is morally appropriate to withhold therapy from a particular patient because that patient has refused to receive that therapy. They may judge that it is morally appropriate to warn a third party about a threat posed by a patient even if the patient demands confidentiality. They may judge that a particular patient in an ICU should be discharged from the ICU to the floor because demands of justice require that a place be made for a patient with a greater need for the ICU bed. That bioethicists make such judgments about particular actions should come as no surprise. One of the major reasons for the emergence of bioethics is just that such judgments regularly need to be made in the world of high technology medicine.

Bioethicists regularly make moral judgments about the moral appropriateness of particular social policies. They may judge that it is morally appropriate to allocate additional funds to better prenatal care rather than to additional beds in neonatal ICUs. They may judge that it is morally appropriate to weaken some of the restrictions on involuntary civil commitment so as to aid some segments of the homeless population efficiently. They may judge that it is morally appropriate to allocate scarce organs without reference to the 'social worth' of the recipient. That bioethicists make such judgments about particular social policies should come as no surprise. One of the main reasons for the emergence of bioethics is just that such judgments regularly need to be made in the world of limited resources.

What is the basis for such judgments? How are they to be justified? How can they be defended against those who would make different judgments? Questions such as these explore the epistemological basis for bioethics. Epistemology is, after all, the study of knowledge. It is the study of how we know that various judgments are true or false. Questions such as these force bioethicists to develop an epistemology for their discipline.

If one looks at standard practice in bioethics, one would be tempted to answer these questions in the following fashion: there are a variety of

1

Baruch A. Brody (ed.), Moral Theory and Moral Judgments in Medical Ethics, 1–12.
© *1988 by Kluwer Academic Publishers.*

principles that constitute the foundation of all bioethical judgments. These include such principles as beneficence, non-maleficence, autonomy, the right to life, justice, and confidentiality. Bioethicists justify their judgments about particular actions or particular policies by reference to these principles. They constitute the basis of bioethical knowledge.

There is no doubt that bioethicists often proceed in this fashion. Nevertheless, there are good reasons for thinking that these principles are not the true foundations of justified judgments in bioethics. There are good reasons for believing that we must go beyond them if we are to find the appropriate epistemological foundations for bioethics. After all, these principles often conflict with each other, their scope and implications are unclear, they are themselves open to challenge, and they cannot explain how bioethics fits into a complete picture of the moral life. These problems can be resolved only if the principles of bioethics are integrated into some larger theoretical framework. We need moral theories and not just bioethical principles.

What is the problem of conflicting bioethical principles and how can an appeal to moral theory help deal with this problem? It is a truism that the above-mentioned principles of bioethics can lead to conflicting judgments about particular actions or social policies. Beneficence may tell us to treat a patient in a certain way because that form of treatment will produce the best results for that patient (judged by the patient's own values and goals), while autonomy may tell us to eschew that form of treatment because the patient, for one reason or another, is refusing that form of therapy. Confidentiality may call on us to keep information about a patient secret, while non-maleficence may call on us to reveal that information so that others may not be harmed. The right to life may demand that a particular patient should be allowed to keep for a long time his or her place in the ICU because it offers the best chance for life, while justice may suggest that the bed should be reallocated to several others, each of whom has a better chance of benefiting from the reallocation of that place in the ICU. The problem of conflicting principles is the problem of what to do when the principles of bioethics lead to different conclusions about particular cases. One solution to this problem is to develop a lexical ordering of the principles of bioethics. Adopting this solution means ordering the principles so that there is one whose implications are followed in all relevant cases, a second whose implications are followed when the first is irrelevant, a third whose implications are followed when the first and second are irrelevant, etc. Such a solution is attractive because of its simplicity, but it might not be acceptable because it is not easy to think of a principle that takes precedence in all cases over all combinations of opposing principles. A second solution to this problem is to develop a scale for weighing the significance of the conflicting principles in a given case and for concluding which action should be adopted because it is supported by the weightier considerations in that case. Such a solution seems more realistic than the lexical ordering approach, but the development of such a scale is a problematic task. Still other, more complex solutions are possible. Which is the best solution to this problem of conflicting principles of bioethics? We need a moral theory to answer that question. This is the first reason for concluding that the principles of bioethics are not the true foundations of justified judgment in bioethics.

What is the problem of the unclear scope and implications of the principles of bioethics and how can an appeal to moral theory help deal with that problem? The scope of a bioethical principle is the range of cases in which it applies. The implications of a bioethical principle are the conclusions to be derived from that principle in those cases in which it applies. It is clear from a review of the discussions in bioethics that there are major unclarities about the scope and implications of each of the principles. Consider, for example, the principle of autonomy. Does it apply to fourteen-year-olds, and if it does, does it apply to them with as much force as it applies to adults? Does it apply to very depressed patients, and if it does, does it apply to them with as much force as it applies to others? Consider, as a second example, the principle of the right to life. Does it apply to fetuses and/or to newborn children, and if it does, does it apply to them with as much force as it applies to adults? Does it apply to severely demented patients and/or to persistent vegetative patients, and if it does, does it apply to them with as much force as it applies to those with fuller cognitive capacities? These questions are illustrative of the many crucial questions about the scope of the principles of bioethics. Consider, as a third example, the principle of beneficence. Does it require doing what is best for the patient regardless of what that means to others, or does it involve taking into account the results for others? If the latter, which others should be considered? The family? The health care providers? The rest of society? How should the interests of these many parties be balanced? Consider, as a final example, the principle of justice. Does it mean treating everyone equally? Does it just mean insuring that everyone has equal access to some basic minimum of health care, and if so, how do we determine what is that basic minimum? These questions are illustrative of the many crucial questions about the implications of the principles of bioethics. How shall we deal with this problem of the unclear scope and implications of the principles of bioethics? It seems that we need a moral theory to help us deal with this problem. That is the second reason for concluding that the principles of bioethics are not the true foundations of justified judgment in bioethics.

What is the problem of the challenge to bioethical principles and how can an appeal to moral theory help deal with that problem? Bioethicists tend to assume that everyone accepts the validity of the standard principles of bioethics. Even if that is so, we need to be sensitive to the possibility that this is an unjustified consensus. More realistically, however, we need to recognize that there are real challenges to the validity of these principles. The principle of autonomy is a simple example of this. It is clear that the literature of bioethics assumes that everyone accepts its validity, even if there are disagreements about its scope and implications. Discussions with clinicians make it equally clear that many are dubious about its validity. They want to do what is best for their patients, and that, they believe, sometimes means disregarding patients' expressed wishes. How can one respond to this often felt but not often articulated challenge to the principle of autonomy? I see no choice but to argue for the principle of autonomy by appealing to some more fundamental moral theory. The principle of justice presents an even better, although more complex example of this need for moral theory. In truth, there is no single principle of justice. There are libertarian principles of justice in health care, egalitarian principles of justice in health care, social-contractarian principles of justice in health care, etc. For any particular principle of justice in health care, there are many who would challenge its validity. How can one respond to such challenges? I see no choice but to argue for some principle of justice in health care by appealing to some more fundamental moral and political theory. In short, there are challenges to the validity of the principles of bioethics, and it seems that we will need a moral theory to help us deal with these challenges. This is the third reason for concluding that the principles of bioethics are not the true foundations of justified judgments in bioethics.

What is the problem of how bioethics fits into a complete picture of the moral life and how can an appeal to moral theory help deal with that problem? Bioethical principles are normally understood as principles governing the relation between health care providers (all providers, not just doctors) and health care recipients (all recipients, not just patients in offices and hospitals). Sometimes – and this is an improvement – they are understood as principles governing the relation between providers, recipients, and other affected individuals. We often forget, however, that nobody is just a health care provider or a health care recipient. Providers and recipients are human beings who play many other roles and who have many other relations, roles and relations bringing with them opportunities as well as obligations. The principles of bioethics do not address the question of how providers and recipients are to fit health care into the broader context of their lives. Non-maleficence, for example, tells providers that they should not harm their patients. Harm comes, of course, in many forms, and neglect is one of those forms. Does the provider harmfully neglect a patient when he or she attends to his role as a spouse, a parent or child, a friend, a citizen, an advocate of a cause, or a pursuer of some other goal? In some cases, the answer to the question is no. There are time, energy, and resources available to do all of these things. In other cases, the answer to the question is yes. How is one to balance one's role as provider against these other roles? No principle of bioethics (including the principle of non-maleficence) answers this question. Justice, to take another example, tells us to distribute the resources employed in health care in a just fashion. There are, however, many other goods besides health care. Before we can apply the principles of justice to the distribution of available health care resources, we need to figure out how much of our social resources should be allocated to health care and how much should be allocated to these other goods. That is a question that cannot be solved merely by appealing to principles of bioethics. We need an overarching moral theory that allocates a proper place in the full lives of individuals to the principles of bioethics and that provides a morally appropriate setting in which those principles are to operate. This, then, is the final reason for concluding that the principles of bioethics are not the true foundations of justified judgments in bioethics.

Bioethics needs, therefore, to be grounded in moral theory. Which moral theory? How will this grounding process work? Are we beginning on a never-ending search for ultimate foundations? We shall look at these questions in the next section.

II. THE PROBLEMS OF WORKING WITH MORAL THEORIES

The history of moral philosophy can be fruitfully understood as a history of the emergence of a wide variety of moral appeals, each of which has significant plausibility as well as significant internal and external problems. It is necessary for our argument to review at this point both a wide variety of theories (each with its major appeal) and some of the internal problems each faces. The theories we shall review at this point are: consequentialism, contractarianism, natural rights theory, Kant's respect for persons theory, virtue theory, theological ethics, and Marxism.

The basic theme of consequentialism is that actions and social policies are right insofar as they result in the most favorable consequences for those affected by the actions, and that actions resulting in less favorable consequences for those affected are wrong. Classical utilitarianism, the most familiar version of consequentialism, is an attempt to fill in some of the details of this theme. It says that we need to count the impact on all those affected equally. It says that we need to consider the consequences of the particular action in question. It says that we use individual subjective utility (which may or may not be identical with the balance of pleasure over pain for each individual) as the metric for assessing consequences. Other versions of consequentialism specify the details differently. They may assess consequences by use of some objective notion of the good. They may consider the consequences of the regular performance of the type of action in question. They may count more heavily the impact on some of those affected than on others affected. One of the major internal problems of consequentialism is the need to specify these details in the most plausible fashion. We shall call this *the specification problem* and it shall be central to our further discussion. There is, however, another internal problem, one which will also be central to our further discussion. This is the problem of the logic of the argument from the specified version of consequentialism to specific consequentialist conclusions. What additional premises are required? How do we know that they are true? We shall call this type of problem *the theory-to-concrete-judgment-problem*. Since consequentialism does not lead to concrete moral judgments without additional premises, it must face this problem.

The basic theme of contractarianism is that actions and social policies are permissible if they are compatible with the set of rules by which rationally self-interested individuals in the right circumstances would agree to order their lives; actions or policies incompatible with those rules are wrong. There are many attempts to fill in the details of this approach. They differ about the rules to be adopted, in part because they differ over the description of the circumstances under which the agreement (the contract) is formed. One of the major internal problems of contractarianism is the specification problem, the need to specify the rules by which actions will be judged. Contractarianism also faces, however, the theory-to-concrete-judgment-problem, since no description of the rules, taken by itself, entails any specific conclusions about particular cases without additional premises. What are these additional premises? How do we know that they are true?

The basic theme of natural rights theory is that particular actions and social policies are permissible if they do not violate the rights of any individuals; actions and policies that do involve the violation of rights are morally impermissible. Naturally, there are many different versions of natural rights theory, since there are many different accounts of what are the rights possessed by individuals. John Locke talks in terms of the rights to life, liberty, and property. Other versions of natural rights theory have added additional rights to this list and/or subtracted some from the list. John Locke thought that all human beings have these rights. Others have argued that members of other species have them as well and/or that only some human beings have those rights. One of the major internal problems of natural rights theory has been the specification problem, the need to specify in the most plausible fashion the nature of the rights in question and the possessors of those rights. There is, however, another internal problem faced by natural rights theory, the theory-to-concrete-judgment-problem. What does it mean to violate the rights of an individual? What additional premises are required before we can judge that such a right has been violated? How do we know that they are true?

The basic theme of Kant's theory of respect for persons is that persons are morally special and must be treated with a respect to which non-persons are not entitled. This is often expressed by the claim that persons must be treated as ends in themselves and not merely as means. One of the major internal problems of this theory is to specify in the most plausible way possible the details of such an approach. What are the criteria for personhood? Are all and only the members of our species persons, or are some humans non-persons while other non-humans are persons? What is demanded by respect? Is it simply a matter of not violating the rights of persons? Does it also involve a commitment to furthering the interests of persons? The theory of respect for persons has major specification problems. It also faces, however, a serious theory-to-concrete-judgment-problem. No matter how many specifications are provided, the specified theory will not entail any judgment about specific actions or policies. Additional premises, depending on the specifications, will be required. What additional premises are required? How do we know that they are true?

The basis theme of virtue theory is that morality calls on individuals to develop character traits, the virtues, and to act in accordance with those traits of character. Right actions in particular cases are those actions typically performed by virtuous people, while actions typically eschewed by such people are wrong. It is clear that there will be many different versions of virtue theory, each solving the specification problem differently by offering a different account of the virtues. Is moderation a virtuous form of practical wisdom or is it an inability to commit ourself? Are chastity and/or fidelity virtues or are they just a choice of one of many permissible lifestyles? Even if its specification problem is solved, however, virtue theory faces its version of the theory-to-concrete-judgment-problem. What additional premises are required before we can conclude that a particular action is right because virtuous people would typically perform that action in those circumstances? How do we know that these premises are true?

The basic theme of theological ethics is that the rightness and wrongness of actions are at least in part due to the relation between human beings and God created by and/or expressed by that action. Morally right actions create and/or express theologically appropriate relations between human beings and God; actions that create and/or express theologically inappropriate relations are morally wrong. Different forms of theological ethics specify the appropriate relation differently. For some, it is a question of obedience to the will of God. Actions are right if one is obedient to the will of God in performing them because God has commanded their performance. Other forms of theological ethics place less emphasis on following revealed commands of God and more emphasis on such relations as imitating the ways of God or expressing one's gratitude and loyalty to God. There are, then, different ways of specifying the details of a theological ethic. But even once the specification problem has been resolved, any theological ethic will face a version of the theory-to-concrete-judgment-problem. What additional premises will be needed in order to move from such a specified theory to judgments about concrete situations? How do we know that these additional premises are true? This latter question may be particularly difficult if the additional premises involve theological components.

We turn finally to Marxist ethics. The basic theme of this approach is difficult to articulate, particularly because there is some question about whether Marxism generates any ethical system at all. Still, many have attempted to identify basic themes of Marxist ethics such as an avoidance of exploitative relations, of alienation, etc. Given the very abstract nature of these themes, it is not surprising that any Marxist ethics will have to face difficult specification problems and theory-to-concrete-judgment-problems.

There is a definite pattern that has emerged in our survey. Each of the moral approaches we have considered requires considerable specification before it can be treated as a fully articulated theory. Each will require additional premises before it yields concrete moral judgments, and the nature and epistemic status of these premises is unclear. All of these internal problems must be resolved before any of these theories can be used in the various ways we suggested in Part I of this essay.

This leads me to the major point of this survey. Part I claimed that bioethics needs to appeal to moral theories to deal with various problems that cannot be resolved by an appeal to the standard principles of bioethics. Many would object that such a suggestion is problematic because of a problem external to any particular theory, viz., the problem of choosing which of the many moral theories to employ. The point of this part of the Introduction is that there are still other and perhaps more immediate problems, the internal problems of specification and of theory-to-concrete-judgments, faced by each of the theories in question. Until those internal problems are resolved, none of the theories can be employed in the ways suggested in Part I, and we will not have to worry about which of the theories to employ.

The conference out of which this volume grew was devoted to an examination of these internal problems in many (although not all) of the above-mentioned moral theories. In the final section of this introduction, we will examine the conclusions reached and their potential implications for the use of moral theory in bioethics.

III. THE CONTRIBUTIONS OF THE PAPERS

The first section of this book is devoted to an examination of these issues as they arise in the context of utilitarian theory. Professor L. W. Sumner uses the example of the requirement of informed consent to medical experimentation to illustrate how utilitarians should deal with these internal questions.

Sumner notes that most bioethical analyses conclude that research must have a favorable cost-benefit ratio and must be freely consented to by informed subjects. The former requirement is easy to justify by utilitarian considerations. But why should any utilitarian accept the latter requirement? Why not allow research with a favorable cost-benefit ratio (favorable consequences), whether or not the subject consents? Sumner thinks that the answer to this question lies in a proper understanding of how utilitarianism moves from its moral theory to concrete moral judgments.

Sumner's basic argument is that it would be a mistake for utilitarians just to calculate whether the benefits of any piece of research justify the costs. There are, he argues, built-in defects to the process of reviewing research proposals which make it likely that such a direct strategy will lead to many mistaken approvals of research. He argues, therefore, for the adoption of an indirect strategy, one that adds a precommitment to informed consent before research can be performed.

One way of thinking about Sumner's argument is this: the direct strategy suggests that utilitarians move from their theory to the approval of specific moral judgments (e.g., the permissibility of a specific research project) by adding a factual premise about the favorable consequences of a particular action (e.g., allowing that research project). Sumner argues that this strategy should not be adopted because of structural considerations that will often lead to mistaken beliefs about these factual premises. Utilitarians must complicate their move from theory to concrete judgments through indirect strategies that help them avoid these errors.

Professors W. Ruddick and J. Reiman challenge Sumner's attempt to reconcile utilitarian theory with research ethics practice. Ruddick argues that there are additional elements of I.R.B. practice that Sumner cannot justify. Reiman argues that there are alternative indirect strategies that may do better than the complete commitment to informed consent, and that there are cases where that requirement will lead to too many denials of research protocols. The reader will have to judge whether they have successfully refuted the details of Sumner's argument. What is clear, however, is that Sumner has shown that utilitarians should not necessarily solve the theory-to-concrete-judgment-problem by adding to their theory premises about which actions will lead to the best results.

The second section of this volume is devoted to an examination of these issues as they arise in the context of natural rights theory. Natural rights theorists, as pointed out above, place their central emphasis on avoiding violating the rights of any individuals. Professor Eric Mack uses the question of whether there is a difference between causing a death and allowing someone to die to illustrate how natural rights theories should deal with our internal questions.

Mack's basic claim is that natural rights theorists can only move from their theory to the moral condemnation of particular actions with the help of causal judgments that particular actions cause the loss of that to which a person has a right because violating a right means causing the loss of that to which one has a right. This is what explains the moral difference between killing and allowing to die, a difference crucial for bioethical theory. He goes on to argue that these causal premises need to take into account his principle of antecedent peril as opposed to the much discussed principle of double effect. If Mack is right, bioethicists who appeal to natural rights (and so many do make these appeals) will have to become causal casuistrists.

Professor Gruzalski challenges Mack's causal assumptions. He argues that omissions can be the cause of a death. In particular, he argues that omitting to employ medical technology that is efficacious in preventing death is causing the death of the patient. If Gruzalski is right, Mack's analysis of the theory to concrete judgment problem for natural-rights theory will not justify the claim that allowing to die is morally permissible because the person's right to life has not been violated. Professor Levine raises an even more fundamental objection to Mack's analysis. He argues that we can only tell whether someone caused the loss of a right by first determining whether it is a violation of that right. If Levine is right, then Mack has offered a fundamentally incorrect solution to the theory-to-concrete-judgment-problem for natural rights theory.

The third section of this book is devoted to an examination of these issues as they arise in the context of Marxist theory. As was noted above, Marxist theory has major specification problems as well as theory-to-concrete-judgment-problems. Professors Buchanan and Mahowald sharply disagree about how that theory should be specified.

Professor Buchanan believes that Marxism is essentially a consequentialist moral approach, one that assesses all actions and social policies by whether or not they promote a set of intrinsic goods (community, individual development, and freedom). This analysis of the basic specification of Marxist moral theory leads Buchanan to the surprising conclusion that Marxists should approve of the corporatization of modern medicine, of the emergence of large corporate for-profit group practices. The very undesirable features of such a system – where life and health are commodities to be bought and sold – may help lead to a recognition of the failure of market solutions and to the emergence of a new social order.

Professor Mahowald believes that Marxism represents a conception of an ideal and that actions and institutions are morally preferable when they move us to approximate that ideal more closely, even if they do not help lead to the realization of that ideal. This analysis of the basic specification of Marxist moral theory leads her to reject Buchanan's views about how a Marxist should analyze the emergence of corporate medicine. Mahowald believes that Marxists should reject the emergence of corporate health care because it moves away from Marxist ideals by causing alienation among competitors and by increasing inequalities among recipients.

The fourth section of this book is devoted to an examination of the issues of specification and of theory-to-concrete-judgments as they arise in the context of Christian moral theory. The example used by Professor Hauerwas to illustrate his analysis is the moral appropriateness of the appeal to litigation as a way of resolving disputes. While his example is given in a non-medical context, its relevance to the world of medicine, where the question of litigation is so important, is obvious.

For Hauerwas, the reconciling work of God in Jesus is central to Christian faith, and this means that Christians must engage in reconciling rather than adversary activities. This leads Hauerwas to conclude that Christians have good reasons for supporting the Mennonite opposition to the use of law as a way for resolving social disputes. Professor Thomas objects to this account of Christian casuistry on two grounds: (1) The ethic of reconciliation and of forgiving may be appropriate in a closed community such as the Mennonite community but would be inappropriate in a large non-closed community; (2) There are too many bioethical issues that focus on matters having nothing to do with reconciliation, and it is unclear how Christian moral theory is to be specified so as to deal with those problems.

The final section of the book examines the move from moral theory to moral judgments from a number of perspectives. Professor Donagan, arguing from a purely Kantian perspective, claims that it is possible to derive from a moral theory principles which, when cojoined with actual historical informa-tion, lead to specific moral conclusions. Professor Strong is less sanguine about such a possibility. Examining utilitarian and contractarian theories, he argues that neither the factual information needed to move from theory-to-concrete-judgment nor the specification of the theory itself is likely to be available. He concludes that bioethicists need to adopt a method of reasoning which he calls the method of case comparison. The reader will need to decide whether Strong's method properly deals with the arguments given in Section I of this introduction about the need to appeal to moral theory. Finally, Professor Devine argues against the priority of the top-down model of moral reasoning presupposed by such authors as Donagan.

As I review the essays in this volume, I am struck by several major conclusions: (1) One of the most fundamental, if not *the* most fundamental, problems of contemporary bioethics is to understand how to use moral theories to deal with concrete moral problems; (2) This problem arises no matter what theoretical perspective is adopted; (3) The essays in this volume are best understood as attempts to begin the discussion of these crucial issues rather than as resolutions of them.

Center for Ethics, Medicine, and Public Issues,   BARUCH A. BRODY
Baylor College of Medicine
Houston, Texas, U.S.A.

SECTION I

DERIVING UTILITARIAN CONSEQUENCES

L. W. SUMNER

UTILITARIAN GOALS AND KANTIAN CONSTRAINTS
(OR: ALWAYS TRUE TO YOU, DARLING IN MY FASHION)

When I was a kid in the fifties, I used to watch a television series called 'I Led Three Lives'. While in my maturer political wisdom I have come to dismiss this potboiler as just another symptom of cold war hysteria, I can still vividly recall how enthralled I was back then by the weekly exploits of one Herbert Philbrick: ordinary citizen, member of the Communist Party, and FBI informer. Little did I dream at that time that one day I too would lead three lives.

One of those lives, that of ordinary citizen, is no more interesting than was Herbert Philbrick's. Both of us are very ordinary citizens. But the remaining two, while less luridly dramatic than Philbrick's, appear to manifest a personality split at least as deep as his. My second life is not remarkable in itself. Like most universities, my university sponsors a good deal of biomedical and social-scientific research which utilizes human subjects. Again like most universities, my university requires all such research to be submitted to ethical review. As a member of our review committee I regularly assess experimental protocols by means of guidelines which impose two different kinds of requirement: (1) that the experiment promise to yield a satisfactory overall ratio of benefits to costs, and (2) that it provide adequate protection for its subjects. A protocol is accepted only if it satisfies both requirements.

So far, so upright. Nothing here to rival Herbert Philbrick's clandestine activities as a member of his local party cell. My split personality emerges only when I reveal my third life – that of the philosophical utilitarian. The creed which informs this life requires me to acknowledge the general welfare as the ultimate standard of right and wrong. It thus apparently requires me to base all of my moral decisions solely on a cost/benefit comparison of the available alternatives. But then, presumably in my second life, I should be deciding whether to accept or reject experimental protocols solely on the basis of their expected cost/benefit ratios. Once the cost/benefit requirement has been satisfied, what is a good utilitarian boy like me doing demanding adequate protection for experimental subjects?

What was a good Communist like Herbert Philbrick doing betraying the party to J. Edgar Hoover? The answer in his case was simple: he was not a good Communist. Instead, he was a loyal, patriotic American. One of his

15

Baruch A. Brody (ed.), Moral Theory and Moral Judgments in Medical Ethics, 15–31.
© *1988 by Kluwer Academic Publishers.*

lives was a deliberate sham, a counterfeit. He suffered from no real conflict
of loyalties because he had only one real loyalty. I would prefer not to resolve
my apparent conflict of loyalties in this Philbrickian fashion. Unlike
Philbrick, I am not merely going through the motions in one of my lives. At
least, I do not think I am. But then, again unlike Philbrick, I must face the
possibility that I really am morally schizoid.

Ever since Socrates, philosophers have made a big deal about the merits of
the examined life. Unfortunately for me, a closer examination of my two
lives merely reinforces the initial impression of their inconsistency. Consider
first my theoretical commitments. Utilitarianism is one form of consequentialism. Consequentialist theories form a family by virtue of their common
moral structure: roughly speaking, that the best (or right) thing to do is
always whatever will produce the greatest net value. All members of the
family therefore share a commitment to some maximizing goal. If we want to
keep the boundary between consequentialist and nonconsequentialist theories
from being trivialized, we will doubtless have to impose some conditions on
the values which define a consequentialist goal (e.g., that they not be agent-
relative or occasion-relative, that they not be lexically ordered, etc.). But for
our present purposes we may safely ignore these further complications and
simply assume that particular versions of consequentialism are individuated
by means of their substantive goals. Then the goal espoused by utilitarians is
unique in being both welfarist and aggregative. To say that it is welfarist is to
say that nothing but individual welfare is valuable for its own sake, thus that
for moral purposes all gains and losses are increments and decrements in the
well-being of individuals. Finally, to say that the utilitarian goal is aggregative is to say that it is formed by simply summing these gains and losses.
Thus, on this view the best (or right) thing to do is always whatever will
produce the greatest net sum of welfare, thus whatever will yield the most
favorable cost/benefit ratio.

Now contrast with this the procedure which I regularly follow in assessing
an experimental protocol. The guidelines with which our review committee
operates agree with similar guidelines elsewhere in distinguishing two
different kinds of consideration which bear upon the acceptability of a
protocol ([2], ch. 4; cf. [4], Part C, [9], ch. 4). The first of these is a
cost/benefit balancing, in which the main category of cost consists of the
harms to which experimental subjects will be exposed, while the main
category of benefit consists of the payoffs, either for the subjects themselves
or for society at large, yielded by the results of the experiment. A protocol
must, at this stage of deliberation, promise an acceptable ratio of benefits to

costs. Our guidelines define an acceptable ratio in the following way: 'the foreseeable overall benefit of the proposed research to science, scholarship, understanding, etc., and to the subjects, must significantly outweigh the foreseeable risks subjects may be invited to take' ([2], p. 21). A protocol whose cost/benefit ratio is deemed unacceptable will be given no further consideration.

Once it has cleared this first hurdle, a protocol must then satisfy a number of further conditions designed to protect the welfare and autonomy of research subjects. Some of these conditions govern such matters as confidentiality, remuneration, and the protection of special categories of subjects, but the most prominent and most stringent of them is the requirement that subjects be adequately informed of the nature and purpose of the experiment, including its anticipated risks and benefits, that they should consent to participation freely (without coercion or duress of any sort), and that they should be able to terminate their participation whenever they wish (without a penalty of any sort). This requirement of informed consent is not treated in the guidelines as just another item in the cost/benefit balancing. For one thing, inroads on the informed consent of subjects are not regarded as just further costs for them which might, in principle, be offset by sufficiently great social benefits. Instead, they are treated as assaults on their dignity or autonomy which are objectionable as a matter of principle. Our guidelines state the matter thus: 'The primary reason for requiring consent is the ethical principle that all persons must be allowed to make decisions and to exercise choice on matters which affect them' ([2], p. 24). This is the language not of a global cost/benefit balancing but of respect for individuals, language which invokes the familiar Kantian demand that persons be treated as ends in themselves and not used as mere means. Thus, considered as a whole, the guidelines operationalize the view that, however favorable an experiment's cost/benefit ratio might be, it is unacceptable if it involves a serious compromise of the integrity of its subjects.

This distinction between the global outlook represented by a cost/benefit balancing and the concern for individual subjects manifested, *inter alia*, by the requirement of informed consent maps very roughly onto the distinction between scientific and ethical review. When an experimental protocol is assessed for its scientific merits, the primary issue is whether or not it promises to yield results which will be both scientifically valid and sufficiently important to warrant funding. Thus, at the stage of scientific review questions are already being raised concerning the experiment's expected benefits. A protocol whose design is scientifically flawed is given no further consideration; the funding of bad science is assumed to be unethical. Thus, when a protocol comes up for serious ethical review, a substantial part of the cost/benefit analysis has already been executed. In practice, the process of ethical review concentrates largely on safeguarding the subjects, and especially on ensuring their properly informed consent.

Before we proceed any further, incidentally, I should forestall one possible misapprehension. As it happens, I had no hand in drafting the guidelines which our review committee applies. Nonetheless, I do not work within them reluctantly or *faute de mieux*. I do not regard them as flawed standards which, however regrettable, are preferable to none at all. Were I asked to design a set of guidelines, the results would be similar to our present set in all essential respects. The standards we use are in this sense *my* standards.

But then the schism which appears to divide my moral theory from my moral practice is unmistakable. My theory tells me that the right thing to do is always whatever will yield the most favorable cost/benefit ratio. In practice, on the other hand, I reject experimental protocols with a favorable cost/benefit ratio if they propose to violate informed consent. My moral practice thus imposes constraints on the pursuit of the goal which is the foundation of my moral theory. My theory and my practice appear to be fundamentally at odds.

Perhaps they really are fundamentally at odds and I really am morally schizoid. The more Stalinist of my fellow utilitarians think so, since they see my moral practice as acknowledging the force of individualist Kantian intuitions which lack a utilitarian, and thus a moral, justification. On their view only my inability to rise above the conventional morality of my culture prevents me from bringing my moral practice into line with my moral theory. On the other hand, the more zealous of my deontologically minded opponents, while sharing the diagnosis of split personality, will find in my practice some welcome evidence that my moral sensibilities have not been completely corrupted by my allegiance to an evil theory. While the former faction thinks I should change my practice, the latter thinks I should change my theory. But both agree that my practice is inconsistent with my theory.

One possible solution would be to take the utilitarian and Kantian ingredients in my moral practice as reflecting two equally fundamental and irreducible aspects of the moral point of view. Were I to pursue this route, then I would need to abandon the ideal of a single unified moral framework. Perhaps that ideal is unrealizable and the only adequate moral theories are mixed theories. But before settling for that solution, I want to explore a different possibility, namely that the practical inconsistency to which I have confessed is merely apparent. More particularly, I want to explore the possibility that the appearance of inconsistency depends on our acceptance of a seductively simple picture of the relationship between moral theory and moral practice. If this picture turns out in the end to be untenable, then the unity of my moral life may turn out in the end to be salvageable.

As it applies to utilitarianism, the picture I have in mind is so familiar as to seem truistic. The theory provides me with an ultimate goal, namely, doing on each particular occasion whatever will produce the best outcome. Suppose we then ask how on each occasion I should set about trying to achieve this goal. The answer seems obvious: among the various alternatives open to me I should try to find the one which will produce the best outcome. Thus, my moral decision procedure should be deductive, indeed syllogistic: of the alternatives open to me I should choose the one with the best outcome, this alternative will have the best outcome, therefore I should choose this alternative. In short, I should set about doing the best I can on each occasion by trying on each occasion to do the best I can. Of course, in order to locate the best alternative, I may not always need to undertake a full cost/benefit comparison of all the available options. Instead, I may often be able to draw on past experience, including the shared, cumulative past experience which is stored in our commonsense moral rules. But reliance on these rules will be no more than a surrogate for the full inquiry, and I will have no reason whatever for conforming to them whenever it is clear that, all things considered, violating them will yield a better outcome.

Now it seems to me that this is a very attractive picture, and that its attractiveness has always been the main source of the enormous appeal of act-utilitarianism. After all, once I have accepted promoting the general welfare as my ultimate goal how could I ever have adequate reason to do anything except whatever will best promote the general welfare? If I attend to any other considerations, except as devices to help me determine which course of action will best achieve my basic goal, am I not betraying my commitment to that goal? To those of a utilitarian turn of mind, act-utilitarianism has always seemed the most straightforward and tough-minded version of the theory. Stalinist utilitarians are all act-utilitarians, out to expose their revisionist colleagues as dupes and wimps.

The picture is attractive in part precisely because it seems so truistic. We have difficulty evaluating it because we have difficulty imagining what a rival picture might be like. In order to overcome this obstacle, let us re-examine the structure of a utilitarian theory. Begin with the ground floor, which consists of the goal which makes utilitarianism unique. Here the theory tells us that the right thing to do is whatever will maximize the net sum of welfare. Now what is the function of this principle? What does it do? The answer seems to be that it provides an ultimate criterion of right and wrong. And it does this by telling us that, whenever an act has a certain empirical property (yielding a greater net sum of welfare than any of its alternatives), then it also has a certain moral property (being the right thing to do).[1] Now there is an obvious sense in which this criterion is objective, since it tells us not when a course of action appears to be right from the vantage point of some subject, or when some subject would justifiably believe it to be right, but when it really is right. Alternatively, we might say that it tells us what would appear to be right from the vantage point of an omniscient observer, or what such an observer would justifiably believe to be right. However we choose to explicate the notion, in the old-fashioned (and now somewhat disused) terminology, it is a criterion of objective rather than subjective rightness. Thus, it determines what the right answer is, whether or not anyone is ever actually in a position to discover it.

What it does not do is tell us how to discover the right answer. That is, while it provides a target to aim at, it specifies no strategy for hitting it. Thus, it needs to be supplemented by some decision making procedure which we can use when we are confronted by practical problems. Whatever shape this procedure might take, we should expect it to be adapted both to our peculiarities as moral agents and to the circumstances in which we must make moral choices. Thus, just as the basic criterion reflects, as it were, the epistemic position of an omniscient observer, the strategy for satisfying that criterion must reflect our epistemic position.

A utilitarian moral theory must therefore contain both an objective and a subjective component: that is, a criterion which determines what is right, and a strategy for discovering what is right. But there is no reason to think that this inventory applies only to utilitarianism. The generalization to other forms of consequentialism is trivial, since all consequentialist theories share the feature of stipulating some basic goal which then serves as their objective criterion. But nonconsequentialist theories must also aim both to discriminate right from wrong and to tell us how to achieve the former and avoid the latter. Thus, in their own fashion they too must begin by providing a criterion and end by providing a strategy.

We know what the utilitarian criterion of right and wrong is. But what is its recommended strategy for satisfying this criterion in particular cases? We are now in a position to see how the simple, seductive picture sketched earlier constitutes one possible answer to this question. After all, the straightforward way of satisfying the criterion which tells us that the right thing to do is whatever will maximize welfare is just to seek on each occasion the course of action which will maximize welfare. On this view of the matter the theory's decision making strategy simply consists of the injunction to satisfy the theory's ultimate criterion. Because on this strategy we try to satisfy the criterion by just aiming to satisfy the criterion, we may call it the straightforward or direct strategy.

This account of a utilitarian decision strategy has some obvious merits. For one thing, since the theory's basic criterion does double duty as its practical procedure, the account is economical of theoretical resources. For another, since on this account all of the theory's practical implications are derivable from its criterion of right and wrong plus empirical truths about the world, there is no possibility of genuine inconsistency between theory and practice. Thus, practical schisms, like the one between my two moral lives, are entirely avoided. On this view, when I assess experimental protocols, I should base my decision exclusively on the outcome of a cost/benefit analysis. Of course, in carrying out this analysis I should take seriously the costs which are likely to result from violating the autonomy or integrity of experimental subjects. These costs are typically of three sorts. First, subjects may come to suffer harms which would have been avoided had they been informed in advance of the risks of participation and given the option of declining to volunteer. Second, even when this is not the case, we must recognize that people typically attach a great deal of importance to having effective control over their lives, and thus resent being mere tools in the hands of others. Given this fact, obtaining subjects by force or fraud will seriously compromise their sense of self-worth, and on any plausible account of welfare this must count as a sizeable cost. Third, even if in this particular case violating informed consent would generate neither of these two sorts of cost, by setting a precedent it might generate them in future cases.

These considerations suffice to show that if my committee employed the direct strategy, we would still attach considerable importance to securing the informed consent of experimental subjects. Indeed, we would be likely to treat informed consent as a requirement to be satisfied in all normal cases. But it seems unlikely that the direct strategy could justify assigning it the role which it actually plays in our deliberations. On this strategy once the costs of violating informed consent have been included in the overall cost/benefit equation, the moral weight of this consideration has been entirely exhausted. This leaves open the possibility that those costs might be outweighed by sufficiently great benefits, so that a protocol which violated informed consent might for all that have an acceptable cost/benefit ratio. However, approving such a protocol is not a possibility which we would take seriously. For us informed consent is a (virtually) non-negotiable demand, which must be satisfied whatever a protocol's expected cost/benefit ratio. We therefore treat informed consent not just as one item in the cost/benefit balance sheet but as an independent constraint, so that we enforce the requirement even when we have good reason to think that, all things considered, violating it would produce a net balance of benefits over costs. Of this practice the direct strategy can make no sense.

However, if we are now in a position to see that the direct strategy is one possible utilitarian decision making procedure, we are also in a position to see that it is not the only one. For let us ask ourselves how, as utilitarians, we should choose among competing strategies. To this question there seems no answer except to appeal once again to the theory's basic criterion. That criterion tells us that the right thing to do is always the welfare-maximizing thing. It therefore furnishes the standard for evaluating competing strategies: one strategy is better than another just in case it is a more reliable means of identifying the welfare-maximizing alternative. In selecting a strategy we cannot fall back on some already established strategy (or if we do, then we will need some strategy for selecting it, and then some further strategy, and then...). Sooner or later we will have no choice but to favor that strategy which promises to be the most successful. One possibility is that we will succeed most often at doing the welfare-maximizing thing if we simply aim on each occasion at doing the welfare-maximizing thing. This is the hypothesis which, if true, would support the direct strategy. *But it might not be true.* In any case, it is an empirical hypothesis. Thus, the fact that the direct strategy is direct – that is, that it replicates on the practical level the theory's ultimate criterion – is itself no point in its favor. The basis for choosing among competing strategies is not theoretical symmetry or economy but success rate. As utilitarians with the goal of promoting the general welfare we must favor that strategy, whatever it is, which best enables us to achieve that goal. And it might not be the direct strategy.

Any indirect strategy will consist of something other than just aiming at doing our best on each occasion. It will therefore propose some more complex set of procedures, or rules, or guidelines designed to enable us to achieve our goal more reliably, if less directly. Clearly, there are many possible indirect strategies. What we now know is that we should favor the direct strategy only if its success rate promises to be higher than any of its indirect competitors. We have accomplished something just by showing that it isn't obvious that the direct strategy is the one to choose. But how can we go further? How could we ever carry out a cost/benefit comparison of competing decision making procedures? And if we could, what would the optimal strategy look like? I will not pretend that I know the answers to these questions. I will therefore confine myself in what remains to two modest objectives. The first is to provide some general reasons for thinking that the direct strategy is unlikely to be our best bet. The second is to provide some more specific reasons for thinking that the role which informed consent plays in my moral practice is likely to be one ingredient in a promising indirect strategy. If I can establish this much, then I will have gone some distance toward unifying my moral life.

We can begin to see the implausibility of the direct strategy if we ask what the best case for the strategy would be. Which conditions would have to be satisfied by a decision context in order for the direct strategy to be plainly indicated? With no pretention to completeness, I can think of three such conditions:

1. Unlimited domain of options. If there are no predetermined or externally imposed constraints on the set of available alternatives then, in principle at least, new options can always be devised, and old ones further refined, in order to yield better outcomes. All that is fixed for us is our maximizing goal; we are free to pursue any pathway, whatever it may be, which promises to get us to it efficiently. This ability to manipulate and expand the feasible set results in turn from our control over the agenda. Where someone else determines the available alternatives, and the order in which they are to be considered, we may be able to do little more than accept or reject each as it comes along. By contrast, where we are the initiators, we are free to present new alternatives at any time, and to adopt any procedure we like for deciding among them.

2. Perfect information. Of course, the absolutely best case would be decision making under certainty about the outcomes of all options. This would require omniscience. But we could get by with something less, namely decision making under risk with reliable objective probabilities. In either case, the process of acquiring information must itself be costless.

3. Infallible information processing. Assume, for the sake of the present inquiry, that the goal of maximizing aggregate welfare is itself coherent and determinate. Then, once we have reliable information about the individual gains and losses which will result from each alternative, we still need to generate overall cost/benefit ratios for each. This will require both freedom from bias and formidable computational skills. Furthermore, information processing, like information gathering, must itself be costless.

If we combine these three conditions, we get a profile of the ideal agent for the direct strategy: someone who is extremely powerful, highly knowledge-able, exceptionally bright, and rigorously impartial. Does this remind you of anyone you know? If I were such a creature, then I would be pretty confident that I could identify the maximizing option in most decision contexts. I would therefore regard the direct strategy as my best bet. (I leave aside here complications for the direct strategy which may be caused by coordination problems.) Since the direct strategy involves just directly trying to satisfy the theory's basic objective criterion, this result should not be surprising. For we have already observed that this criterion, by virtue of being objective, takes the viewpoint of an omniscient observer. If such an observer is also om-nipotent, hyperrational, and impersonally benevolent, then he/she is ideally equipped to hit the target of maximizing welfare by aiming directly at it.

It would be tedious to dwell on the many respects in which our world falls short of this decision-theoretic utopia. I will therefore confine myself to contrasting with it the decision context in which my review committee operates. First off, we have only a limited degree of agenda control. We are not ourselves the initiators of the proposals which come before us. Thus, our options are pretty well limited to accepting or rejecting a proposal. We can, of course, impose (or negotiate with the investigator) conditions which must be satisfied if a protocol is to be accepted. But beyond this we have little power to amend or redesign a protocol. Furthermore, we are confined to considering those proposals that happen to come along. The process by which research projects are generated in the first place is sensitive to a large number of contingencies: the career pressure to which researchers are exposed, the dominant ideology within a scientific domain, the structure and funding of research institutions, the vagaries of public demand and political agendas, the priorities of granting agencies, and so on. We are free only to decide whether the proposals which are regarded as scientifically respectable, by the prevailing standards of the discipline, are also ethically acceptable. We have no power to suggest that an entire line of inquiry has become bankrupt, nor that research priorities should be fundamentally rethought, nor that the funds which are being poured into research could be better utilized in some other fashion.

Indeed, one feature of our review committee, which it shares with most committees elsewhere, serves to guarantee that these deeper issues will seldom be examined. The committee responsible for assessing a particular protocol will contain a majority of members who are themselves researchers in the domain in question, though not connected in any direct way with the proposal under consideration.[2] The rationale behind this arrangement is that only experts in the field can determine the scientific merits of a protocol. While this is doubtless true, the upshot is that the process of scientific review basically consists in determining whether the protocol satisfies the standards of experimental design which are currently accepted in the domain in question, and which therefore are likely to be common ground between the initiator of the proposal and its scientific assessors. By the very nature of the case, challenges to the viability of an entire research domain are unlikely to be raised, or to be taken seriously if they are raised.

In the second place, our access to information is as limited as the scope of our powers. If we were to conduct a full cost/benefit analysis, we would need reliable information concerning both the benefits promised by the research and the risks to which subjects will be exposed. For both sorts of information we are largely dependent on the initiator of the proposal, who of course is an advocate of acceptance rather than an impartial arbitrator. The danger here is not generally deliberate distortion but rather selective perception. Since investigators should be expected to believe in the validity of their own proposals, it would not be surprising if they tended to overstate the importance of the expected results and understate the risks to the subjects. On the benefit side a protocol will of course identify the broad area of inquiry and describe the contribution to it intended by this particular experiment. These are claims which the scientific members of our committee should be in a position to assess, but for the reasons given above their very expertise in the area is likely to mean that they share the investigator's belief in the importance of the expected outcome. In practice, therefore, their role is largely confined to checking the validity of the investigator's planned procedure. Furthermore, once our committee has passed a protocol, we have little or no further involvement in the experiment. While investigators are mandated to report any significant departures from the approved protocol, lay members of the committee have no real opportunity to determine whether the benefits so confidently predicted beforehand are ever realized after the fact. Our acceptance of these predictions, typically advanced by investigator and scientific assessors alike, is largely an act of faith. Meanwhile, on the cost side we are dependent on risk assessments which are furnished by the party who will be imposing them rather than the parties who will be exposed to them. Since the investigator is the initiator of the proposal, there is an institutional channel through which that side of the case can be made. By contrast, the subjects, who will only be recruited once the protocol has been approved, are in the nature of the case unorganized and unrepresented. In principle this structural bias in favor of the investigator could be mitigated somewhat by appointing a counterbalancing advocate of the subjects' interests.[3] But our committee has no such advocate.

Finally, those of us who have the task of processing all of this imperfect information bring to it all of our own idiosyncrasies and prior commitments. When we attempt to compare a protocol's expected benefits and costs, we make no pretence of using a precise metric. Instead, we work with highly impressionistic labels, such as 'significant' and 'negligible', behind which it is easy to conceal the influence of one's preconceptions. Furthermore, the deadlines under which we operate and the outside pressures imposed by our other duties conspire to limit the duration of our deliberations, and thus the extent of both our information-gathering and our information-processing. In the end the cost/benefit ratio which we project for a protocol is much more likely to be a matter of intuitive guesswork than the product of a rigorous quantitative analysis.

For all of these reasons my role as member of the review committee is a far cry from that of the ideal utilitarian administrator with unlimited opportunities to channel social energies down optimal paths. Were I such an administrator, then I would indeed make all my social decisions by means of the direct strategy of straightforward maximization. The practical limitations of my decision context, however, induce me to depart from the direct strategy in two distinct ways. The first is a retreat from maximizing to something much closer to satisficing. Since in evaluating a protocol my committee's options are pretty well confined to acceptance or rejection, my concern is not with whether it is the best possible research initiative, or the best possible use of the proposed funding, but only with whether it passes some absolute standard. Furthermore, the defects in our cost/benefit information, plus the fact that risks to subjects are generally more predictable than experimental benefits, make it reasonable to set this standard fairly high. Thus, my committee's first test, namely, that a protocol's expected benefits must 'significantly outweigh' its expected costs.

The second departure is toward what Jon Elster has called precommitment ([3], ch. 2). Precommitment is an indirect strategy for coping with weakness of will or limitation of resolve. It is indicated when some goal is antecedently judged clearly optimal but one has reason to fear that, at the moment of decision, one will choose the path which frustrates achievement of that goal. Roughly speaking, to precommit is to increase the likelihood of choosing the antecedently preferred option when the particular occasions for choice arise, by manipulating one's environment so as to reduce either the feasibility or the desirability of the competing options. Although it can take a number of forms, two of the most common involve making the seductive option either physically impossible or much less desirable. Classic cases include the strategies of weak-willed smokers who try to boost their chances of quitting either by placing themselves in situations in which tobacco will be unavailable or by licensing their friends to ridicule them in the event of their backsliding.

The many defects of the decision context faced by my review committee render precommitment an attractive option. Being aware of these defects, I know that if we attempt a full cost/benefit analysis of each experimental protocol we will very often make mistakes, thereby permitting unnecessary costs to be imposed on research subjects. Furthermore, the probability of these costly mistakes will remain very high even after we have shifted from the comparative/maximizing to the absolute/satisficing version of the cost/benefit test. However, being also aware of my own utilitarian tendencies, I know that the temptation to make the attempt might be irresistible on each particular occasion. Thus, I will do well to join with my fellow committee members in precommiting ourselves so as to reduce or eliminate this temptation. This we do by announcing in advance additional standards of acceptability for protocols which function as constraints on the cost/benefit test. Thus our second test, namely, that however favorable a protocol's cost/benefit ratio might appear to be, it must also satisfy the further requirement of informed consent. By adopting this constraint we oblige ourselves not to treat informed consent as just another entry in the cost/benefit balance sheet, and thus oblige ourselves not to sacrifice informed consent, even where doing so seems compatible with yielding an acceptable cost/benefit ratio. We also effectively decentralize risk assessment, thereby counterbalancing both the investigator's perception of risk and our own, by giving veto power to the prospective subjects.

My rationale for endorsing this precommitment, in advance of considering particular cases, rests largely on my lack of confidence that I will be able to project costs and benefits accurately in those cases. At the stage when I am designing the standards which I will later be committed to applying in particular cases, I can choose to treat informed consent either as an item in the cost/benefit balancing or as an independent constraint. Because of the many impediments which will afflict my decision context in particular cases, my judgment is that, if I allow myself to sacrifice informed consent whenever doing so seems (on balance) beneficial, then I will often sacrifice it when doing so is in fact (on balance) harmful. If this judgment is correct, then I will produce better results on the whole if I treat informed consent as an independent constraint; thus I do not assess protocols exclusively on the basis of their expected cost/benefit ratios.

It is, therefore, my recognition both of my own limitations and of the imperfections inherent in the review process which lead me to prefer an indirect to a direct strategy. Since the two strategies will often appear indistinguishable, it is important to appreciate the crucial difference between them. For this purpose, imagine that you are assessing protocols and that you encounter one which proposes to bypass the informed consent of its subjects. On the best evidence available to you, and giving full weight to all of the expected costs of bypassing consent (both short term and long term), it appears that this experiment will yield benefits which will outweigh its costs. If you are employing the direct strategy, you will have no reason to reject the protocol, whereas if you are employing an indirect strategy (of the sort I have proposed), then you will have such a reason. The two strategies will therefore support different decisions in all cases which satisfy the foregoing conditions.

Given this divergence, your choice of a strategy will depend in large part on your confidence in your ability to make accurate forecasts of resultant cost/benefit ratios. Your objective criterion of right and wrong tells you that the right thing to do is whatever will yield the best outcome. It thus tells you that, whenever your decision in a particular case turns out not to yield the best outcome, you have made a mistake.[4] The better strategy is the one which will lead you to make the fewer (or the less costly) mistakes. If you are a perfect predictor of actual resultant cost/benefit ratios, then the direct strategy will lead you to make fewer mistakes. But if you are a highly fallible predictor of actual resultant cost/benefit ratios, then an indirect strategy (of the sort I have proposed) may lead you to make fewer mistakes. To see why this might be so, it is useful to distinguish between two different kinds of mistake. Whenever you accept a protocol which turns out not to yield a favorable cost/benefit ratio, let us call that mistake a *false positive*. Any case in which you reject a protocol which would have turned out to yield a favorable cost/benefit ratio is therefore a *false negative*.[5] Given the cost/benefit structure of research on human subjects, every false positive will impose unnecessary costs on the subjects of the experiment, while every false negative will impose unnecessary costs on the potential beneficiaries of the experiment. There may be no reason to think that the former costs are in themselves either more or less serious than the latter when they actually occur. But, as we have seen, there is reason to think that they are more predictable, thus that they are more avoidable. In that case, you are likely to make fewer mistakes if you aim to avoid false positives. Since false positives are the mistakes which will result from a direct strategy, you are likely to make fewer mistakes if you employ some indirect strategy.

Unfortunately, this clear division between the two strategies is blurred somewhat by the realities of my moral practice. For simplicity, I have spoken so far as though our committee treats informed consent as utterly non-negotiable, thus refusing either to weaken the requirement or to waive it altogether in any circumstances. But in fact we allow at least two different inroads on informed consent. Where subjects are competent to give or withhold consent, we permit a protocol to incorporate some deception, as long as (a) the subjects are fully debriefed afterwards, and (b) they are exposed to no more than a negligible risk. And where subjects are not competent to consent, we permit investigators to secure proxy consent, as long as (a) the subjects themselves stand to benefit from the results of the experiment, or (b) they are exposed to no more than a negligible risk.[6] In both of these departures from informed consent our practice is similar to that of other committees.[7] However, in both of them we are allowing some tradeoffs between cost/benefit on the one hand and informed consent on the other. Thus, our strategy is more complex than I have thus far allowed. But it is still an indirect strategy, and it is still the one whose employment in particular cases seems to me likely to yield the best results over the long run.

I began this exercise in self-criticism by likening my practical predicament to that of my erstwhile hero, Herbert Philbrick. I also allowed as how I had no wish to reconcile my two moral lives by the Philbrickian device of conducting one of them as an elaborate sham. It may now seem that I have taken Philbrick's escape route after all. For if the story I have told is convincing, then my lives are consistent only because my moral practice has been orchestrated by my moral theory, just as Philbrick's activities as a Communist were orchestrated by his membership in the FBI. In both cases the appearance of divided loyalty is deceptive, because each of us has but one ultimate loyalty. In this respect Philbrick and I are indeed alike. But there remains this crucial difference. In order for Philbrick to achieve his FBI objectives efficiently, he has to appear to be a sincere Communist, but he does not actually have to be one. This is why his life as a Communist can be

a mere sham: he need only convince others, not himself. But in order for me
to achieve my utilitarian objectives efficiently, I must do more than merely
appear to be sincere in my commitment to informed consent as an independent constraint; I must really be sincere in that commitment.[8] I must therefore
be able to convince myself as well as others. By comparison with this feat,
Philbrick's charade was mere child's play.

NOTES

[1] For expository ease I here presuppose a particularly simple utilitarian connection between
welfare and the right. There are more complex, and probably also more interesting, possibilities;
for a discussion of these issues see [8]. My present purpose requires only that an ultimate
utilitarian criterion of the right will make it some function of the maximization of welfare.

[2] This domination of review committees by researchers in the field is very common; see [5],
pp. 57–58.

[3] For a proposal along these lines, see [7], pp. 30–31.

[4] Strictly speaking, we can never know for certain that our decision has turned out for the worse,
for we can only project how the alternative(s) might have fared. But we can know for certain that
it has turned out badly, and that is often enough to justify our conviction that we could have done
better.

[5] I owe this way of thinking about the question to Jim Child.

[6] These conditions are a simplified version of the guidelines in [2], pp. 28–30, 34–36.

[7] See, for instance, [4], pp. 12–13, and [9], pp. 23–24, 30–31.

[8] There is much debate in the literature on the extent to which indirect strategies such as
precommitments require agents to behave irrationally. For some good recent discussions see [3],
ch. 2, [6], ch. 1, and the papers by David Gauthier and Edward F. McClennen in [1]. Nothing in
my case for a particular indirect strategy depends on resolving this issue one way or another.

BIBLIOGRAPHY

[1]   Campbell, Richmond, and Sowden, Lanning (eds.): 1985, *Paradoxes of Rationality and
      Cooperation: Prisoner's Dilemma and Newcomb's Problem*, University of British
      Columbia Press, Vancouver.
[2]   Dickens, Bernard M. (ed.): 1979, *Guidelines on the Use of Human Subjects*, Office of
      Research Administration, University of Toronto, Toronto.
[3]   Elster, Jon: 1984, *Ulysses and the Sirens: Studies in Rationality and Irrationality*, rev. ed.,
      Cambridge University Press, Cambridge.
[4]   The National Commission for the Protection of Human Subjects of Biomedical and
      Behavioral Research: 1978, *The Belmont Report: Ethical Principles and Guidelines for the
      Protection of Human Subjects of Research*, DHEW Publication No. (OS) 78–0012,
      Washington, D.C.
[5]   The National Commission for the Protection of Human Subjects of Biomedical and
      Behavioral Research: 1978, *Report and Recommendations: Institutional Review Boards*,

DHEW Publication No. (OS) 78–0008, Washington, D.C.

[6]   Parfit, Derek: 1984, *Reasons and Persons*, Clarendon Press, Oxford.

[7]   Robertson, John A.: 1979, 'Ten Ways to Improve IRB's: A Letter to the Secretary of DHEW', *The Hastings Center Report* 9, 29–33.

[8]   Sumner, L. W.: 1979, 'The Good and the Right', in Wesley E. Cooper, *et al.* (eds.), *New Essays on John Stuart Mill and Utilitarianism*, Canadian Association for Publishing in Philosophy, Guelph.

[9]   Working Group on Human Experimentation: 1978, *Ethical Considerations in Research Involving Human Subjects*, Medical Research Council Report No. 6, Ottawa.

University of Toronto
Toronto, Ontario, Canada

WILLIAM RUDDICK

UTILITARIANS AMONG THE OPTIMISTS

To paraphrase one of *my* childhood serials, can a Utilitarian from a small cloistered discipline find happiness on a review board of worldly research scientists? Wayne Sumner thinks that he can; I have my doubts.[1]

There are at least three obstacles to a happy companionable marriage: Autonomy, Equity, and Evidence. Sumner believes he can in good faith take the IRB vow of Autonomy: commitment to informed consent can, he argues, be justified as an 'indirect strategy' for maximizing Utility within the constraints of IRB procedures. Research subjects' welfare may be so maximized, but, for Utilitarians, the interests of all those who are involved in, or affected by the research must be considered. Boards are allowed to consider only a fraction of possible harms and benefits to other people. If the interests of all parties affected were considered, informed consent may not maximize Utility. Secondly, boards are increasingly concerned with *equitable* selection of research subjects: the burden of experiment must cease to fall primarily on people who are infirm, institutionalized, or poor. I doubt that Equity can be justified as an indirect strategy, even within the narrow range of harms and benefits which boards currently consider. Thirdly, with little regard for supporting evidence, boards make assumptions about the prospective harms and benefits which they do consider. This practice is, by Utilitarian standards, cavalier optimism.

In short, it seems that Utilitarians cannot expect much sympathy or help from most board members. It will be a tense marriage of opposites at best. Let us examine these apparent conflicts more deeply.

On Sumner's showing, Utilitarians may adopt non-Utilitarian constraints to compensate for practical limits on information and calculation. Thus, in such constraining circumstances, a near-absolute policy of informed consent can be adopted as 'an indirect strategy' for maximizing, or at least 'satisficing' welfare.[2]

Externally imposed regulations may, as in the United States, provide Utilitarians with less subtle justification for adopting informed consent constraints on cost/benefit judgments. Legal risks and costs may add negative utility enough to protect informed consent from all but the most arrogant,

33

Baruch A. Brody (ed.), Moral Theory and Moral Judgments in Medical Ethics, 33–39.
© *1988 by Kluwer Academic Publishers.*

confident researcher. Malpractice suits, or loss of research funds outweigh the prospective benefits of almost any experiment, however promising. Indeed, cynics see informed consent in American research as protection for clinicians from litigious patients, not as the protection for vulnerable patients intended in the initial regulations.

Cynics will have a harder time with the more recent concern that research subjects be chosen equitably.[3] So, too, will Utilitarians. Sumner's means of accommodation will, I think, not work here. There are clear advantages to using prisoners, soldiers, the mentally infirm, or poor people in various phases of drug testing. There are obvious costs, without compensations in utility, to reduced use of these groups. (The fruitful Willowbrook hepatitis studies in the 1960's, for example, could not now be carried out on institution-alized children, in spite of predicted – and realized – benefits for the subjects, and for other children and adults.) A Utilitarian could not support these restrictions on the grounds that non-ideal circumstances make direct cost/benefit judgments highly fallible. Nor is it likely that a researcher indifferent to equity would run afoul of the law or lose funding, or even professional respect. So, there are no imposed, external sanctions severe enough to make equity a reasonable 'indirect strategy' for Utilitarian researchers.

Equity aside, are Utilitarians justified in even adopting IRB informed consent policies? It is not enough that 'precommitment' to informed consent compensates for some temptations and liabilities under which Utilitarians labor, or even that subjects are thereby benefited. Utilitarians must also take into account the costs and benefits of this policy for others engaged in, or affected in the research – researchers already burdened by bureaucracy and third-party regulations, or patients who might well benefit from research now hampered by consent regulations.

Of course, IRBs are not able to take account of such affected interests. By law and inclination they are concerned with only a very narrow range of benefits and harms, or, rather, with a very narrow range of *prospective* benefits and harms. Under the heading of risks, only harms to the subject are to be considered. Possible harms to researchers, or to 'society' are excluded. Moreover, of the harms to the subjects, only 'significant' harms are to be entered into the balance for weighing against benefits.

Some of these exclusions make Utilitarian sense. Minor harms may be too slight to make a difference. Even a large number of minor harms (for example, pains and bruises from venipunctures) will not overwhelm a project with the standard promise of contributions to knowledge and therapy. As for risks to research personnel, it may be assumed that committee review would not improve upon the investigators' own self-interested precautions.

Harms to society are, clearly, more difficult to define and predict and perhaps fall outside an IRB's competence. And yet members have some knowledge of the uses and misuses to which new therapies might be put. For example, IRBs might well predict how a new tranquilizer would be marketed by the drug house sponsoring the research under consideration. IRB members would, or could have information on the adverse effects of testing on relations within a hospital – on doctor-doctor, or doctor-nurse collaborations, as well as on doctor-patient relations. Their impressions of such social harms, specific and general, could be augmented by medical sociologists on the board. To assess social harm would undoubtedly complicate IRB deliberations, as well as IRB budgets, but the epistemic obstacles are not formidable. More information could be gathered and weighed, if the current IRB mandate allowed for inclusion of possible social harms.[4]

The class of allowable benefits is somewhat wider: Possible benefits to knowledge or to society may enter the calculus. Why social benefits, but not social harms? Perhaps committees are better able to predict social benefits of research. And, yet, committees rarely seek information or deliberate upon the promised benefits of research, unless the promises are clearly exaggerated. Nor do IRBs make regular retrospective enquiries. Researchers are supposed to report 'unexpected, serious adverse reactions' during testing,[5] but there is no comparable request for reports of positive responses, expected or unexpected.

This apparent indifference to evidence of benefits may spring from two assumptions shared by many board members (on medical IRBs): first, that every clinical trial, if carefully designed and executed, will yield knowledge, and second, that any contribution to knowledge adds, sooner or later, to therapeutic progress. These assumptions are embodied in the very categories of deliberation: IRBs do not consider *Possible* Benefits, but Promised, or Anticipated Benefits.[6] (By contrast, possible harms to patients are always counted as Risks, even when they are 'foreseeable' or virtually certain – for reasons suggested below.)

There are familiar reasons to question these sanguine assumptions. Results of testing are often inconclusive or negative. Since such results are often not published, they can be of use only to the researchers themselves in designing their next set of experiments, or in deciding to abandon that line of investigation altogether. Of those results which are published or circulated, only a fraction are cited by other researchers, sometimes solely as evidence of conscientious knowledge of the literature. Of clear contributions to knowledge, we might wonder how many contribute to new therapies. And, of course, new therapies often prove in time to have fewer desirable effects, or more side effects than initial testing and use revealed. (Thalidomide, DES, cytotoxic cancer drugs and X-radiation are the best known of many remedies which proved pathogenic.)

A third, less questionable assumption is also at work: IRBs assume that funders, public and private, carefully assess the projects they support. New projects often begin as pilot projects, whose further funding requires impressive initial results. Scrutiny of later stages in a series of projects may be less exacting, especially if the senior investigator or laboratory is well regarded. Nonetheless, each claim of prospective benefits is based on, and invites retrospective assessment of prior work. (It is said to be a common practice to submit, as if prospective, results already secured. Funding then becomes a covert reward rather than a gamble.) Moreover, certain funding agencies (NIH) conduct occasional general reviews of larger areas of research.

However reasonable this third assumption of closer review by others, IRBs cannot substitute these judgments for their own. These reviews often use simple indices of harm and benefit, or – as in the case of drug houses – primarily financial measures. But profits are no measure of therapeutic benefit in a market generated in part by advertising and excessive medication. Nor are research and legal costs a measure of the kinds of costs IRBs should be considering.

Even if more comprehensive enquiries into costs and benefits were undertaken, the results might be inconclusive: causal judgments can be as elusive as judgments of harms and benefits. Yet without general and specific retrospective assessments, we have no way of assessing Utilitarian strategies, direct or indirect. Informed consent may, as Wayne Sumner suggests, reduce the number of mistaken risk/benefit judgements. But how would we know, if there are not attempts or ways of assessing benefits? If an archer's target is never closely inspected, we have no way of telling whether the 'indirect strategy' of aiming slightly above the bull's eye is better than aiming at it.

Clearly, IRBs are not staffed by Utilitarians: their range of harms and benefits is too narrow, and their attitude to probabilities and evidence too cavalier. Nor, contrary to rhetorical appearance, are they Kantians: their commitment to autonomy is doubtful, and too strongly enforced by legal sanctions to be easily tested. (I recall board member remarks about 'the good old days', when 'we could give newborns a sodium overload without asking anyone.')

For want of a ready label, we might call them Optimists. Like Utilitarians they look to the future, but confidence not calculation is their hallmark. Optimists are often indifferent to evidence. Their confidence is not closely tied to probabilities empirically determined. They are more interested in possibilities. If something *can* be done, they will do it. ('The difficult takes time; the impossible a little longer'.)

In some respects Optimism is like an ethical theory. Optimism does not provide a criterion of the Good, but it encourages a choice of goals uncompromised by prior regard for means. As for strategies for achieving a goal so selected, Optimism, as a 'cognitive stance,' encourages a confidence that takes evidence at its most favorable, supported by assumptions for which there may be little or no evidence. For the Optimist, the proverbial glass is half-full, not half-empty, because the Optimist is confident that a half glass is enough to satisfy thirst, or even that the glass is being filled, not emptied (by a charitable or Invisible Hand).

Optimism dismisses as irrelevant much of the negative evidence others would insistently take account of. Thus, like all theories, Optimism is a way of reducing or avoiding uncertainty in matters which do not easily lend themselves to objective assessments. Like political and religious creeds, Optimism provides permission for action in circumstances which would confuse or discourage 'realists.'[7]

Optimists have much in common with political agents like Herbert Philbrick. How great was the 'menace of Worldwide Communism' to the 'American Way of Life'? In Philbrick's eyes, the threat was great enough to use morally objectionable practices to infiltrate the American Communist Party, a small and aging political remnant of the Thirties. To speak now of 'Cold Warrior hysteria' is to reject the Cold Warriors' Manichean analysis of America and its adversaries. Manicheanism simplifies the world to mortal struggle between two Powers of Light and Darkness. To transcend it is to complicate our political thought and hamper political action.

Indeed, some board members may see themselves as part of the War on Disease (or Ignorance); more exactly, part of the recruitment of subject-soldiers. They may sincerely oppose conscription, but may not look too closely at the ways in which volunteers are secured so long as the formalities of informed consent are followed by hospital and college recruiters. Likewise, they may regard as subversive the very kinds of enquiry Utilitarians would make in arriving at cost/benefit assessments, prospective or retrospective.

Wayne Sumner raises the question as to whether Utilitarians can share a committee's commitment to informed consent. My doubts lead to a more general question, namely, Can a Utilitarian serve on committees dominated by Optimists? Optimists will not care to gather or weigh the kinds of evidence Sumner needs to test his hope that informed consent may prove an 'indirect strategy'. Nor will Optimists help him fully assess particular projects for cost/benefit ratios, since Optimists tend to treat all possible benefits, however unlikely, as promised or anticipated, and all harms, however likely, as mere risks.

Whether Optimists or not, many board members are barely reconstructed Paternalists. As such, they will not share a Utilitarian's need for a wider range of evidence than current regulations allow. Their concern as Paternalists is simply with what is good and bad for their patient-subjects, including (of course) participation in clinical decisions.[8] Indeed, Paternalists would tend to ignore even allowable benefits for knowledge or for future patients.

I would not want Utilitarians to resign from IRBs on these grounds. On the contrary, boards no doubt benefit from having people who are sensitive to a range of interests which Paternalists neglect and Optimists skew. Utilitarians do, however, face here (as elsewhere) an issue of candor for Utilitarians: Should they make clear their commitment to a wider range of harms and benefits, more carefully investigated and weighed? Or should they pretend allegiance to IRB procedures, while subtly trying to improve the range, description, and evidence for harms and benefits under consideration?

A larger issue, for Utilitarians, is whether they can justify membership on committees which deviate far more than circumstances dictate from the Utilitarian ideal. Since these deviations do not constitute immoral practice, the problem is not one of Dirty Hands. But it is one of Troubled Minds, troubled by a lack of consistency between ethical theory and moral practices.

In judging practices by Utilitarianism, or any of the standard ethical theories, we must take into account not only the principles philosophers label and debate, but also the less systematized attitudes by which people simplify data and decisions. If we confine our analysis to the familiar options (Utilitarian, Kantian, Natural Law, etc.), we are likely to mistake the moral and political character of the practices we wish to understand. And, as participants, we are likely to strive for a consistency of theory and practice which legal and institutional realities cannot satisfy.

Perhaps the lesson for Applied Ethics is: Consistency is the hobgoblin not only of little minds, but of large, abstract minds as well.

NOTES

[1] My own first-hand experience of IRBs has been supplemented by helpful talks with John Arras, Dr. Robert Levine, Ruth Macklin, and Peter Williams. But we are all most familiar with American medical center IRBs, which may differ somewhat from the University review board Sumner serves in Canada.

[2] Did Philbrick justify his 'un-American' political activities by appealing to the ways in which the Communist Party deviated from 'ideal' American politics? His more fervent admirers argued that a party which would curtail the civil liberties of others was entitled to none of their own – an argument which might appeal to those who prize consistency of theory and practice, even imposed consistency, more than civil liberties.

[3] Equity was first urged in [1].

[4] For a discussion of this exclusion, see [3].

[5] For an exchange on problems of defining 'adverse effects', see [2], p. 23 and Appendix G.

[6] Original terminology was less sanguine: the early 1966 regulations spoke of 'possible' benefits.

[7] Realism, like Pessimism, is a contrasting 'cognitive stance'. Realists are more attentive to circumstances than are Pessimists, but both are, by contrast with Optimists, given to inaction.

[8] For an attempt to give a paternalist account of informed consent, see [4].

BIBLIOGRAPHY

[1]   The National Commission for the Protection of Human Subjects of Biomedical and Behavioral Research: 1978, *Report and Recommendations: Institutional Review Boards*, DHEW Publication No. (OS) 78–0008, Washington, D.C.

[2]   The President's Commission for the Study of Ethical Problems in Medicine and Biomedical and Behavioral Research: 1983, *Implementing Human Research Regulations*, Second Biennial Report, DHEW Publication No. 83–600504, Washington, D.C.

[3]   Schwartz, R. L.: 1983, 'Institutional Review of Medical Research: Cost-Benefit Analysis, Risk-Benefit Analysis, and 'The Possible Effects of Research on Public Policy'' *The Journal of Legal Medicine* 4, 143–166.

[4]   Weiss, G.: 1985, 'Paternalism Modernized', *The Journal of Medical Ethics* 11, 184–186.

New York University
New York, N.Y.

JEFFREY REIMAN

UTILITARIANISM AND THE INFORMED CONSENT REQUIREMENT (OR: SHOULD UTILITARIANS BE ALLOWED ON MEDICAL RESEARCH ETHICAL REVIEW BOARDS?)

Utilitarianism holds that aggregate welfare (or happiness) is the ultimate standard of right and wrong. This theory determines what is right, among the courses of action possible, by summing the gains and losses to welfare likely to result from each course of action. The right or best thing to do is the course of action that is likely to produce the greatest net sum of welfare. The problem referred to in my subtitle arises because research ethical review boards tend to insist that, to win approval, research projects involving human subjects must obtain the informed consent of those subjects. Moreover, and this is the rub, this requirement is for all intents and purposes absolute. Lack of informed consent is not treated as a welfare loss that can be compensated for by other welfare gains. Informed consent is a requirement independent of welfare gain-and-loss calculations, such that, even where there is reason to believe that a research project would serve to maximize net welfare, the review boards will not approve it unless there is provision for the informed consent of subjects. In short, these boards will do something that seems decidedly *un*utilitarian: They will recommend a course of action (non-performance of a research project) though it is likely to produce less welfare than an alternative possible action (performance).

Service on such review boards, then, poses a problem for individuals with utilitarian moral sympathies. These individuals will have to be untrue to themselves when they go along with the board's absolute insistence on informed consent, and, accordingly, the boards will have to be wary lest their utilitarians subvert that absolutism. But perhaps the problem is only apparent. Perhaps it is possible for utilitarians honestly to embrace an absolute requirement of informed consent, and thus for review boards to embrace their utilitarian members without anxiety. To address this question, consider the case of L. W. Sumner, card-carrying utilitarian moral philosopher and member of his university's research ethical review committee. Sumner's attempt to reconcile his sincere participation on this committee with his utilitarianism is recounted in his autobiographical essay, 'Utilitarian Goals and Kantian Constraints (Or: Always True to You, Darling, in My Fashion)'.[1] Determining whether this attempted reconciliation succeeds will

Baruch A. Brody (ed.), Moral Theory and Moral Judgments in Medical Ethics, 41–51.
© *1988 by Kluwer Academic Publishers.*

help to bring out some important features of the ethical review of research, and the particular problems posed by and for utilitarianism. I shall argue that Sumner's attempt to defend the compatibility of his utilitarianism with his endorsement of an absolute requirement of informed consent fails. And, I shall go on to show that the unresolved tension that remains is more serious with respect to medical research than to social science research.

The point of this exercise goes beyond refuting Sumner. I will argue that the strategy that Sumner uses to try to reconcile utilitarianism and the informed consent requirement is not idiosyncratic to him – it is necessarily the only strategy that has a chance. Accordingly, my aim in refuting Sumner is to show that utilitarianism is congenitally unable to account for the absolute insistence that research subjects only have done to them what they have informedly consented to – and the case of medical research only throws this inability into greater relief. The implication of my argument is that absolute insistence on informed consent will require just the sort of Kantian (or Kantian-like) commitment to the absolute value of human autonomy or dignity that utilitarians can never make. And for those of us who believe that research review boards ought to insist on informed consent as an absolute requirement, it will be appropriate to wonder whether utilitarians should serve on research ethical review boards in general, and in particular on boards that review medical research.

As do many others, Sumner's committee qualifies the requirement of informed consent only in allowing some deception of research subjects where necessary to the research and where risk to the subjects is negligible. Since, even with this qualification, Sumner's committee will reject many welfare-maximizing research proposals that lack informed consent, the qualification is irrelevant to the problem of reconciling Sumner's committee work with his utilitarianism. Sumner writes that his committee does not regard infringements on subjects' informed consent as

just further costs for them which might, in principle, be offset by sufficiently great social benefits. Instead, they are treated as assaults on their dignity or autonomy which are objectionable as a matter of principle. Our guidelines state the matter thus: 'The primary reason for requiring consent is the ethical principle that all persons must be allowed to make decisions and to exercise choice on matters which affect them.' This is the language not of a global cost/benefit balancing but of respect for individuals, language which invokes the familiar Kantian demand that persons be treated as ends in themselves and not used as mere means ([3], p. 17).

Thus, even with the allowance for deception, Sumner's committee treats the informed consent requirement as effectively absolute, and, consequently, for the most part, Sumner leaves the qualification aside and tries to show that insisting on informed consent as an absolute requirement is compatible with utilitarianism. This is appropriate, since we can think of the limited allowance of deception as a proviso built into the informed consent requirement. Then, it remains the case that committees like Sumner's treat *that* requirement (with its built-in proviso) as effectively absolute in the way that poses problems for utilitarianism. Thus, I shall follow Sumner in treating the requirement as absolute even though it contains limited provisions for its relaxation.[2] Furthermore, Sumner's account makes no distinction between review of medical and social science research, and thus I shall temporarily ignore this distinction.

Before considering how well Sumner succeeds, it is worth pausing to state some of the conditions on what would count as success here. The first thing to note is that, if to succeed Sumner must show that he can endorse the informed consent requirement on the grounds of respect for individuals independently of global cost/benefit considerations, Sumner's attempted reconciliation cannot possibly succeed. If, that is, sincere participation in his committee's review work requires believing – as Kantian moral theorists do – that people are absolutely entitled to informed consent because they are human or rational or ends-in-themselves or autonomous or whatever, Sumner cannot possibly participate sincerely (a point he confesses, albeit obliquely, in the final sentence of his essay). He must always believe that the informed consent requirement is a means to maximum aggregate welfare for all individuals, not something owed to each individual human being because of his or her nature. To be an absolute, then, the requirement must be an absolutely necessary means. Therefore, what success is available to Sumner lies in showing that *always* insisting on the requirement is the best means to maximizing net welfare.

Second, obviously rigged solutions must be excluded from the outset. For example, inner moral schism might be patched over by taking the costs (to welfare) of violating informed consent to be infinite or so high as always to outweigh all possible benefits that might result. But the arbitrariness of this moral price-gouging is apparent, and shows the solution to be no more than an ad hoc attempt to buy Kantian gold with inflated utilitarian currency.

Sumner's argument for the compatibility of the informed consent requirement and utilitarianism takes the form of distinguishing a direct and an indirect strategy for pursuing the utilitarian goal of maximum welfare. The direct strategy rules out treating informed consent as an absolute, but the indirect strategy does not. Since the indirect strategy is good utilitarianism, the problem of inner schism is only apparent, and Sumner and his review board colleagues can rest easy. Sumner begins by identifying the 'direct strategy' for satisfying utilitarianism's criterion of right and wrong:

the straightforward way of satisfying the criterion which tells us that the right thing to do is whatever will maximize welfare is just to seek on each occasion the course of action which will maximize welfare. On this view of the matter the theory's decisionmaking strategy simply consists of the injunction to satisfy the theory's ultimate criterion. Because on this strategy we try to satisfy the criterion by just aiming to satisfy the criterion, we may call it the straightforward or direct strategy ([3], pp. 20–21).

On the direct strategy, says Sumner, 'when I assess experimental protocols I should base my decision exclusively on the outcome of a cost/benefit analysis'.

But, he goes on to argue, there is nothing inherently superior about the direct strategy. Indeed, for utilitarians, no strategy has inherent primacy. What matters is 'success rate', and it is not necessarily the case that the direct strategy has the best success rate. If some alternative were more likely than the direct strategy to succeed in maximizing welfare, then it would be the decisionmaking strategy that utilitarians are required to adopt. And any alternative to the direct strategy is an indirect strategy. Writes Sumner, 'Any indirect strategy will consist of something other than just aiming at doing our best on each occasion. It will therefore propose some more complex set of procedures, or rules, or guidelines designed to enable us to achieve our goal more reliably, if less directly. Clearly there are many possible indirect strategies'. The indirect strategy that Sumner will defend is *precommitment to requiring informed consent*. 'Precommitment' is the practice of deciding in advance to hold to some policy irrespective of the appeal of alternatives that present themselves at any particular moment. This is the sort of thing that Odysseus did in forbidding his men in advance from obeying his commands to untie him while within hearing range of the Sirens, and it is the sort of thing that alcoholics and dieters do in promising in advance to resist the temptation to take just one little drink or bite no matter how appealing and harmless it seems. Precommitment to requiring informed consent, then, means committing oneself in advance to insisting on it as a requirement for approving any research proposal, no matter what or how appealing its cost/benefit prognosis is.

What is important to note here is that the 'precommitment to informed consent strategy' (PICS) is only one possible indirect strategy. It will help in evaluating Sumner's argument for the PICS if we identify some possible alternatives. Call one, the 'enormous gains exception strategy' (EGES), and another, the 'citizens' review panel strategy' (CRPS). On the EGES, we precommit ourselves to requiring informed consent *except* in those cases in which we have good reason to think that the benefits of a research proposal (that lacks provision for informed consent) seem not merely to outweigh its costs significantly, but enormously. On the CRPS, we precommit ourselves to allowing any (otherwise acceptable) proposal which either provides for informed consent *or* obtains the approval of a randomly-selected group of citizens, none of whom are researchers and some of whom are former research subjects. A third indirect strategy (EGES-CRPS) would combine features of the first two, such that proposals, for which anticipation of enormous gains argued for relaxing the informed consent requirement, would have to secure approval by the citizens' panel. Note, in passing, that I have no quarrel with the rationality of precommitment as such. The three alternatives to the PICS are all precommitment strategies.

Bearing these alternative indirect strategies in mind will help us see what Sumner must prove to succeed in his quest for inner peace. Since there are any number of indirect strategies, Sumner must give us, not just an argument for replacing the direct with an indirect strategy, but an argument for that particular indirect strategy that takes the form of precommitment to requiring informed consent. And that argument must demonstrate that always using that particular strategy is the best way to maximize welfare. To prove that, Sumner must prove that always using the PICS is better than always using any other indirect strategy, which includes the EGES, the CRPS, and the EGES-CRPS. Thus we can evaluate Sumner's success by determining whether the advantages he claims for the PICS are superior to those likely to result from these alternatives.

Sumner's argument for the PICS is based on the fact that he and his fellow committee members are fallible. Therefore,

if we attempt a full cost/benefit analysis of each experimental protocol we will very often make mistakes, thereby permitting unnecessary costs to be imposed on research subjects... However, being also aware of my own utilitarian tendencies, I know that the temptation to make the attempt might be irresistible on each particular occasion. Thus, I will do well to join my fellow committee members in precommitting ourselves so as to reduce or eliminate this temptation. This we do by announcing in advance ... that however favorable a protocol's cost/benefit ratio might appear to be, it must also satisfy the further requirement of informed consent ([3], p. 27).

This serves to 'decentralize risk assessment, thereby counterbalancing both the investigator's perception of risk and our own, by giving veto power to the prospective subjects' ([3], p. 27). In short, Sumner contends that he could, in good utilitarian conscience, adopt the informed consent requirement because doing so is likely to improve his success rate in identifying those proposals that really do serve maximum welfare. Writes Sumner,

My rationale for endorsing this precommitment, in advance of considering particular cases, rests largely on my lack of confidence that I will be able to project costs and benefits accurately in those cases.... Because of the many impediments which will afflict my decision context in particular cases, my judgment is that, if I allow myself to sacrifice informed consent whenever doing so seems (on balance) beneficial then I will often sacrifice it when doing so is in fact (on balance) harmful. If this judgment is correct then I will produce better results on the whole if I treat informed consent as an independent constraint... ([3], pp. 27–8).

This argument for utilitarian embrace of the PICS fails on at least three grounds. I shall take these up roughly in order of ascending gravity. I contend that each alone is capable of dooming Sumner's hopes for inner moral integration. For ease of identification, I shall number the paragraphs in which the three objections are introduced.

1. In the just-quoted paragraph, the conclusion simply does not follow. From the fact that, in light of my fallibility, 'I will often sacrifice [informed consent] when doing so is ... harmful', it does not follow that 'I will produce better results on the whole if I treat informed consent as an independent constraint.' This doesn't follow because we don't know *how often* sacrifice will be harmful or *how* harmful, and we don't know *how often* sacrifice will be beneficial and *how* beneficial. That is, even if I often sacrifice informed consent with harmful results, I will sometimes sacrifice it with beneficial results. Sumner isn't arguing that we are always mistaken, only that we 'often' are. But, if, for example, I will often sacrifice consent harmfully but only with minor harm, and if I will more often sacrifice consent beneficially and with great benefit, then it follows that I will on the whole do worse by treating informed consent as an independent constraint. Since Sumner gives no argument for believing that the consequences will not work out this way, his conclusion is unsupported. Moreover, even if he did have such an argument, he would not have shown that the PICS is superior to the EGES. It seems plausible to expect that in some cases the benefits to be derived from projects that deny informed consent are enormous, and that when we have good reason to think they are, we will have good reason to think that, even if we are underestimating the costs to subjects, the likely outcome of the project will still be to maximize net welfare. If we were prepared to follow the PICS in every case except those which promised enormous gains, we would spare ourselves most of the errors that the PICS protects against without having to forego the enormous gains of the exceptions. Since, though fallible, we are not crazy or stupid or blind, there seems every reason to think that the EGES will give even a better success rate that the PICS. At the very least, Sumner

has failed to prove otherwise and thus failed to prove that *always* using the PICS is the best strategy for maximizing welfare overall.

2. The PICS can only reliably improve our success rate, if the mistakes we are most likely to make (or if the worst mistakes we are likely to make) are those of underestimating the costs to research subjects. The PICS will not protect us against underestimating the benefits of research, since these are not generally directed toward the subjects. And Sumner recognizes that mistakes go both ways. While it is possible to underestimate the costs to subjects, it is also possible to underestimate the benefits to others. The first mistake imposes unnecessary costs on the research subjects, while the second imposes unnecessary costs on the potential beneficiaries of the research. And, concedes Sumner, 'There may be no reason to think that the former costs are in themselves either more or less serious than the latter when they actually occur' ([3], p. 29). This, of course, makes the insistence on informed consent by subjects (in the absence of any representation of potential beneficiaries) seem a rather lopsided strategy, likely to lead to as many mistakes as it prevents. Sumner's response to this is to maintain that costs to subjects 'are more predictable, thus ... more avoidable' ([3], p. 29). This he takes to imply that we will make fewer mistakes by protecting ourselves against underestimating costs to subjects than by protecting ourselves against underestimating costs to beneficiaries. And since the first sort 'are the mistakes which will result from a direct strategy, you are likely to make fewer mistakes if you employ some [!] indirect strategy' ([3], p. 29).

There are two problems here. Recognizing the apparent one-sidedness of protecting ourselves exclusively against underestimating costs to subjects, Sumner replies by pointing out that costs to subjects 'are more predictable', from which he infers that we will make fewer mistakes by protecting ourselves against them. This is a *non sequitur*. The fact that costs to subjects are more predictable should imply that we (on the review board) will have less trouble seeing them, and thus be less in need of protecting ourselves against underestimating them. In addition, as the surprising tentativeness of Sumner's concluding line hints, even if it followed from the penultimate line, that would only prove the appropriateness of *some* indirect strategy, not of *the* PICS. While the PICS might protect us against underestimating the costs to subjects, it opens the possibility that some beneficial research will be prevented because prospective subjects overestimate the risks to them of participating. Even if our most urgent need is to protect against underestimating risks to subjects, the costs of preventing such beneficial research are not negligible. It seems plausible to expect that the citizens' panel described earlier would be as unlikely as prospective subjects to underestimate risks to the subjects, and less likely than prospective subjects to overestimate those risks. If this is correct, then the CRPS is likely to be superior to the PICS in improving our success rate. And then, again, since Sumner has given us no reason to think the contrary, he has failed to defend the claim that *always* using the PICS is the best way to maximize welfare.

3. We now reach the problem with the gravest implications for utilitarianism with regard to the ethical review of research. To sharpen the issue, suppose now that problems (1) and (2) don't exist. That is, contrary to the arguments I have made, suppose that Sumner has proven that it is more important that utilitarians protect against underestimating costs to subjects than against underestimating benefits, and that the best way to do this is by adopting the informed consent requirement. Even so, inner harmony is still beyond Sumner's reach, and that of any utilitarian on a board that insists on the informed consent requirement. Sumner illustrates the force of the PICS by stating that a utilitarian using the direct strategy will accept, and a utilitarian using the PICS will reject, a research project 'which proposes to bypass the informed consent of its subjects', but which nonetheless there is evidence to believe 'will yield benefits beyond its costs' ([3], p. 28). And, he contends that a utilitarian will adopt a policy of rejecting such proposals because insisting on consent is protection against inaccurate cost/benefit estimates, and thus this policy is more likely to yield maximum welfare than allowing consent to be bypassed. But, note that the informed consent requirement will do more than protect against underestimates of costs to subjects. *It will also effectively prohibit research in which the costs to subjects have been estimated correctly as high.* And since some of this research might still produce great benefits, a utilitarian is going to have a hard time swallowing this prohibition.

The point here is that there are really two sorts of research proposal that requiring informed consent will torpedo, and in only one sort is underestimation of costs to subjects relevant. The other sort is that in which the costs to subjects are, for all intents and purposes, known – let's say they are admitted, documented, and illustrated in the research proposal. The researchers maintain, however, that the benefits to be obtained from the research are potentially enormous – great enough, and even probable enough, to outweigh the *recognized and high* costs to subjects. Presumably, few people free and sane enough to consent meaningfully at all will consent to participation in such research. Thus, to commit oneself to the informed consent requirement as an absolute is to commit oneself in effect to an absolute prohibition of such research. But how can a utilitarian make that commitment? Surely the claim that we may be underestimating the costs to the subjects cannot support such a commitment. Here there is no question of protecting ourselves against such an underestimation – the prospective subjects will refuse consent precisely because they agree with the researchers' estimate. Nor, of course, can requiring consent be any corrective to overestimating the benefits. The simple point is that, in cases like these, and there need only be a few real ones, requiring informed consent gives no help in achieving maximum welfare. In such cases, one can only insist on informed consent if one holds the Kantian (or Kantian-like) view that there is something gravely wrong with imposing costs on people against their wills no matter how great the benefit. And no self-respecting utilitarian can accept that.

It is here that the special nature of medical research is germane. The reason is that in such research – particularly experiments aimed at curing terrible diseases – the costs to research subjects may be high and known, and the potential benefits enormous and probable. What benefits could social science research promise that could match even a small chance of, say, curing cancer? How many people benefit from the Salk vaccine? Millions, billions, probably trillions! How many would benefit from a similar 'vaccine' against cancer? Suppose that scientists were reliably close to discovering such a vaccine, but needed to perform an experiment in which some small number of people were unknowingly injected with cancer cells. As far as I can see, utilitarianism simply has no resources to justify prohibiting such research, and thus no grounds for insisting that such research only be performed on consenting subjects.

Moreover, I think this is generally true regarding promising medical research. First of all, improved health is uncontroversially a benefit – a claim that cannot so easily be made about the increments of esoteric knowledge which much social science research promises. And, advances in maintaining health not only benefit the living but those who will be born in the future. The fact is that the number of people who stand to benefit substantially from promising medical research that imposes costs on a few subjects is astronomical. Consequently, on a utilitarian reckoning, it will almost always be right to allow medical research that has a good chance of leading to a cure, even if that research will require imposing suffering or even death on a few unfortunate subjects against their wills. It follows that, at least with regard to medical research, no utilitarian can embrace an absolute requirement of informed consent.

The general lesson here is this: Sumner's attempted reconciliation testifies

to the fact that utilitarianism's only chance at justifying an absolute requirement of informed consent is as a hedge against faulty cost/benefit estimates.
This is not idiosyncratic to Sumner; it is necessarily the only strategy
available to any utilitarian. Since utilitarians cannot give up their commitment to maximum aggregate welfare as the criterion of the rightness of any
moral principle, they can only embrace principles independently of their
reckoning of aggregate welfare *on the grounds that by doing so they will do
better at getting maximum welfare than by proceeding on straight reckoning
of the costs and gains to welfare.* But they can only hope to do better than
straight reckoning *on the assumption that their straight reckoning is likely to
be faulty.* Then the only way that an independent constraint can be justified
for a utilitarian is *as a means to correct for faulty cost/benefit estimates.* But
to earn this justification, the alternative must correct for faulty cost/benefit
estimates *without also imposing additional impediments to achieving
maximum welfare.* And that is why utilitarians like Sumner cannot embrace
the informed consent requirement. The requirement does too much. As the
case of promising medical research brings out most clearly, in addition to
protecting against incorrect estimates, the requirement will prohibit research
that is highly beneficial to many and highly costly to a few *where there is no
question of the accuracy of the estimates.* The PICS (as Kantian constraints
do generally) must amount to overkill from a utilitarian perspective.

If the PICS is to block research with favorable cost/benefit estimates where
there is no problem about the correctness of those estimates, it follows that
the PICS cannot be justified on cost/benefit terms at all. Which is to say, it
cannot be justified on utilitarian grounds. Rather it will have to be justified in
terms like those Sumner's committee states in its guidelines, namely, that
people are entitled in principle to exercise choice over their fates, no matter
what benefits can be derived from denying them that choice. But then, if
informed consent is required on those grounds, we must expect conscientious
utilitarians to be inwardly divided when they serve on social science research
ethical review boards, and a fortiori on medical research ethical review
boards.[3] Such inner division may be tolerable, and utilitarians might in fact
be able to be good board-members and play by the Kantian rules. If not, for
medical research boards in particular, no utilitarians need apply.

NOTES

[1] All quotations in my text are from this essay. See [3].

[2] See note 3, below.

[3] It is reasonable to suspect that Kantians will have one problem on such boards that utilitarians can escape. This is the problem of research that requires deception of its subjects, for example, psychological research in which the subject's full knowledge of the nature of the experiment would prevent the researcher from eliciting the subject's spontaneous reactions. Think here, for example, of Stanley Milgram's important research on obedience (see [1]). Since one cannot consent to what one doesn't truly understand, such deception undermines the consent requirement (even where subjects give an uncoerced 'yes' to participating in the experiment as they *mis* understand it). Those who take the Kantian (or kindred) view that persons must be treated in ways that are compatible with their autonomous control over their destinies will have to regard such deception as generally wrong, and thus have problems about participating on research review boards that allow it. But the problems here are not fatal. I have argued elsewhere that some limited deception in research can be compatible with respecting the autonomy of research subjects, when it can be reasonably maintained that the subjects would have willed the deception, much as the deception involved in setting up a surprise party can be compatible with respecting the autonomy of the surprise on similar grounds. See [2].

BIBLIOGRAPHY

[1]   Milgram, S.: 1963, 'Behavioral Study of Obedience', *Journal of Abnormal and Social Psychology* **67**, 371–378.

[2]   Reiman, Jeffrey H.: 1979, 'Research Subjects, Political Subjects, and Human Subjects', in C. B. Klockars and F. O'Connor (eds.), *Deviance and Decency: The Ethics of Research with Human Subjects*, Sage Publications, Bevery Hills and London.

[3]   Sumner, L. W.: 1987, 'Utilitarian Goals and Kantian Constraints (Or: Always True to You, Darling, in My Fashion)', in this volume, pp. 15–31.

The American University
Washington, D.C.

REPLY TO RUDDICK AND REIMAN

William Ruddick thinks that as a utilitarian I am too good to serve on my review committee, while Jeffrey Reiman thinks that I am not good enough. Since my experience leads me to conclude that Ruddick's pessimism about the operations of such committees is as unwarranted as Reiman's optimism, I judge the contest between them a standoff.

What I welcome from both are the complications which they introduce into my relatively simple story. Both urge, and I agree, that when all relevant factors are taken into account, determining the optimal utilitarian strategy is at least terribly difficult, and perhaps for all practical purposes impossible. Neither disputes my contention that a direct strategy is unlikely to be optimal. If even this much is agreed, then we must radically rethink the relations which are standardly assumed to hold between utilitarian goals and deontological constraints. However, as Reiman rightly insists, it is one thing to claim that some constrained strategy or other will be optimal and quite another to defend a particular package of goals, procedures, and constraints. I am certain that direct cost/benefit balancing would be one of the worst strategies for my committee, as would the complete suppression of such balancing; I am much less certain that our actual practice is the best we can do.

The problem here is the familiar one of large-scale institutional design. Even if we all shared a commitment to a utilitarian goal, how could we ever contour the institutional structure, substantive guidelines, and operational procedures of review committees in such a way as to best achieve that goal? I shall limit myself to two observations. The first is prompted by Ruddick's mention of equity in the selection of research subjects. Since their basic goal is aggregative, utilitarians have notorious difficulties with equity. Were I to try to defend equity on utilitarian grounds, I would argue that we should wherever possible avoid imposing additional misery on those sections of the populace which are already badly disadvantaged. But suppose that this appeal were unpersuasive. One option then open to me would be to argue that equity is less important than it is often thought to be. But another would be to accommodate it by building it into my basic goal. I offer no opinion on which of these would be the more desirable direction for me to pursue, or why. I

53

Baruch A. Brody (ed.), Moral Theory and Moral Judgments in Medical Ethics, 53–54.
© *1988 by Kluwer Academic Publishers.*

merely point out that while the resulting framework would no longer be utilitarian, it would still be consequentialist. Thus, it would still be consonant with my main theoretical aim, which is to show that the value of deontological constraints lies in their service of consequentialist goals.

Complicating our theoretical goal would, however, also complicate our practical problem of institutional design. My second observation is that the intractability of this problem is less damaging to utilitarianism (or consequentialism) than is usually supposed. For one thing, the actual practice of establishing the rules of the game for review committees always involves a balancing of competing values – chiefly social benefits against costs to subjects, but other values as well. This balancing is, however, often merely intuitive. Utilitarians should be understood as counselling that we take this process seriously, substituting for guesswork the best empirical evidence concerning the costs and benefits of research available to us. Even if we do take it seriously, we can of course never be certain that we have found the right answer. Thus, we should regard the process as open-ended, and our institutions as subject to periodic revision in the light of accumulated experience. If we can never manage to devise the ideal institution, at least we can try to improve our actual institutions through a continuing series of incremental reforms. Seen from this angle, the problems which utilitarians encounter in seeking an optimal decisionmaking strategy are those which are inherent in the design of any significant social institution. Since one criterion of adequacy for a moral framework is that it should not oversimplify complex problems, this result seems to count in favor of utilitarianism rather than against it.

University of Toronto
Toronto, Ontario, Canada

SECTION II

NATURAL RIGHT CASUISTRY

ERIC MACK

MORAL RIGHTS AND CAUSAL CASUISTRY

1. INTRODUCTION

The primary goal of this essay is to examine the character of and problems within the translation of a particular type of moral doctrine into the sort of particular moral judgments we all must make as professional moralists and even as human beings. In particular, I shall be examining the translation or application of certain of the moral dictates of the type of individualistic moral rights theory which is now commonly designated as 'libertarian'. However, I shall approach this issue of the application of moral dictates to concrete cases within the context of medical ethics and, more specifically, within the context of life-and-death medical decisions. This means that I shall not be concerned with the application to concrete cases of the whole panoply of libertarian rights, e.g., rights to this or that economic good. I will only be concerned with instances in which the relevant right is the right to life and the relevant question is whether a physician's (or nurse's, etc.) action violates this right to life. I believe that the main claim which I wish to make about the application of this right to life to concrete medical cases applies very broadly to the application to specific cases of libertarian-type rights at large. That main claim is that the identification of the rights involved in particular cases, i.e., the identification of what the relevant parties have rights to, only provides half of what is needed to reach a judgment about the moral permissibility or impermissibility of a particular action. The other half of what is needed is knowledge of whether the action under consideration would *violate* the identified right(s).

Consider Dr. Alice and potential patient Alyosha.[1] Let us allow that Alyosha possesses a right to life. Were Alice to sneak up behind Alyosha and slit his throat, she would be violating this right – absent some surprising story about Alice's being engaged in preemptive defense or just retribution. But it can also easily be true that there be some action on Alice's part such that, if Alice performs that action Alyosha will die, whereas if Alice acts in some other way Alyosha will not die, and yet it is not true that if Alice performs the first action (and, as predicted, Alyosha dies) she *violates* Alyosha's right to

57

life. For instance, the following might be the situation: Alice is in Delhi getting ready for a dinner party. Alyosha is in Bombay dying for lack of the services of a surgeon with Alice's skills. If Alice goes to her dinner party, Alyosha will die, whereas he will live if she rushes to his aid. Nevertheless, Alice's going to the dinner party in Delhi does not *violate* Alyosha's right to life – or so, at least, I maintain.

If I am correct, what this case illustrates is that one cannot move immediately from an identification of the relevant right to a determination of the permissibility or impermissibility of an action touching on that right. The interesting task for the translation of a rights doctrine into judgments about concrete cases is the specification of how one agent's action must be connected with another agent's loss of some rightfully held object or condition (e.g., the second agent's life) for the first agent's action to count as a violation of that second agent's right.

Alice's action (or inaction) will constitute a *violation* of Alyosha's right to R only if her action (or inaction), *in a sufficiently robust sense, causes* Alyosha's loss of R. One's theory of the violation of rights will, then, be the product of one's causal casuistry. Causal casuistry especially focuses on actions which satisfy the following condition: Had the agent not performed the action in question or had the agent not failed to act (but, instead, acted in some other specific way), the second party would not have lost R. For the satisfaction of this condition is at least necessary for the agent's robustly causing the second party's loss of R and, hence, being a violation of the second party's right to R. Causal casuistry as such seeks to determine whether any further causal condition has to be satisfied (whether any further feature of the causal structure must obtain) before the primary causal responsibility for the loss of R can be reasonably assigned to that agent. A *restrictive* causal casuistry of the sort I shall be pursuing seeks to identify ways in which an action (or inaction) can satisfy this precondition – as Dr. Alice's trip to the dinner party does – and yet not be a violation of rights.

It should be useful to see the place of causal casuistry within the broad context of the clash between consequentialist and deontological moral theories. Consequentialism is, of course, the view that actions are right insofar as they produce (tend to produce, contribute to the coordinated production of) that possible set of upshots which is ranked most highly by the upshotist's favorite gauge for ranking sets of upshots and are wrong insofar as they diverge from the production of the best upshots.[2] Deontologists deny this strict determination of rightness and wrongness in actions on the basis of the ranking of the possible sets of upshots of actions.

A certain type of Kantian deontologist might proceed by blanketly rejecting the relevance of the value or disvalue of an action's upshots to its evaluation as right or wrong. Upshots count for nothing. Rightness and wrongness is entirely a matter of the state of the agent's will, his subjectivity, what maxim he is acting under, etc. But most deontologists want to say that actions can be right in virtue of the values they create and can be wrong in virtue of the evils they produce (or the values they destroy). This requires, to concentrate on the side of wrongs, evils and values destroyed, that for certain actions not all the upshots of that action – more pointedly, not all the upshots which the particular deontologist himself recognizes as evils – be allowed to count towards that action's negative evaluation.

Moralists with a deontological orientation have been especially fond of one or another or both of two principles which effectively discount the significance of some of an action's upshots for the moral assessment of that action. And both of these principles appear prominently in the literature on medical ethics. One principle – let us call it the Causing versus Allowing Principle (CA) – asserts that there is a morally significant difference between *causing* a death and *allowing* a death. The difference is such that it may be morally impermissible for a physician to cause the death of a patient while, in an otherwise perfectly parallel case, it would be morally permissible for a physician to allow a patient to die. For instance, though it may be permissible for Dr. Alice to attend that party and thereby let Alyosha die, it would not be permissible for her to rush to Bombay and slit his throat (even if the latter would engender a less painful death). The other principle – the Principle of Double Effect (DE) – asserts that there is a significant moral distinction between causing a *foreseen* death and causing a death with the *intention* of doing so. The difference is such that it may be morally permissible for a physician to act in a way which she knows will result in a patient's death while, in an otherwise perfectly parallel case, it would not be morally permissible for a physician intentionally to cause a patient's death. For instance, it may be permissible for Dr. Alice to administer a drug to relieve a patient's great pain, even though she knows that this will shorten the patient's life, while it would not be permissible (everything else being equal) to administer a drug with the intention of (for the sake of) hastening that patient's death.

It is crucial to note that CA does not assert that causing death is always wrong or that allowing death is always permissible. Causing death in accordance with a patient's request may well be permissible while allowing death contrary to a patient's instructions may well be impermissible (see [1]).

Similarly, no one would maintain that it is permissible to bring about death as long as one does not intend that death. And few would maintain that all intentional causings of requested deaths are impermissible. But CA and DE are each commonly thought to play an important role in defining the initial boundaries between actions which violate rights and those which do not, even though some party suffers a loss of a righful condition. Special voluntary relationships, including the contractual and quasi-contractual relationships between physicians (nurses, etc.) and their patients, can redraw these initial boundaries. Had Alice agreed to be in Bombay to treat Alyosha, then of course her going to the dinner party instead would be impermissible – a violation of Alyosha's contractual right to her medical services.

CA allows for a non-upshotist application of a theory of value which itself could well be shared by the upshotist. Thus, we have the familiar cases of choice between allowing five people in need of organ transplants to die while allowing a healthy potential donor of the needed organs to pass out of our clutches, and preventing the death of those five by fatally dismembering the healthy donor. The shared theory of value can say that each life at stake is of equal commensurable value so that a world in which the five live and the one dies ranks more highly on the value scale than a world in which the five die and the one lives. But the advocate of CA maintains that refraining from saving the five is less wrong (along the crucial moral dimension) than the killing of the one. For only by refraining does one avoid *causing* death. Similarly, the advocate of DE may also share the doctrine of the equal commensurable value of each life at stake while arguing in favor of inaction – the upshot of which ranks lower than the upshot of organ redistribution. For, in saving the five through organ redistribution, the death of that person is intended as one's means – one's course of action would be built upon the use of the one as one's means – while no one's death is intended, as a means or as an end, when the five are allowed to die.

Now CA is much more obviously a principle of causal casuistry than is DE. The former is not a moral dictate. It asserts that allowing is not a species of causing. And, while not itself a moral dictate, it provides a bridge for moving from moral claims about rights (e.g., Alyosha's right to life) to judgments in concrete cases about whether a given action or omission (Alice's not traveling to Bombay) is a violation of rights. Fortunately, however, I will not have to discuss the senses in which DE is, or is not, a principle of causal casuistry. For I shall be proposing a substitute for DE. I shall be proposing, as its replacement, the Principle of Antecedent Peril (AP). And this principle will better fit the profile of a principle of causal casuistry.

Whereas I shall only briefly discuss CA, I shall spend more time discussing the relative merits of DE and AP and the reasons for preferring the latter.

II. TITLE-BASED VS. ACTION-BASED RIGHTS

Unfortunately, before discussing these principles which hook up with ascriptions of rights and allow us to arrive at particular judgments regarding the violation of rights, something must be said about the structure of those rights ascriptions themselves. These remarks about the structure of the rights ascriptions themselves clarify the need to supplement the judgments of rights if one is to arrive at judgments about the permissibility or impermissibility of specific actions. Theories of non-contractual rights proceeding along libertarian lines can be classified as either 'action-based' theories or 'title-based' theories (see [10]). The action-based theories seek to specify, as the most basic ascription of rights, what sorts of actions persons have rights to perform or (more commonly) what sorts of actions persons have rights against. So someone arguing that the most basic right is a right to liberty, i.e., a right against liberty-denying, coercive, actions by others, would fall into the 'action-based' camp. In contrast, someone maintaining that a person's most basic rights were rights over his own body, person and/or life, would fall into the title-based camp.

The action-based program of specifying those actions against which (or to which) persons have rights seems to avoid the need for a separate enterprise of causal casuistry. (This is why I had to use the idioms of title-based theory when I introduced the distinction between one's theory of rights and one's theory of their violation.) For it seems that, from the very statement of Alyosha's action-based rights against Alice, along with a list of the actions performed (or not performed) by Alice, one could determine whether Alice has violated some right of Alyosha. But on two levels we should anticipate the rights theorist being driven back to the title-based approach and to the need for an associated causal casuistry. On the most abstract level, it appears that the action-based approach is parasitic upon the title-based approach in that the crucial notions employed in the former must, it seems, be defined on the basis of the latter. Thus, for instance, the advocate of a fundamental right against liberty-denying actions must specify what counts as liberty-denying in terms of some more basic theory of title-based rights. A necessary precondition of an action counting as liberty-denying for Alyosha is that but for the action Alyosha would still possess or enjoy some R to which he had a right.[3] But not every action which is such that, but for it, Alyosha would still possess or enjoy R violates Alyosha's rights. Hence the need for causal casuistry.

On a less abstract level, consider the action-based strategy of speaking of a right against being killed rather than of a right to life. The common claim is that the 'right against being killed' does not suggest, as the 'right to life' does, that refraining from, e.g., the saving of the five in need of transplants violates the rights of those five. But opting for 'the right not to be killed' over 'the right to life' avoids suggesting that refraining violates rights only so long as a particular bit of causal casuistry is implicitly assumed. In particular what has to be implicitly assumed is precisely that such a refraining is not a killing; that such a refraining is not simply another way of causing death on a causal par with poisoning or throat-slitting. But as soon as this assumption is challenged – as it has been all over the philosophical literature in recent years – the only way to maintain that the refraining does not violate the rights of the five is to argue explicitly for the contrary proposition within causal casuistry, viz., that the refraining does not violate the rights of the five because it does not (even non-robustly) cause their loss of life. But if one does accept this proposition of restrictive causal casuistry, i.e., if one does accept CA, then there is no need to speak of the relevant right as the action-based right not to be killed. That right is the title-based right to life, and it is not violated (says the advocate of CA) by the non-prevention of the loss of life.

Clearly a major issue within causal casuistry is whether inactions or omissions or refrainings cause those evils (or those goods!) which would not have existed had the relevant agents acted in certain specific ways instead of not acting, omitting, or refraining. What I call Jewish causal casuistry, i.e., the impulse to hold people responsible for as many evils as possible, affirms negative causation. Through Jewish causal casuistry, a libertarian-like theory of rights to the effect that individuals have rights to their (respective) bodies and lives yields the conclusion that every (knowing) failure to prevent bodily injury or death violates rights. Since every action which prevents harms precludes other actions which would prevent other harms, such an expansive causal casuistry pictures us as inescapably and constantly having to judge how much harm we shall do (by action or inaction). The best one can ever hope to do is to minimize the harm one does. Given such an expansive causal casuistry, our moral lives could consist only in a ceaseless effort to avoid unnecessary and inefficient inflictions of injury and death.

III. THE CAUSING VS. ALLOWING PRINCIPLE

I have argued at length elsewhere against doctrines of negative causation, against the doctrine that to fail to prevent an untoward upshot is to engage in an alternative method of causing that upshot ([8]). Here I will try to state briefly some of the core reasons against the belief in causation through inaction. Consider again the case of Dr. Alice in Delhi and Alyosha in Bombay. To say that Alice can prevent Alyosha's death is to say that she can intervene into some current, ongoing train of events which otherwise will cause Alyosha's death. That chain of events is causally sufficient for Alyosha's death. Those events do not have to be re-enforced or enhanced by Alice's non-intervention in order for them to eventuate in Alyosha's death. This is made clear by recognizing that, had Alice never existed and, hence, had the possibility of her non-intervention never arisen, that chain of events would threaten Alyosha's life in precisely the same way. Alice's presence in the world with the capacity to intervene in no way alters the causal sufficiency of that independently existing train of events for bringing about Alyosha's death. Thus, when that chain of events does bring about Alyosha's death, it is that chain of events, not that chain plus Alice's omission which causes that death.

To say that Alice can avert Alyosha's death is to say that she can (and knows she can) intervene against certain of the conditions which otherwise will jointly cause Alyosha's death. If the total set of conditions, some of which she can nullify, were not causally sufficient for Alyosha's death, we would not say that she can *avert* that death. It is, therefore, inconsistent to say both that Alice can avert Alyosha's death and that, if she does not do so, her omission joins those other causal conditions making for Alyosha's death without which they would not have been causally sufficient. Our very conception of averting upshots builds on the picture that sometimes causal processes are at work in the world and we can either remain outside of those processes or intervene to disrupt or nullify them. When Alice does not intervene, she does (or does not do) just that. Hence, she remains outside of those causal processes which eventuate in Alyosha's death. Perhaps she can be morally criticized for not intervening, for letting those causal processes bring about what they were causally sufficient to bring about, for not undercutting their causal sufficiency for Alyosha's death. Her non-intervention may show a moral callousness. And, of course, if she was positively obligated to go to Alyosha's aid (by, e.g., having agreed to perform the needed surgery), then her failure to aid would violate Alyosha's positive right to her medical aid. But in the case of simple non-intervention (where no positive duty has been created), it is an error to ascribe causal responsibility for Alyosha's death to Alice. To possess the unexercised capacity to prevent untoward events is not to be causally responsible for those untoward events. Alyosha and his unhappy fate to the contrary notwithstanding, (causally-based) guilt for evils requires more than presence in the world with a capacity to avert those evils. It is because of CA that, although had Alice acted differently Alyosha would not have lost a rightful condition (*viz.*, his life), Alice does not violate Alyosha's rights. It is through CA that we can arrive at a specific judgment about Alice's conduct which we could not arrive at merely on the basis of recognizing Alyosha's right to life.

IV. THE PRINCIPLE OF DOUBLE EFFECT

I turn now to the pursuit of a second principle of causal casuistry – the Principle of Antecedent Peril. In this section I work toward this principle by considering the merits and demerits of the more commonly discussed Principle of Double Effect. I place emphasis on and vindicate the significance of DE's central distinction between intended and merely foreseen effects. But I also point to certain implications of DE which may not seem plausible. In the next section I present and defend an alternative principle AP, which: (a) provides an explanation for the significance of the intended vs. foreseen distinction; (b) fits the profile of a principle of causal casuistry; and (c) avoids the most problematic of DE's implications.

To begin the discussion of DE, consider two cases in each of which you act with the ultimate goal of saving the lives of New Yorkers. Both are, in a sense, public health cases. In the first case, a swarm of mosquitos is approaching New York City from the North. If allowed to arrive in New York, they will transmit a fatal disease to all New Yorkers. Unfortunately, there is only one way to prevent this catastrophe. The swarm can be sprayed as it crosses central Massachusetts. But it is foreseen that this spraying will not destroy the entire swarm. A remnant will be deflected on to Worcester, MA, infecting and causing the death of all of Worcester's population. Nevertheless, you proceed with the spraying.[4] In the second case, the entire population of New York has already been infected with a disease which will be fatal unless they are treated with a medication which can only be made out of the vital organs of the inhabitants of Worcester. The Worcesterians can be dismembered and processed painlessly and without anxiety-producing warning. You proceed to produce the vitally needed medication.

DE, on reflection quite correctly, draws a bright moral line between these two actions. It allows the first in which the Worcesterian deaths are foreseen but are in no way aimed at or employed as your means. But it disallows the second in which the deadly processing of the Worcesterians is aimed at, is employed as your means. The plausibility of DE and its implications in these cases is connected with the idea that what one is doing (or what one is characterized as doing for the purpose of moral evaluation) is crucially determined by what one's intention is. In dismembering the citizens of Worcester one would be bringing about the deaths of innocent bystanders in a way in which one would not be were one to spray that swarm or otherwise deflect it on to Worcester. The two instances of causally contributing to the deaths of innocents would be different in kind because their *intended* effects would be different in kind. An intended effect of an action is not what the agent happens to envisage at the moment of action. Rather, it is a goal – albeit, perhaps, only an intermediate goal employed for some further end – which calls forth and contours the agent's action. Thus, it is characterized as a 'direct' effect of the action: it is that toward which the act is directed. In contrast, a 'second' effect is incidental to the action, in that it plays no role in calling it forth or guiding its structure. The agent would be acting in precisely the same way even if that second effect were not an upshot of his activity. Incidental as it is to the action and its structure, an unintended effect is merely an 'indirect' effect of that action.

For instance, your spraying that mosquito swarm is not in any way done in response to the existence of Worcesterians. But quite the contrary is true vis-a-vis the Worcesterians if you choose to save the New Yorkers by utilizing the Worcesterians' bodies. In the first case, you act precisely as you would had there been no Worcesterians. In the second case, your plan of action is directed at those unfortunates. You do what you do in order to get hold of them and process their internal organs. Were they to become aware of your plans and attempt to flee, you would have to change your plans in order to capture them. Although dismembering the Worcesterians is not something you would be pursuing as an ultimate end, this dismemberment would be sought by you as your chosen means to the end of saving the New Yorkers. If you save the New Yorkers through pursuit of the Worcesterians, you must, in some sense, take it to be a good thing that the Worcesterians are there to be used as your means. In contrast, choosing to save the New Yorkers by spraying the mosquito swarm (and deflecting its remnants) in no way involves your taking the presence of the ill-fated Worcesterians to be a good thing.

DE has been subject to a number of well-known criticisms. One crucial family of criticisms focuses on the question of how morally significant is the difference between acting such that a death foreseen by you ensues and acting such that a death intended by you ensues. After all – despite what has just been said in the way of distinguishing the two cases of saving New Yorkers – in both cases, were you to choose to act, you would be willing (under the circumstances) to have the Worcesterians die, while in neither case would you be happy about these deaths. It is sometimes suggested that our inclination to differentiate morally between cases such as these is not due to any morally significant difference between intended and (merely) foreseen untoward upshots. Rather, it is suggested that this inclination to differentiate merely reflects different degrees of causal proximity between the actions under consideration and their respective fatal upshots, and that such differences in causal proximity are not morally significant.

Consider, however, a minor variant of the mosquito threat to New York. Suppose that you spray such a swarm and, in the process, divert its remnants to Worcester *for the sake of causing the deaths of the Worcesterians*. You act with the intention of causing those deaths and make use of the swarm and the deflecting effect of your spraying devices to bring about those deaths. The deaths of the Worcesterians is what you are aiming at, is that toward which you are directing your action. It is the purpose which calls forth and contours your action (though it need not be your ultimate purpose). In the sense of causal distance employed in the objection to the significance of the intended vs. foreseen distinction, the causal distance between each of your deflecting acts and its upshot for the Worcesterians is the same. But this equality of causal distance does not eliminate the sense that there is a significant moral difference between the actions such that the first of these acts is permissible while the second of these acts is impermissible – a difference which it is reasonable to continue to believe is linked to the foreseen vs. intended distinction.

So far so good for DE. But it has long been noted, even by philosophers prepared to be sympathetic with DE, that DE seems to allow other savings of lives which are accompanied by foreseen (but not intended deaths) which should not be allowed. Consider the following case: Bob and Barbie are critically ill roommates in a hospital. You can save them only by the release into their room of a gas which is fatal to anyone not suffering from their particular disease. Unfortunately, Beau is the third roommate. He has recently returned to health and is about to be discharged. But the gas must be released immediately, before Beau can leave the room, if it is to save Bob and Barbie. You release that fatal (to Beau) gas.[5] Now, if any evil effect is foreseen but not intended, in the general spirit of DE, it is the death of Beau in this example. DE seems to allow your so causing the death of Beau. But I take it that your causing this death is *not* permissible. But how can one maintain that this causing of death is impermissible, while spraying/deflecting the mosquito swarm on the way to New York is permissible?

It is, of course, true in this gassing, as in the dismemberment of the Worcesterians, that you would be *causing* death and not merely failing to prevent death. An advocate of CA may claim that this is why these two acts are impermissible in contrast to the permissibility of Dr. Alice's failing to save Alyosha. But this point cannot be too comforting to the advocate of DE who, after all, sets out to argue that sometimes it is permissible to contribute causally to an innocent bystander's death – e.g., to the foreseen but unintended deaths of the Worcesterians. In fact, a principle like DE can be seen as modifying the stringency of CA. For CA, combined with an assignment of serious (i.e., at least fairly absolute) rights to life, seems to rule out any causal contribution to the death of innocent bystanders, while a principle such as DE maintains that certain types of contribution to such deaths may not be impermissible. Indeed, perhaps the most famous (notorious?) use of DE in a medical context has been to argue to a special group of *exceptions* to a general moral ban on killing fetuses. It is argued that, while in general it is wrong to kill fetuses because this is causing or intentionally causing the death of innocent *persons*, it is permissible to administer medical treatment to a seriously ill pregnant woman even if it is known that the medical treatment will result in the death of the fetus. (The key, of course, for the advocate of DE is that the medical treatment be precisely, or at least essentially,[6] what would have been administered to the woman even had she not been pregnant.) Since DE and principles like it have the function of modifying CA, CA can hardly be invoked to limit (modify) the implications of DE.

So we have a dual problem with the implications of DE. First, DE properly allows certain actions which causally contribute to deaths of innocent bystanders and thus requires exceptions to a moral drawn from CA that one must refrain from foreseen causal contribution to the deaths of innocent bystanders. But since it is at least dubious that DE is a principle of causal casuistry, it is hard to see how an exception based upon DE can link up with and modify the moral drawn from CA. Far better if we had a principle which identified the acts properly allowed by DE as causally insignificant contributions to losses of rights. For then we could see how such acts would not violate the moral rule against (robustly) causally contributing to the deaths of innocent bystanders. Second, DE improperly allows certain other actions which causally contribute to the deaths of innocents, e.g., Beau. What is needed, therefore, is an alternative principle which discriminates between the acts properly and improperly allowed by DE.

V. THE PRINCIPLE OF ANTECEDENT PERIL

I turn now to the alternative to DE, the Principle of Antecedent Peril (AP). I want to show how AP provides a causally casuistic account of the moral line between the two cases of unfortunate Worcesterians. And, at the same time, AP does not yield the permissibility of your indirectly gassing poor Beau. In their *Causation in the Law* [7],[7] Hart and Honoré discuss what types of intermediate events between the occurrence of an earlier event X and a later event Y 'negatives' the causal connection between X and Y. It is clear that, even when such negativing obtains, X may remain a necessary causal condition of Y. It is the status of antecedent cause X as the primary or substantial cause of Y that is negatived. If such a negativing of causal connection does not occur, then primary causal responsibility for Y continues to go back to X and not merely to some event (or action) which mediates the causal connection between X and Y.

Hart and Honoré hold that, except in special cases such as those involving inducement, intervening voluntary actions negative causal connections. One of their examples is as follows. If I put poison in Jones' coffee and, unaware of this poison, Jones drinks the coffee and dies, then I have killed Jones. However, if Jones is aware of the poison and, nevertheless, 'deliberately' drinks the coffee, he is a suicide. I will not have killed Jones (absent some elaborate truth about my having preyed upon his psychological weakness and peculiarities).

The hard question is whether Jones' being aware of the poison and, hence, his *foreseeing* his death should he drink the coffee suffices for his 'deliberate' act of drinking the poisoned coffee to break the causal chain going back to my poisoning of the coffee. Or does Jones have to drink that coffee with the *intention* of ingesting the poison for the connection between my poisoning the coffee and Jones' death to be negatived? If intermediate intention, but not intermediate foresight, negatives causal connection, then when you deflect the swarm to Worcester with the intention of infecting its inhabitants you negative the causal link back to the swarm itself while, in contrast, when you deflect the swarm away from New York with the (mere) foresight that its remnant will infect Worcester you do not negative the causal connection back to the antecedent peril. So, if intermediate intention, but not intermediate foresight, negatives causal connection, primary causal responsibility will lie with you when you intend the infection of the Worcesterians, while, in contrast, when you deflect the swarm away from New York with the (mere) foresight of Worcesterian fatalities, primary causal responsibility lies with the antecedent peril, the swarm itself.

Unfortunately, Hart and Honoré themselves seem to hold that even intermediate foresight negatives causal connection. For they seem to hold that for Jones to take the poison 'deliberately', and thereby break the causal connection, it is enough that he know the poison is there in his coffee ([4], p. 12; see also [3]). On this basis one would have to say that in each swarm-deflection case primary causal responsibility goes back only to you, the intermediate agent. Thus, on their specific version of the doctrine that deliberate intermediate action negatives causal connection, one could not distinguish between your causal responsibility in these two cases. In both, in virtue of your intermediate action, the antecedent peril would be causally off the hook. But I dispute their particular interpretation of negativing intervening events.

I maintain that Jones deliberately consumes the poison in a way that breaks the link between my poisoning the coffee and his death only if Jones *intends* to consume the poison. It is difficult, in the example as given, to imagine Jones bringing about his foreseen death by poison without the intention of doing so. So let us slightly change the case. Suppose the poison causes a painful one week illness from which the victim fully recovers. Suppose also that Jones has, prior to the poisoning, negotiated a contract with some third party to receive a $10,000 payment for drinking that coffee which sits before him. Now it is easy to imagine that Jones might knowingly consume the poison, foreseeing the painful illness, without at all intending to consume the poison or undergo the illness. He drinks coffee in order to collect the $10,000 – just as he would have, had the poison never been placed in the coffee. Although he foresees the consumption of the poison and the illness, neither prospect plays any (positive) role in guiding or explaining his action [8].[8]

Suppose Jones does consume that unhappily poisoned coffee. He does not thereby deliberately bring about the illness through a voluntary act which negatives my causal responsibility for his subsequent suffering. I remain primarily causally responsible for his painful illness. Similarly, if I construct a chamber of horrors along the route through which someone must pass if he is to escape a concentration camp, the causal responsibility for his injuries in that chamber is mine even when he knows full well what awaits him on that route. Only if Jones or the prisoner act with the intention of undergoing those painful episodes do their actions negative the chain of responsibility leading back to me. Intending an untoward effect, but not (merely) foreseeing it, negatives the causal link back to the antecedent perilous condition and its author. Only if Jones and the escapee are masochists am I causally off the hook.

AP and DE both employ the distinction between intended and foreseen effects. But the former, unlike the latter, is a principle of causal casuistry. AP, unlike DE, speaks to the issue of whether an agent's action is the primary cause of some untoward upshot. Even if that untoward upshot is the loss of a rightful condition – e.g., the Worcesterians' loss of their lives – an agent's causal role in that loss may fall sufficiently short of being robust that the agent cannot be said *to violate the rights* of the unfortunate losers. Only when the causal connection back to the antecedent peril is negatived by the agent's actions so that the primary causal responsibility only passes back to that agent, is that agent's causal role sufficiently robust for us to say that he does violate the rights of those who have lost their lives.

The relevance of the intended vs. foreseen distinction within the doctrine of AP is that an act with the intended result of a death will undercut (negative) the causal status of the inevitably injurious setting which presented that death as a possible intended result, while an act with the (merely) foreseen result of a death will not undercut (negative) the causal status of the horrible setting. The theoretical intuition is that when people are confronted with inescapably death-dealing circumstances, responsibility for ensuing deaths can be attributed to the circumstances (or, better yet, if possible, to an author of those circumstances), and hence not to the intermediate agents, as long as the ensuing deaths are not intended by the relevant agents. When one is acting within such an imposed and inescapably death-dealing context, one's action does not negate the situation's primary causal responsibility for an ensuing death unless that death (or the wrongful injury or risk which produced it) is a formative goal of one's action.[9]

AP, then, provides an explanation for the significance of the intended vs. foreseen distinction. Moreover, since it is a principle of causal casuistry, we can readily understand how it can modify the Causing vs. Allowing Principle. It allows us to identify certain instances of playing a causal role in bringing about the loss of a rightful condition in which the primary causal responsibility still rests with an antecedent peril so that the intermediate agent should not be said to violate rights.

Furthermore, AP provides an explanation for why the standard (i.e., non-intentional) deflection cases are so easy, i.e., why it is easy for us to accept the permissibility of your deflecting the remnant of the swarm away from New York and of Judith Thomson's trolley passenger's act of turning the runaway trolley away from the track with five innocents trapped on it onto a track with one innocent trapped on it. For, in these cases, there is a clear sense in which the very dangerous condition which threatened the New Yorkers or threatened the five is what, in fact, causes the Worcesterians' death or the death of the one. AP is an improvement over DE because it accommodates our sense that a major part of what vindicates you and the trolley passenger is your each being confronted with an inevitably deadly situation.

What, however, does AP tell us about the gassing of poor Beau who unfortunately shares that hospital room with Bob and Barbie? DE is questionable precisely because it allows the indirect gassing of Beau. But especially when one is thinking in terms of DE, it is hard to see how to allow the spraying/deflection of the mosquito swarm with foreknowledge of the deaths in Worcester and still disallow the unintended gassing of Beau. But, in light of the causal focus of AP, one can differentiate these two cases. There are two respects, in the case of Beau's death, that the role of an independent antecedent peril is less than the role of such a peril in the deaths of the Worcesterians. First, in the case of Beau's death, you would not be deflecting an already oncoming gas away from Bob and Barbie and (unfortunately and incidentally) on to Beau. You would be *introducing* the gas. Although, but for your spraying the swarm as it moves toward New York, its remnant would not arrive in Worcester, there is still a clear sense in which the dangerous mosquitos which infect the Worcesterians are not introduced by you. (In Thomson's language, you only play a role in distributing this pre-existing evil.[10])

Second, in the case of your gassing Beau it is natural for us to suppose that you are a physician or other health professional working in association with the hospital and that, therefore, either you or others with whom you are institutionally associated are responsible for Beau's being in that room. You cannot claim, therefore, that poor Beau just happens to be there precisely as the unfortunate Worcesterians just happen to be in the swarm's deflection path. It is partially because of your prior actions, or those with whom you are institutionally associated, that the release of the gas is perilous for Beau. Thus, there are two respects in which your causal connection with Beau's death would be tighter, more significant, more robust, than it would be with the deaths of the Worcesterians. I believe that, although it is hard to say with precision why, this more robust causal connection is the basis for our sense that releasing the gas which eventuates in Beau's death is impermissible (is a violation of Beau's right to life) while, horrendous as it is, the spraying/deflection of the swarm on to Worcester which effectuates in the death of its inhabitants is permissible (is not a violation of their rights to life).[11]

VI. CONCLUSION

It is a mistake to think that, in all cases of reaching specific moral judgments about particular actions, one need only instantiate some general moral dictate. This is not true with regard to judgments about whether a particular action violates rights. One's moral dictates will indicate whether someone's right is at stake, whether a prospective loss would be the loss of a rightful condition. But, in order to determine whether some agent counts as violating rights, one must also determine the causal relationship (or lack thereof) between that agent's acts or omissions and the other party's loss. Only if the agent robustly causes the loss can it be said that he has violated the second party's rights. I have tried to illustrate this complementary structure of moral principles and causal casuistry by stating, utilizing and defending two principles of causal casuistry, the Allowing vs. Causing Principle and the Principle of Antecedent Peril. The latter principle, in particular, needs much more clarification than I have provided in this essay, in which my primary goal has been to illustrate the need for *some* principles of causal casuistry if ascriptions of rights are going to be translated into concrete judgments about the permissibility or impermissibility of particular actions.

NOTES

[1] I speak of 'potential' patient Alyosha to emphasize that Alice and Alyosha have not entered into any special voluntary relationship which generates a special obligation on Alice's part to come to Alyosha's aid. The belief that positive obligations to aid and, correlatively, positive rights to aid only arise through special voluntary relationships is, of course, a crucial component of the libertarian rights view, the application of which to concrete cases we are investigating in this essay.

[2] Since the deontologist's contention will precisely be that certain of the upshots which the consequentialist wants to count should not count as consequences of the actions being evaluated,

and since the label 'consequentialism' inherently suggests that these upshots are consequences, fairness bids us to adopt a more neutral label of 'upshotism'.

[3] Both hostile and friendly commentators on libertarian rights theory have argued that a right against coercion (or against interference or to liberty) cannot be the most fundamental libertarian right because coercion (or interference or liberty) must itself be defined in terms of some independent specification of (title-based) rights. See, e.g., [5] and [6].

[4] Cases involving the deflection of a danger or evil from its original path but on to equally innocent bystanders, especially on to the long-suffering inhabitants of Worcester, are extensively discussed in [1]. The original deflection of the runaway trolley case, along with the original case of saving the five through transplants made possible by harvesting organs from a sixth (unwilling) person appears in [2].

[5] The case is a slight variant of a case described by Foot in [1].

[6] The 'essentially' is supposed to allow us to slide past the following complication. The pregnant woman's independent medical problem would normally be treated with drug A. But the pregnancy itself so changes her body chemistry that drug A would be ineffective as a treatment for her problem. So the indicated treatment becomes drug B – not 'precisely' what would have been done had she not been pregnant. And, worse yet, imagine that only drug B is fatal to fetuses.

[7] See [4], especially Chapter III, 'Causation and Responsibility', pp. 58–78 and Chapter VI, 'The Law of Tort: Causing Harm', pp. 126–170. The next several paragraphs draw heavily on [9].

[8] Contrast this with the case in which Jones has been promised $ 10,000.00 if he consumes poison and, to his great good fortune, I come along and dump some otherwise unavailable poison into his coffee. He then drinks the potion before him (partially at least) in order to collect on this promise. Here I will not have imposed the poisoning upon Jones.

[9] Even such intention on the part of the intermediate agent may not shift responsibility to that agent. An intermediate intentional act resulting in death may not negative the primary causal responsibility of a diabolical first agent who has thoroughly and purposively orchestrated the intermediary agent's activity. See the discussion of Jim and the commandant in [9].

[10] More, but I am unsure what, should be said about our sense that, while it is permissible to 'distribute' an evil to A rather than to B and even rather than merely to let it fall on B, it is not permissible to redistribute it from A to B. It is not, e.g., permissible to extract the infecting agent out of A to whom it has already been (permissibly or 'naturally') 'distributed' if that extraction puts the infecting agent into B.

[11] In [9], I extend this analysis, in the name of a Principle of Antecedent Causation, to foreseen, but unintended deaths which occur in the course of self-defensive actions. The problem is that only in fantasy cases can one's deployment of defensive force consist in deflecting toward the aggressors the dangerous missiles which they have introduced. If one could do so, then as long as one directed that deflection at the aggressors and one had played no role in the innocent bystanders being fatally close to those aggressors, one would have a case precisely parallel to the tragic, but permissible, deflection of the swarm on to Worcester. One would not have introduced the dangerous stuff as one would have in the gassing case. But do real world defenders who, in responding to acts of aggression and directing their destructive efforts at the aggressor's forces, utilize their own (counterforce) weapons count as introducing new perils (as you do in the gassing case)? And if this is so, is such defensive action impermissible even when it is directed solely at aggressors and the defenders are not responsible for the location of the innocents?

74   ERIC MACK

BIBLIOGRAPHY

[1] Foot, P.: 1977, 'Euthanasia', *Philosophy and Public Affairs* **6**, 85–122.
[2] Foot, P.: 1975, 'The Problem of Abortion and the Doctrine of Double Effect', in J. H. Rachels (ed.), *Moral Problems*, Second Edition, Harper and Row, New York, pp. 59–70.
[3] Hart, H. L. A.: 1968, 'Intuition and Responsibility', *Punishment and Responsibility*, Oxford University Press, Oxford.
[4] Hart, H. L. A. and Honoré, A. M.: 1959, *Causation of the Law*, Clarendon Press, Oxford.
[5] Kelley, D.: 1984, 'Life, Liberty and Property', *Social Philosophy and Policy* **1**, 108–118.
[6] LaFollette, H.: 1978, 'Why Libertarianism is Mistaken,' in J. Arthur and W. Shaw (eds.), *Justice and Economic Distribution*, Prentice-Hall, Englewood-Cliffs, N.J., pp. 194–206.
[7] Mack, E.: 1980, 'Bad Samaritan and Causation of Harm', *Philosophy and Public Affairs* **9**, 230–239.
[8] Mack, E.: 1984, 'Deontologism, Negative Causation and the Duty to Rescue', in E. Regis (ed.), *Gewirth's Ethical Relativism*, University of Chicago Press, Chicago, pp. 147–166.
[9] Mack, E.: 1986, 'Three Ways of Killing Innocent Bystanders: Some Conundrums Concerning the Morality of War', *Social Philosophy and Policy* **3**, 1–26.
[10] Steiner, H.: 1977, 'The Structure of a Set of Compossible Rights', *The Journal of Philosophy* **74**, 767–775.
[11] Thomson, J.: 1976, 'Killing, Letting Die and the Trolley Problem', *The Monist* **59**, 204–217.

Tulane University
New Orleans, Louisiana

BART K. GRUZALSKI

DEATH BY OMISSION

In his 'Moral Rights and Causal Casuistry', Professor Eric Mack articulates a theory of what he calls 'causal casuistry' that he labels 'restrictive'.[1] One of the central principles of Mack's 'restrictive' view of causality is the 'Causing versus Allowing Principle' (hereafter, 'CA') according to which 'there is a morally significant difference between *causing* a death and *allowing* a death' ([10], p. 59). I shall argue that CA is false and that the view of causality articulated by Professor Mack disguises the richness and complexity of what we do or fail to do.

I. MACK'S DEFENSE OF THE VIEW THAT OMISSIONS ARE NOT CAUSES

As part of his support of CA Professor Mack defends the underlying theoretical claim that to fail to prevent an event by performing an alternative action is not to cause that event. If this underlying theoretical claim is false, then so is CA, since allowing a death will be one way of causing it. Professor Mack defends this crucial claim as follows:

To say that Alice can prevent Alyosha's death is to say that she can intervene into some current, ongoing train of events which otherwise will cause Alyosha's death. That chain of events is causally sufficient for Alyosha's death. Those events do not have to be re-enforced or enhanced by Alice's non-intervention in order for them to eventuate in Alyosha's death. This is made clear by recognizing that, had Alice never existed and, hence, had the possibility of her non-intervention never arisen, that chain of events would threaten Alyosha's life in precisely the same way. Alice's presence in the world with the capacity to intervene in no way alters the causal sufficiency of that independently existing train of events for bringing about Alyosha's death. Thus, when that chain of events does bring about Alyosha's death, it is that chain of events, not that chain plus Alice's omission, which causes that death ([10], p. 63).

The causal principle allegedly supported by the example – that the act of allowing a death is never a cause of that death – is open to counterexample. To show that this general causal claim is false, we will focus on the following variation of the above example (in Mack's own variation Alyosha is an adult in one city and Alice a physician in another who chooses to go to a party rather than save him). Suppose that Alyosha is a three-month-old infant who has been found by Alice in a hotel room which she has rented for the evening

75

Baruch A. Brody (ed.), Moral Theory and Moral Judgments in Medical Ethics, 75–85.
© *1988 by Kluwer Academic Publishers.*

and that the infant will die if it is not given water within a few hours. If Alice fails to provide water for the infant or in some other way to get help for the infant, there is no question that her failure to aid the infant is a cause of the infant's death.[2] The same causal story applies if Alyosha happens to be a kitten in Alice's apartment, or a plant, or any living creature that was not able to prevent its own death without some help or cooperation from Alice. In short, the general causal claim imbedded in the example – that allowing a death is not a way of causing that death – is false, at least over the range of cases just examined.

There is a more specific causal claim in Mack's discussion of the above example that is also false. Mack writes that "Alice's presence in the world with the capacity to intervene in no way alters the causal sufficiency of that independently existing train of events for bringing about Alyosha's death" ([10], p. 63). However, contrary to Mack's claim, that Alice has the option to prevent Alyosha's death *does* alter the potential causal sufficiency of the *otherwise* independently existing train of events that would have brought about the death. If Alice were to intervene, these causal factors would not be causally sufficient to bring about the death, the death would not occur and, hence, it follows that Alice's non-intervention is required for the death to come about.[3] The underlying problem with Mack's view of causality is that it bypasses the background situations within which we find ourselves and which imbue our actions and omissions with causal efficacy. On his view we have a "picture that sometimes causal processes are at work in the world and we can either remain outside of those processes or intervene to disrupt or nullify them. When Alice does not intervene, she does (or does not do) just that. Hence, she remains outside of those causal processes which eventuate in Alyosha's death" ([10], p. 63). But by remaining outside of *those specific causal processes*, which really serve as a background for her own choice of action, Alice does cause the death in question. Mack seems to assume that an action or omission can be the cause of an event only if it is causally sufficient for that event all by itself. But actions or omissions do not cause events all by themselves, rather they do so *only* against the background of real conditions that imbue the agent's action with a causal efficacy – even if that causal efficacy is not voluntarily chosen.

II. THE ORTHODOX ACCOUNT OF CAUSES AND BACKGROUND CONDITIONS

Consider the following noncontroversial example. When we say that striking the match caused the fire we are not saying that striking the match alone caused the fire – after all, if there had been no oxygen present or if the fuel had been soaking wet there would have been no fire even if the match had been struck. Rather, in these ordinary causal contexts when we say that X was the cause of Y we are distinguishing the factor X from the other causally relevant factors which we sometimes refer to as 'background conditions'. In our match example, striking the match causes the fire only against the background of a number of causally relevant conditions that include oxygen and a suitable fuel. Or consider a second example. When we say that Alex's way of pulling out of his driveway caused the accident, we are not pretending that the truck coming up the street was not also a causal factor in the accident. Rather, the truck's coming down the road, along with a long list of conditions that include each driver's reaction time and the relevant braking times, constitute the background conditions against which Alex's careless action is properly identified as *the cause* of the accident.

According to recent accounts of how to distinguish between causes and background conditions, a causal factor is correctly regarded as the cause of some event only if it differentiates the situation in which the effect occurs (the *effect-situation*) from similar actual or hypothetical situations (*comparison-situations*) that include all the other causally relevant factors in the effect-situation.[4] For example, suppose someone wants to know why Jones became overwhelmingly grief-stricken after the destruction of the shuttle Challenger, whereas most other citizens who were not working on the project or who did not know any of the victims personally only felt sad and shocked. In this context of inquiry we are asking what factor differentiates Jones from these other citizens who were not deeply grief-stricken. Such a factor might be, for example, that Jones had an unresolved grief that expressed itself in the context of the nation's grief over the loss of the shuttle. Of course, many other factors contributed to the effect: that humans grieve when we suffer losses, that the shuttle's destruction was a perceived loss, and so on. These other factors are not themselves the cause, for they do not, whereas Jones' unresolved grief does, allow us to differentiate the effect-situation in which Jones experienced overwhelming grief from the comparison-situations in which people did not experience overwhelming grief but were aware of the shuttle disaster. Rather, these causal factors are the background conditions against which we can and do identify Jones' unresolved grief over a previous loss as the cause of his overwhelming grief at the destruction of the shuttle. This rough explanation of how causes are identified, although incomplete, allows us to return to our more controversial examples.

If we follow Mack's view, there is a *causal* difference between causing a patient's death and simply letting a patient die whose life could be extended. But consider a patient who is suffering from an end-stage carcinoma and is ready to die. Suppose that this patient contracts pneumonia, the pneumonia is untreated, and the patient dies. What is the cause of the patient's death? What we identify as the cause of death will depend on our selection of comparison-situations. If we are comparing this patient with others with an advanced carcinoma, we would identify the pneumonia as the differentiating factor and would properly identify the pneumonia as the cause of death. On the other hand, if we compared this patient with others who had an advanced carcinoma *and* pneumonia, we would properly identify the failure to treat the pneumonia as the differentiating factor and thus as the cause of death. Both choices of comparison situations are appropriate. If we are asking what physiological disease caused the death, we identify the pneumonia as the cause. If we are asking what (if any) social factor caused the death, we identify the failure to treat as the cause. There is no oddity in identifying both a physiological event and an action or omission as the cause of death [2]. For example, we would have no problem in doing so in a similar case if the carcinoma were treatable and the failure to treat the pneumonia were either an oversight or a deliberate act. In the modified example, as in the original example, the failure to treat *and* the pneumonia are each correctly identified as causes of death.

The conclusion of our discussion of the orthodox account of causality is that the theoretical underpinning of CA is false. There is no moral difference between causing versus simply permitting a death to occur *because* permitting a death to occur is a way of causing that death. Granted, we do tend to feel that allowing a creature to die is less morally significant than causing the creature's death by smashing, cutting, or shooting, but this feeling can be explained. First, most deaths caused by smashing, cutting or shooting are unexpected, violent, and against the victim's wishes, whereas most 'lettings die' of which we take note are benevolently motivated and are often at the wishes of the deceased.[5] Second, and as I've discussed elsewhere ([7], p. 97), in learning about the morality of causing death we first learn about smashing and cutting, and only later about the more subtle but equally efficacious ways of causing death by starvation and dehydration. That we first learn not to cut and smash, and only later not to starve or dehydrate, also helps explain the feeling that the former ways of causing death are more odious than the latter. Nonetheless, to fail to prevent an event by performing an alternative action *is* to cause the event in question.

It may be objected that this conclusion rests on cases like our revision of the Alyosha example, but when we consider Mack's original example we are not inclined to believe that Alice has caused Alyosha's death even given the background conditions of her action. According to the objection, there were many doctors who could have saved Alyosha's life, as well as many other people and other possible intervening processes, and it is arbitrary to pick out Alice's omission as the culprit. We are more inclined to say that Alyosha died because of 'natural causes' and, if we need to add more, that he was in a society in which people are frequently allowed to die of preventable causes. But these observations will not save Mack's theoretical claim. It may be that there are many people in Alice's situation equally responsible – much as the omissions of each of two parents may each be properly identified as the cause of a child's death. Furthermore, it is difficult to feel certain about the causal connections between Alice, who is in one city, and Alyosha, who is in another, and this tends to undermine any intuitive certainty that Alyosha would not have died had Alice tried to help him. If we cannot feel certain about that, we obviously cannot expect to feel certain that Alice caused Alyosha's death. However, if we can firmly implant in our imaginations the presupposed background conditions against which Alyosha dies only if Alice does not help him, and does not die if she does, then the case is no different causally than the revised case in which Alyosha finds a severely dehydrated three-month-old infant in her hotel room. She can, in both cases, omit helping Alyosha, but in each case the result is a death which, given the background conditions, is caused by her omission.[6]

III. THE CAUSAL EFFICACY OF OMISSIONS IN THE MEDICAL CONTEXT

Another objection to our account focuses on the fact that many of the examples we used in its support assume the person, whose failure to act causes a death, had an obligation to care for the victim of his or her failure to act.[7] It is true that we supported the orthodox account with cases in which people cause harm by not feeding their pets, by not watering their plants, and by not taking care of themselves or their families. The objection focuses on these cases by claiming that a failure to act causes a preventable death (or other event) *only* when there was a *background obligation* to act in the way in question. When we are talking about pets, plants, ourselves, or family we are talking about entities for which we have an obligation to care, and in those cases the failure to care does differentiate between the situation in which this obligation is properly carried out and the situation in which it is not. To generalize from these examples to all cases in which omissions can be identified as differentiating between situations in which the effect occurs from other situations in which the effect does not occur is to miss the fact that omissions are properly labelled as causes only when the background conditions include the obligation to care. Take that away, according to the objection, and omissions are not causes.

There are two responses to this objection. The first is that this discussion and the examples about which we are concerned, including the pneumonia example above, occur in the *medical context* in which *there is a presumption of the obligation to care for the patient*. The objection has no force in this context, since whenever some deterioration is preventable it is under the control of the medical staff in a situation in which there is an obligation to care [9], pp. 35–36). As a dying physician wrote in the *New England Journal of Medicine*, "attention from the first breath of life through the last breath is the doctor's work; the last breath is no less important than the first" [16]. As this quotation emphasizes, in the medical context the events of dying that are preventable are no longer some causal process happening independently of the medical staff and its actions but are part of the physician's obligations toward the patient. The obligation to care for a patient may, in fact, obligate the staff not to prevent the patient's death, and such an obligation is consistent with the causal claim that the lack of prevention of an avoidable death is a cause of that death. It is for this very reason that what is commonly referred to as voluntary *active* euthanasia is not morally more or less significant in itself than voluntary *passive* euthanasia. As others have pointed out, in some cases so-called active euthanasia may, for reasons of patient preference and the avoidance of unwanted suffering, be morally preferable [13]. Although this is not the place to begin a full-fledged discussion of euthanasia, it is relevant to point out that deaths are often to be caused by a medical staff, if only by non-intervention, especially when the patient wants to die and is end-stage. The main point of this discussion, however, is not to raise the issues about conditions under which it is morally permissible to cause the deaths of a patient by omission or commission, but rather that *in the medical context there are background obligations for patient care against which permitting an avoidable death is a way of causing that death.*

There is a second, more abstract response to this objection.[8] If we are looking for a value-neutral way of distinguishing between omissions that are causally relevant and those that are not, we need to choose one in which we have not already presupposed the obligations in question in the background conditions. This means that we need to select our comparison-situations in such a way that our selection procedure does not rely on any presumed moral obligation. One candidate suggested for such a selection procedure is: in a moral context of inquiry, a situation is a comparison-situation if the kind of effect occurring in the effect-situation is avoidable in the proposed comparison-situation given the agent's skills and the available technology. The reason supporting this value-neutral selection procedure is that we want to know the causal situation *prior to* making moral assessments, and if our causal story presupposes a moral account, that becomes impossible. If we limit our causal judgments by the limitations of presupposed moral obligations, then we prevent ourselves from being able to assess omissions we currently consider to be morally neutral. If we did that we would turn moral theory from a way of exploring what we are to do into an apology for what society, or custom, dictates.[9]

IV. WHY VIEWING OMISSIONS AS CAUSES IS UNFAMILIAR

The view of the world that is revealed by the above analysis of singular causal explanation is not complex, but it is somewhat unfamiliar. It is in part unfamiliar because it requires us to appreciate and apply accurately an *analysis* of what it means to identify a causal factor as a cause of some event. This analysis, albeit clear and well established both in the law and in common usage ([9], [11]), is not as familiar as the naive view that for something to be the cause of an event it must be independently sufficient, all by itself, for that event. Stabbing someone through the heart is typically sufficient to cause death, whereas failing to provide fluids is not – someone else might provide fluids, including the person or animal itself. It takes a degree of clarity to see that the act of failing to provide fluids, given certain background conditions, is as much a cause of death as severing heart muscle. It also takes a development in clarity to realize that no factor is independently sufficient to cause death. A causal factor is sufficient for a death only given those background conditions against which the effect in fact will occur. Even stabbing someone through the heart, given conditions in which there is sophisticated medical expertise available (and perhaps a heart suitable for transplanting), might not result in death.

The view that omissions can cause death is also unfamiliar because we tend to learn of it only after we have learned about more obvious causal connections. Smashing a bird's head with a stone is obviously the cause of its death, or at least obvious enough that once a person experiences that kind of killing he or she will tend to be aware of the causal efficacy of throwing stones at birds or other animals. Children do have to learn that small animals are vulnerable to serious injury and even death from being tossed about, having things thrown at them, and so on. But this learning is much more straightforward and obvious than the fact that death can be caused by not feeding or providing adequate water for these animals. The difference in degree between these ways of causing death explains in part why we think of the most obvious forms of causing death – e.g., crushing or stabbing – as 'causing death', and the less obvious ways of causing death as 'letting die'.

An additional explanation of why our intuitions do not initially correspond with the orthodox causal account is due to the advances of modern medicine. For thousands of years parents have known that it is possible, by failing to give fluids to a child, to cause that child to die. But recently modern medicine has provided techniques which are as equally efficacious as water in preventing the deaths of children, and so by failing to provide these techniques we in fact cause these deaths. But our tradition-based causal *intuitions* do not automatically take these medical advances into account, and so we are likely to *feel* more comfortable in identifying failing to provide an infant with fluids as the cause of death than in identifying failing to provide renal dialysis as the cause.[10] Yet both acts are causes of death, and that we are less familiar with some of the current causally efficacious ways of preventing death does not undermine their causal efficacy.

Finally, it is worth pointing out that the view that omissions are never causes is often quite convenient for us and thus a degree of self-deception makes it harder for us to see clearly that this view is false. We begin by learning that smashing a pet's head is a way of causing its death, and only later that failing to feed the pet is equally a way of causing its death. But such learning only comes later, and often only at the cost of giving up many beliefs that are otherwise convenient for us – specifically that we are responsible for events that we could prevent, although often at the cost of extra awareness, effort, or sacrifice. Just as the child learns that starving a pet is a way of causing its death, so we learn that failing to prevent a death in the medical context is to cause it. Just as the child's lesson brings new responsibilities and illuminations, so does ours.

Our conclusion is that the idea of a causal casuistry or a category of rights outside of which we might act with impunity is an illusion, along with the notion that some causes are more 'robust' than others. A cause produces an effect given certain background conditions, however much or little our intuitions label it 'robust'. As a result, we have many more responsibilities than the libertarian would have us think, largely because we live in a world that is causally more complex and subtle than the libertarian wants to believe or wants us to believe. These subtleties and complexities add a great deal of responsibility that we might like to avoid by pretending we are not causally responsible for what we can prevent, but that self-serving view is false. Although we typically do not choose the background conditions of our actions, these conditions in which we find ourselves empower us and allow us to be causally efficacious, even if against our own choices, and so imbue our omissions with consequences that are morally significant.[11]

V. THE ETHICAL DIMENSIONS OF OMISSIONS

Nothing written above has any immediate implications for whether it is morally permissible, obligatory, or wrong to cause a particular patient to die by omitting treatment. We have explored *only* the causal ramifications of letting patients die and have seen that letting a patient die is one way to cause that patient's death. Whether the act is right or wrong is another matter, but a matter which does rest in an important way on the causal story above. Because an omission can be the cause of a patient's death, a death can be as much a consequence of a failure to intervene as it can be a consequence of a stabbing, shooting, or poisoning. From a rights-based or libertarian point of view (as articulated by Professor Mack), the rightness or wrongness of causing a death by omitting to prevent it will be a function of the particular right in question, and that is no easy matter to work out. People have a right to life, but some also claim that we have a right to control the destiny of our own bodies as well as a right to die. How all of this is worked out by some particular rights-theorist would be a topic which would carry us far beyond this discussion.[12] My conclusion is simply that omitting treatment is one way to cause death. This conclusion and the discussion which leads to it may enrich our understanding of what we do and what we fail to do.

NOTES

[1] In itself this is surprising, for the causal character of our actions is something to be discovered and, *whatever* it is, it cannot be restrictive – just as the laws of chemistry or the laws of physics

cannot be restrictive. 'Restrictive' is an evaluative term that has no proper meaning in a characterization of the nature of chemistry, physics, or causality.

[2] We are assuming that Alice has not in any way voluntarily contracted to care for the infant, or otherwise entered into any voluntary relationship either with the infant or a proxy for the infant.

[3] These observations undermine Mack's statement that "it is, therefore, inconsistent to say both that Alice can avert Alyosha's death and that, if she does not do so, her omission joins those other causal conditions making for Alyosha's death without which they would not have been causally sufficient" ([10], p. 63). This statement is false. It is *precisely* because Alice's omission is necessary for Alyosha's death that her omission *is* causally relevant to the death. For example, the conditions in which Alice finds Alyosha in the three-month-old-infant variation of the example *must be* re-enforced and enhanced by Alice's non-intervention in order for them to eventuate in Alyosha's death. If Alice were to intervene, these conditions would no longer be sufficient for Alyosha's death, and he would not die.

[4] For a more detailed account of this analysis of singular causal explanation see [5] and [11]. In this and the next paragraph I follow an argument similar to one which I developed in [7], pp. 94–96.

[5] James Rachels makes this point [13]. Note that we tend to forget about the victims of the Stalin death camps for whom death by bullet would have been merciful.

[6] Mack's unrealistic 'organ redistribution' example also needs a brief comment. He correctly claims that refraining from saving the five unhealthy persons is less wrong than killing one healthy person to save the five. He claims this is so "for only by refraining does one avoid *causing* death." The problem with his claim, however, is that in any realistic setting of which I am aware it would be unlikely that one could save five unhealthy people by killing one healthy person and redistributing his or her organs. Rather, in any realistic example the foreseeable consequences of killing one healthy person in order to try to save five unhealthy persons would typically favor not killing anyone but rather simply letting the five die without any fantastic and disruptive attempts at intervention. The utilitarian account of our obligations in the 'organ redistribution' example are based on this realistic assessment of foreseeable consequences and so coincides with our moral intuitions. See [8], [14], and [16] for more on the general utilitarian account of moral obligation.

[7] I am indebted to Jan Narveson for this objection.

[8] This paragraph is based on an argument I presented in [6], pp. 97–100.

[9] Compare Dewey: "moral theory cannot emerge when there is positive belief as to what is right and what is wrong, for then there is no occasion for reflection" – or at least not for the kind of reflection that might go beyond placing "the standard and rules of conduct in ancestral habit" ([3], pp. 3–5).

[10] I discuss this same example and a similar point in [6], p. 100.

[11] Mack's use of the term 'upshot' for 'consequence' is an attempt to characterize his own account of consequences as neutral, when instead his account is both causally inaccurate as well as a violation of the orthodox analysis of consequences found in the philosophical literature (see [1], [4], [12], and [15]).

[12] It would require an equally lengthy diversion to discuss properly the utilitarian account on which the rightness or wrongness of an action is a function of the foreseeable consequences of that action. See [8], [14], and [16]. Note, however, that on the utilitarian account the moral status of actions is only a function of their *foreseeable* consequences. This moral account is consistent with one typical response we have to the discovery of some evil we could prevent – 'I wish I hadn't seen that'. Once we discover that we can prevent an evil, we thereby discover that our

action has consequences we did not previously foresee. Hence, our action takes on a new causal significance, and we face new responsibilities and obligations that we may wish we did not have.

BIBLIOGRAPHY

[1]   Bergstrom, L.: 1966, *The Alternatives and Consequences of Actions*, Amqvist and Wiksell, Stockholm.
[2]   Benjamin, M.: 1976, 'Death: Where Is Thy Cause?', *Hastings Center Report* 6, 15–16.
[3]   Dewey, J.: 1908, *The Theory of the Moral Life*, Holt, Rinehart, and Winston, Inc., New York.
[4]   Gibbard, A.: 1973, 'Doing No More Harm Than Good', *Philosophical Studies* 34, 158–173.
[5]   Gorovitz, S.: 1965, 'Causal Judgments and Causal Explanations', *The Journal of Philosophy* 25, 695–710.
[6]   Gruzalski, B.: 1980, 'Taking Full Responsibility For Causing Patients To Die', in M. Bradie and M. Brand (eds.), *Action and Responsibility*, 93–101.
[7]   Gruzalski, B.: 1981, 'Killing by Letting Die', *Mind* 90, 91–98.
[8]   Gruzalski, B.: 1981, 'Foreseeable Consequence Utilitarianism', *Australasian Journal of Philosophy* 59, 163–176.
[9]   Hart, H. L. A. and Honoré, A. M.: 1959, *Causation in the Law*, Clarendon Press, Oxford.
[10] Mack, E.: 1988, 'Moral Rights and Causal Casuistry', in this volume.
[11] Martin, R.: 1972, 'Singular Causal Explanation', *Theory and Decision*, 221–237.
[12] Prawitz, D.: 1968, 'A Discussion Note on Utilitarianism', *Theoria* 34, 83.
[13] Rachels, J.: 1975, 'Active and Passive Euthanasia', *New England Journal of Medicine* 87, 78–80.
[14] Rachels, J.: 1986, *The Elements of Moral Philosophy*, Random House, New York.
[15] Sobel, H.: 1974, 'Utilitarianisms: Simple and General', *Inquiry* 20, 394–449.
[16] Stenn, F.: 1980, 'A Plea for Voluntary Euthanasia', *New England Journal of Medicine* 92, 891.
[17] Taylor, P.: 1975, *Principles of Ethics*, Dickenson Publishing Co., Inc., Encino, California.

Northeastern University
Boston, Massachusetts, U.S.A.

MICHAEL P. LEVINE

COFFEE AND CASUISTRY:
IT DOESN'T MATTER WHO CAUSED WHAT

In 'Moral Rights and Causal Casuistry' [2], Eric Mack argues that if I poison your coffee and you know it is poisoned but drink it any way of your own free will, but without intending to be poisoned, for example to collect on a bet, I am causally and morally responsible for your ensuing condition as a result of my poisoning the coffee. This is contrary to the Hart and Honoré [1] position that I am responsible for your ensuing condition if you drink the coffee *without* knowing that it is poisoned, but that once you *do know* it is poisoned, your condition resulting from 'deliberately' drinking the bad brew becomes your causal and moral responsibility. I may remain responsible for ruining your morning coffee, indeed your entire morning, but I am not responsible for the result should you decide to drink it.

Consider the following two principles:

The Principle of Antecedent Peril: The intermediate intention of a causal agent, but not the intermediate foresight, negatives the causal connection between some antecedent peril (i.e., a peril that the agent is not responsible for) and its effect. Therefore, primary causal responsibility will lie with the antecedent peril rather than with oneself if one acts with the intermediate foresight, but without the intermediate intention that the bad effect will result. If the primary causal responsibility lies with the antecedent peril, the intermediate act of a causal agent will not make that agent morally responsible for the effect of the antecedent peril.

Principle of Double Effects: A causal agent is not morally responsible for the foreseen but unintended (bad) effect of an action that results in the good intended effect, so long as that unintended effect is neither an end in itself or (importantly – and perhaps incoherently) a means to the end that is the good effect.[1]

I take it, as I think Mack would, that at first glance most people would be inclined to agree with the Hart/Honoré position. Nevertheless, Mack claims that this position is mistaken if one accepts the Principle of Antecedent Peril (AP). He proposes this as a substitute for the Principle of Double Effect (DE). He argues that AP is acceptable and central to moral casuistry. Furthermore, he argues that it embodies our correct intuitions concerning both (a) the importance of the sometimes morally relevant distinction between 'acting' and 'merely allowing' that is taken up in what he calls the 'Causing versus Allowing Principle' (CA), and (b) the significance of the sometimes morally relevant 'distinction between causing a *forseen* death and causing a death with the *intention* of doing so' either as an end in itself or as a means to an

87

Baruch A. Brody (ed.), Moral Theory and Moral Judgments in Medical Ethics, 87–98.
© *1988 by Kluwer Academic Publishers.*

end, in determining the moral permissibility of an act as it is meant to be captured in DE.[2]

Mack says,

... the identification of the rights involved in particular cases... only provides half of what is needed to reach a judgment about the moral permissibility or impermissibility of a particular action. The other half of what is needed is knowledge of whether the action under consideration would *violate* the identified rights(s)... the interesting task... is the specification of how one agent's action must be connected with another agent's loss of some rightfully held object or condition... for the first agent's action to count as a violation of that second agent's right ([2], p. 57).

Alice violates Alyosha's right to R 'only if her action (or inaction), *in a sufficiently robust sense, causes* Alyosha's loss of R' ([2], pp. 57–8). However, this 'causing' is a necessary but *not* a sufficient condition for Alice's action or inaction being a 'violation' of Alyosha's loss of R.

Causal casuistry as such seeks to determine whether any further causal condition has to be satisfied... before the primary causal responsibility for the loss of R can be reasonably assigned to that agent ([2], p. 58).

I begin by considering Mack's views on negative causation (as presented in [2]) that are relevant to his claim concerning primary causal and moral responsibility for Jones' poisoning. In Section II, I shall argue that Mack's view concerning the centrality of causal casuistry in determining *primary causal responsibility* in the relevant moral sense is mistaken.

I

In [2] Mack briefly states his reasons against a doctrine of negative causation. Such doctrines maintain that allowing x to occur by omitting to do y should itself, for purposes of moral assessment, be counted as a 'cause' of x's occurrence.

To say that Alice can avert Alyosha's death is to say that she can (and knows she can) intervene against certain of the conditions which otherwise jointly cause Alyosha's death. If the total set of conditions, some of which she can nullify, were not causally sufficient for Alyosha's death, we would not say that she can *avert* that death. It is, therefore, inconsistent to say both that Alice can avert Alyosha's death and that, if she does not do so, the omission joins those other causal conditions making for Alyosha's death without which they would not have been causally sufficient ([2], p. 63).

It is true that, 'if the total set of conditions, some of which she can nullify, were not causally sufficient for Alyosha's death, we would not say that she can *avert* that death'. Is it also true that it is 'inconsistent to say both that Alice can avert Alyosha's death and that, if she does not do so, the omission joins those other causal conditions making for Alyosha's death without which they would not have been causally sufficient?' I think not. It *appears* to be inconsistent because the assumption that Alice can *avert* Alyosha's death, that even apart from anything Alice does (or even her very existence) the causal conditions *are* sufficient for Alyosha's death, allegedly conflicts with the assumption that Alice's 'omission joins those other causal conditions making for Alyosha's death without which they would *not* have been causally sufficient'. According to Mack, the assumption that the causal conditions are sufficient for the death, apart from Alice's omissions, conflicts with the assumption that they are not sufficient apart from what Alice does not do.

To generate this apparent inconsistency, Mack has relied upon his notion of what it is to be part of a set of conditions that are causally sufficient for the occurrence of *y*, in circumstances where moral problems such as these arise. He relies upon this notion in such a way as to beg the question concerning whether or not an omission can properly be regarded as a morally relevant part of a set of causally sufficient conditions for the occurrence of *y*, given that the set of causal conditions apart from the omission is causally sufficient for the occurrence of *y*. There are many ways in which to pick out just what the relevant causally sufficient conditions for the occurrence of some *y* is. Mack begs the question as to whether such a condition (omission) is part of a set of morally relevant causally sufficient conditions construed in some other (i.e., non-physicalistic) way – e.g., for the purpose of determining whether Alice is morally responsible, by her omission, for the occurrence of *y*. He does this by refusing to consider any condition (e.g., omission) to be part of a set of morally relevant causally sufficient conditions for the occurrence of *y*, just because its absence would not prevent the occurrence of *y* under *some* physicalistic description of what the relevant causal conditions are.

As long as one does not confine oneself to those conditions that are, in those circumstances, either (a) *necessary* for the occurrence of *y* on some necessitarian account of causation, or (b) on a non-necessitarian or Humean account, regularly conjoined with *y*, then omissions as well as a variety of other non-necessary conditions may properly be regarded as causes. Apart from adherence to either of these two primary competing philosophical analyses of causations, in moral matters as elsewhere, conditions are routinely and matter of factly identified as causes of some specifiable events, though they are not necessary in the circumstances for the event's occurrence. Furthermore, the application of both of these analyses of causation is generally confined to specific *physical* causes of events. Principles of causal casuistry are not needed to determine what the necessary physical conditions are for the occurrence of y. In limiting himself, as Mack has done both in his argument against negative causation and in his argument on behalf of AP, to attributing primary causal responsibility to conditions that are physically necessary in the circumstances for the occurrence of y, he begs the question against those who wish to claim that conditions that are not necessary in that way not only can, but *should* be regarded as primary causes in situations that exhibit certain morally relevant features (e.g., Jones' deliberately drinking coffee he knows that I poisoned).

It is true that y would have occurred apart from any act by Alice, but it does not follow from this that Alice's omission cannot or should not be regarded as part of, even the most important part of, the set of conditions properly regarded as causally sufficient, in the circumstances, for the occurrence of y. This is because what we determine the set of relevant causally sufficient conditions for the occurrence of y to be in a particular instance will depend upon what our interests are concerning that occurrence. These interests may lead us to include some omissions as part of the set of causally sufficient conditions for y in the circumstances, as well as conditions that are present because of actions, chance, etc.

Those who think that omissions are morally relevant *will* want to include some omissions, in some circumstances, as a part of the *properly construed* set of morally relevant causally sufficient conditions for y. For Mack to say that upon some other construal (i.e., a physicalistic construal) of what the causally sufficient conditions for the occurrence of y are (e.g., a construal that leaves out factors such as omissions that others regard as morally relevant features of the situation to be included in the set of morally relevant causally sufficient conditions), omissions are *not* part of the set of causally sufficient conditions for the occurrence of y, is to say nothing of interest to those who claim that the omission is part of the set of (morally relevant) causally sufficient conditions for y. This is because those who claim that the omission is part of the set of morally relevant causally sufficient conditions, do not deny and never intended to deny that y would not occur apart from the omission. They want to point out that, properly construed, (e.g., from the moral point of view), the omission *should* be regarded as one of the members of the set of morally relevant and causally sufficient conditions for the occurrence of y in the circumstances, even if it is not necessary for the occurrence of y in the circumstances.

To say that Alice can *avert y* is to say that 'she can (and knows she can) intervene against certain of the conditions which otherwise will jointly cause' y. But this does *not* mean that by omitting to do something which would prevent y her omission cannot properly be regarded as a morally significant part of the set of conditions causally sufficient for y – even though y would have occurred apart from the omission, or even apart from Alice's very existence. That it *is* so regarded, in certain circumstances, by those who think that there is no morally relevant distinction between 'causing' and 'allowing' in many instances is clear. They may be wrong, but they are not inconsistent as Mack would have it.

Given that there is no inconsistency, what Mack must do is argue for the unacceptability of attributing *moral* relevance to (most) cases of negative causation, rather than argue for the unacceptability of attributing *causal* relevance. The adoption of the strategy of arguing for the unacceptability of attributing *causal* relevance will lead to question begging results, as I think Mack's argument illustrates. My omitting to do something which results in y may be a contributing causal factor of y for which I am morally responsible, if it is legitimate to regard causal conditions resulting in part due to an omission as something I am causally responsible for. Furthermore, it does not matter if one has a necessitarian (or some other non-Humean) account of causation, or some type of regularity account. On either account I can be seen as causally responsible for some condition that contributes, in the circumstances, to y's death. (See [3], Chapters 2, 3, and 5, for many points relevant to my above critique of Mack).

Mack's view as to what can properly be taken as a primary contributing causal factor to an event's occurrence (e.g., omissions cannot be) plays a crucial role in his defense of the Principle of Antecedent Peril, and his subsequent claim that I, the poisoner, am primarily causally responsible for Jones' death should Jones deliberately and knowingly drink the poisoned coffee. I now turn to a consideration of Mack's defence of AP.

II

Mack's motivation for seeking an alternative principle for DE is as follows:

First, DE properly allows certain actions which causally contribute to deaths of innocent bystanders [e.g., spraying the swarm that endangers New York without intending harm to the Worcesterians, but forseeing that it will result in their deaths]. But since it is at least dubious that DE is a principle of causal casuistry, it is hard to see how an exception based upon DE can link up with and modify the moral drawn from CA [i.e., that there is a morally relevant distinction between 'causing' and 'allowing']. Far better if we head a principle which identified the acts properly allowed by DE as *causally insignificant contributions* to losses of rights [my emphasis]. For then we could see how such acts would not violate the moral rule against (robustly) causally contributing to the deaths of innocent bystanders. Second, DE improperly allows certain other actions [e.g., the gassing of Beau – roommate of Bob and Barbie] which causally contribute to the deaths of innocents. What is needed, therefore, is an alternative principle which discriminates between the acts properly and improperly allowed by DE ([2], pp. 67–8).

Mack proposes the Principle of Antecedent Peril (AP) as the alternative to DE. He claims that "AP provides a causally casuistic account of the moral line between the two cases of unfortunate Worcesterians ... and, at the same time, AP does not yield the permissibility of your indirectly gassing poor Beau" (*ibid.*, p. 68) in order to save the lives of his roommates. The two Worcesterian cases are (a) forseeing but not intending the Worcesterians' deaths as a result of spraying, and (b) using them as means to one's end of saving lives (e.g., by directly dismembering them). The case of Beau is that of gassing him 'indirectly' and unintentionally to save the lives of Bob and Barbie who are his roommates. (As Mack points out, on DE the gassing of Beau appears to be permissible, but allowing the killing of Beau, albeit 'unintentionally' and not as a means to one's end, seems clearly wrong).

Mack criticizes Hart and Honoré's view concerning what types of intermediate events between the occurrence of an earlier event X and a later event Y 'negatives' the causal connection between X and Y:

... Hart and Honoré hold that, except in special cases such as those involving inducement, intervening voluntary actions negative causal connections... If such a negativing of causal connection does not occur, then primary causal responsibility for Y continues to go back to X and not merely to some event (or action) which mediates the causal connection between X and Y (*ibid.*, p. 68).

Thus, in the case of the poisoned coffee, the Hart/Honoré position is that if I poison it and Jones drinks it without knowing I poisoned it, then I am responsible for his death. However, "if Jones is aware of the poison and, nevertheless, 'deliberately' drinks the coffee, he is a suicide." Mack says:

The hard question is whether Jones' being aware of the poison and, hence, his *forseeing* his death should he drink the coffee suffices for his 'deliberate' act of drinking the poisoned coffee to break the causal chain going back to my poisoning of the coffee. Or does Jones have to drink it with the *intention* of ingesting the poison for the connection between my poisoning the coffee and Jones' death to be negatived?[3] If intermediate intention, but not intermediate foresight, negatived causal connection, then when you deflect the swarm to Worcester with the intention of infecting its inhabitants you negative the causal link back to the swarm itself while, in contrast, when you deflect the swarm away from New York with the (mere) foresight that its remnant will infect Worcester you do not negative the causal connection back to the antecedent peril. So, if

intermediate intention, but not intermediate foresight, negatives causal connection, primary
causal responsibility will lie with you when you intend the infection... while, in contrast, when
you deflect the swarm away from New York with the (mere) foresight of Worcesterian fatalities,
primary causal responsibility lies with the antecedent peril, the swarm itself *ibid.*, pp. 68–94.[4]
[My notes.]

Does the 'deliberate' act of knowingly drinking the poisoned coffee break
the causal chain 'going back to my poisoning the coffee'? Hart and Honoré
think so, but Mack does not. Jones may *foresee* his death, but unless Jones
had the 'intention' of ingesting the poison, the causal chain is not broken
according to Mack. He says, '... Jones deliberately consumes the poison in a
way that breaks the link between my poisoning the coffee and his death only
if Jones *intends* to consume the poison' (*ibid.*). Therefore, apart from this
intention, primary causal responsibility goes back to the poisoner.

An analysis of intention that says one can deliberately, voluntarily,
uncoerced and knowingly drink poison without 'intending' to get ill, or that
one can deliberately ... etc. jump off a skyscraper without intending to get
hurt may be suspect, since it allows that one's intentions concerning the
known consequences of one's action may be completely independent of what
one's intention is in performing the intended action. However, let us suppose,
as Mack does, that Jones can deliberately and knowingly drink the poisoned
coffee without 'intending' to be poisoned – perhaps (as in Mack's modified
coffee case (*ibid.*) to collect on a bet where this is not regarded as a form of
coercion. If 'intermediate intention, but not intermediate foresight, negatives
causal connection', then Jones' knowingly drinking the poisoned coffee
without *intending* to be poisoned will not negative the causal connection
between the poisoner and Jones. Primary causal responsibility goes back to
the poisoner. Therefore, Mack concludes that Jones is not primarily causally
responsible for his being poisoned, the poisoner is, and so the poisoner is
morally responsible for (causing) the death of Jones.

One who agrees with Hart and Honoré may say that even apart from the
intention of being poisoned, Jones knowingly drinking the poison with the
foresight of death or illness makes Jones primarily causally responsible for
his ensuing condition, even though it is true his death or illness would not
have occurred if not for the antecedent peril – my poisoning his coffee. Is this
view mistaken?

It is important to note that Jones' drinking the coffee is *one of many*
(innumerable) *conditions which are together causally sufficient* in the
circumstances for his being poisoned. What determines the assignment of
'primary causal responsibility' in the morally relevant sense is not where

one's causal contribution occurs in the chain of events leading to the poisoning, but rather where one thinks primary moral responsibility rests for the presence of one or more of the factors that together are causally sufficient, in the circumstances, for the effect. My poisoning the coffee is one of the conditions that are together causally sufficient, in the circumstances, for Jones' death, but so is Jones knowingly and with foresight drinking the coffee. This is why an *omission* may also be cited as the primary *causal* condition in a set of conditions causally sufficient in the circumstance for the occurrence of an event – even if the event would have occurred anyway. An omission can be regarded as a causal condition which is part of a set of causal conditions that are sufficient, in the circumstances, for the occurrence of some event *y*.

It is more plausible to assign causal responsibility, in the relevant moral sense, for Jones' death to Jones himself once he knows about the poison and drinks it deliberately and uncoerced, because at the point at which he decides to drink the coffee he could simply have changed the course of events without any great cost to himself. (I discuss some of the relevant factors in determining the 'cost' below.) Changing the course of events may have caused Jones great inconvenience, for example, if he lost money by not drinking the coffee, or even if he simply liked coffee a great deal. However, while I may be causally responsible, *in part*, for his losing the bet or ruining his coffee etc., as Hart, Honoré, and our intuitions tells us; once Jones deliberately drinks it, then by that very decision and his actually drinking the poisoned coffee the *primary* causal factor (i.e., his uncoerced drinking of it) in the chain of conditions sufficient in those circumstances to his being poisoned, resides with Jones himself – even if he did not *intend* to poison himself by drinking it.

On this account what constitutes the *primary* causal factor, in the morally relevant sense, cannot be determined apart from certain moral considerations – considerations that must be taken into account when developing adequate principles of moral casuistry. The formulation of adequate principles of moral casuistry cannot be prior to a determination of other moral principles that specify what the relevant moral considerations are in determining which causal factors among those present (*or absent*) are the most (morally) relevant in determining culpability. The primary causal factor in the case of Jones is the causal factor that is most morally significant, and this is his drinking it – not my poisoning it – once he knows about the poison etc. – in short, once he drinks it deliberately.

III

One may ask, according to what principle am I able to determine that it is Jones' drinking and not my poisoning his drink that is the primary causal factor in his death. Am I not just doing 'situation' or, what is worse, *ad hoc* ethics?

Without formulating a specific principle, I can specify factors relevant to the formulation of such a principle. There are many situations in which others are morally responsible for something that happens to me. However, if I am able to avoid violations of my rights at little or no cost to myself, then the primary responsibility for any violations that may occur to me resides with myself rather than with the person or persons who may be responsible for the situation that would have resulted in my rights being violated had I not so acted as to avoid them. Furthermore, in determining what the 'little or no cost to myself' is in such situations, any costs that accrue to my action wholly as result of something I have done are not the moral responsibility of the person who would have violated my rights. In other words, assuming I did not know about the bet, I am not morally responsible, at least not wholly or primarily so, for Jones' losing his money should he decide not to drink the coffee. The bet was his own affair. I may be legally responsible, but that is another issue.

Consider another example of Mack's.

... if I construct a chamber of horrors along the route through which someone must pass if he is to escape a concentration camp, the causal responsibility for his injuries in that chamber is mine even when he knows full well what awaits him on that route. Only if Jones or the prisoner act with the intention of undergoing those painful episodes do their actions negative the chain of responsibility leading back to me (*ibid.*, pp. 69–70).

It seems that if we treat this case as Hart and Honoré treat the Jones case, then since the prisoner *knows* what awaits him on route and deliberately chooses to escape anyway, it will be his primary causal responsibility for what befalls him and not mine, even though I constructed the chamber of horrors. However, as Mack correctly points out, there seems to be something wrong with this. Even if our inclination is to hold Jones responsible if he deliberately drinks, we do not want to say that the prisoner is primarily causally responsible for what befalls him along route. On Mack's analysis, the prisoner will not be primarily causally responsible for what befalls him, because he did not *intend* to have those things happen to him, even though he did forsee that they would.

Mack holds that neither Jones nor the prisoner is causally responsible in a

sufficiently robust sense for what happens to him to attribute moral responsibility to himself – thereby getting the poisoner and horror builder off the
hook. Though Hart and Honoré appear to hold that Jones *and* the prisoner
would be primarily causally responsible, I doubt that they would want to
maintain that the prisoner is responsible in the way in which Jones is.
Certainly the prisoner is not 'causally' responsible in any sense that might be
useful for the purposes of determining legal or moral responsibility. Other
factors are involved in attributing blame to the builder of the chamber of
horrors for what befalls the escapee, rather than attributing blame to the
escapee himself because he foresaw the evils about to befall him but escaped
anyway. However, Mack may be correct in claiming that on the Hart/Honoré
account the prisoner is primarily *causally* responsible for what befalls him.

My account of determining primary causal responsibility from among
those conditions and acts (including omissions) that are among the set of
conditions causally sufficient, in the circumstances, for the occurrence of
some event *y* offers a reason why Jones can be held causally and morally
accountable, but not the prisoner. Within a set of developed principles of
causal casuistry, it also offers the basis for determining the morally relevant
distinctions between Mack's three cases of the unfortunate Worcesterians,
and for the impermissibility of gassing poor Beau. Mack's own reasons for
not allowing the gassing of Beau appear *ad hoc* (*ibid.*, pp. 71–2). The first
reason simply is that in the case of Beau we are *introducing* the gas, whereas
in the case of the Worcesterians the swarm is already present. But *why* should
this 'introduction' of the gas make a moral difference? An answer to this
'why' requires reference to moral principles, not to principles of causal
casuistry.

Perhaps more significantly, my account indicates, though in no way
proves, that casuistic principles have a role to play in ethics only in the
context of other considered moral principles. This is because, apart from
these other principles, it is not possible to determine just what the primary
causal condition (i.e., the morally relevant one) is among those conditions
sufficient, in the circumstances, for the occurrence of *y*. A well-developed
casuistry is *derivative* from other more fundamental principles of ethics. A
theory of rights is the basis for only a part of these more fundamental
principles. Thus, the principles discussed by Mack (CA and AP) as principles
of casuistry must be justified in terms of some more basic principles of ethics
if they are to be justified at all. And if they are to be rejected, it will invariably be because they don't square with one or more of these more basic
principles.

Mark claims that DE, unlike AP and CA, is not a principle of causal casuistry at all (*ibid.*, p. 67). I think this is mistaken, since DE is meant to determine causal, and hence moral, responsibility in those situations where 'double effect' arises. At least it is meant to determine this given my broader construal of how a primary cause of some untoward upshot' is to be determined.

In his conclusion Mack says,

... in order to determine whether some agent counts as violating rights, one must also determine the causal relationship (or lack thereof) between that agent's acts or omissions and the other party's loss. Only if the agent robustly causes the loss can it be said that he has violated the second party's right (*ibid.*, p. 72).

In my view this is exactly backwards. In order to determine what the causal relationship is in the morally relevant sense of an agent's act or omission 'causing' the other party's loss, one must first determine whether some agent's act or omission counts as a violation of someone's right. Of course, I suppose it is true that once one determines whether or not an agent's act or omission is a violation of someone's right, then morally speaking there would be no need to determine the causal relationship between 'that agent's acts or omissions and the other party's loss'. Principles of causal casuistry would then be rendered superfluous.[5]

NOTES

[1] This formulation of the principle of double effect is an oversimplification. Additional criteria are needed. According to Robert Young ([14], p. 275), "The following criteria capture the doctrine and help elucidate the talk of permissibility on occasion":

- (a) the act directly aimed at must itself be morally good (or at least morally neutral);
- (b) the purpose must be to achieve the good consequence, the bad (undesired) consequence being only a side effect;
- (c) the good effect must not be achieved by way of the bad, but both must result from the same act;
- (d) the bad result must not be so serious as to outweigh the advantages of the good result.

[2] As Mack notes, both of these principles are used by deontologists, in medical ethics and elsewhere, to "effectively discount the significance of some of an action's upshots for the moral assessment of that action" [2], p. 59.

[3] Mack says: "The relevance of the intended vs. forseen distinction within the doctrine of AP is that an act with the intended result of a death will undercut (negative) the causal status of the inevitably injurious setting which presented that death as a possible intended result, while an act with the (merely) forseen result of a death will not... The theoretical intuition is that when

people are confronted with inescapably death dealing circumstances, responsibility for the ensuing deaths can be attributed to the circumstances (or, better yet, if possible, to an author of those circumstances), and hence not to the intermediate agents, as long as the ensuing deaths are not intended by the relevant agents... one's action does not negate the situation's primary causal responsibility for an ensuing death unless that death... is a formative goal of one's action" ([2], p. 70).

[4] It may seem that the example of the swarm infecting Worcester is an inappropriate one to use for Mack's purpose of explaining the role of AP as a principle of causal casuistry. This is because there is no question of the causal connection going back to the AP (i.e., the swarm) being negatived by the agent's action in the case of the Worcesterians, but only in the case of the New Yorkers, since the swarm is *not* an antecedent peril to Worcester but to New York in the first place. It is only a peril to Worcester *after* the deflection. It is a consequent peril, not an antecedent one. However, this would be to too restrictively define the notion of antecedent peril. The inevitably injurious setting of the swarm headed for New York does present the one who is able to deflect the swarm with the death of the Worcesterians as a possibly intended, and not merely forseen, consequence of spraying the swarm and saving the lives of the New Yorkers. The swarm is an antecedent peril to Worcester merely by the fact that it is headed to New York and that action taken to prevent the death of New Yorkers will result in the deaths of Worcesterians.

[5] My thanks to participants in a philosophy colloquium at La Trobe University, Susan Levine, Michael Stocker and Robert Young whose comments were more helpful and telling than I sometimes knew what to do with.

BIBLIOGRAPHY

[1]   Hart, H. L. A. and Honoré, A. M.: 1959, *Causation in the Law*, Oxford University Press, Oxford.
[2]   Mack, E.: 1988, 'Moral Rights and Causal Casuistry', in this volume, pp. 58–74.
[3]   Mackie, J. L.: 1974, *The Cement of the Universe*, Oxford University Press, Oxford.
[4]   Young, R.: 1976, 'Voluntary and Nonvoluntary Euthanasia', *The Monist*, 59 (1976), 264–83.

La Trobe University
Melbourne, Victoria, Australia

SECTION III

MARX'S THEORY: DERIVING MORAL IMPLICATIONS

ALLEN BUCHANAN

MARXISM AND MORAL JUDGMENT

Here I examine the question: what practical guidance can Marxism provide for resolving what are commonly thought of as concrete moral problems? This cautious formulation does not assume that Marxism is or includes a moral theory or is even compatible with a moral point of view. It leaves open the possibility that, as some defenders of Marx claim, Marx believed that morality is no more than an ideological smokescreen and that, properly speaking, there are no moral problems, only political ones.

If Marxism does provide practical guidance, several additional questions require answers. (1) What is the domain of Marxism's practical guidance in resolving what are commonly thought of as moral problems? Does it only provide guidance for large-scale institutional problems, or can it also aid in the resolution of what are commonly thought of as problems of private morality? (2) If the guidance supplied by Marxism conflicts with the requirements of widely held moral principles, does Marxism offer sound arguments to show that its principles should override? Further, in order to explore either of the preceding questions it will be necessary to answer another: (3) What is the *structure* if Marxism is as a guide to action? More specifically, is Marxism primarily consequentialist in structure, and if so, how does it differ, if at all, from utilitarianism as a consequentialist moral theory? Finally (4), what sorts of intermediate premises are needed to carry us from Marxist principles to concrete practical judgments?

Our first step is an unavoidably controversial one: we must fix upon an interpretation of Marxism as an evaluative perspective – as a source of practical judgments – before we can go any further. An adequate defense of the interpretation I opt for is not feasible in this essay. Since I have developed it in detail elsewhere, here I will only sketch it and then examine its implications for resolving three quite different concrete moral problems.

I. MARX'S EVALUATIVE PERSPECTIVE

I shall focus on Karl Marx's views, not only because those who call themselves Marxists tend to claim his work as authoritative, but also because I believe that, by and large, the writings of Marx still provide the best materials

Baruch A. Brody (ed.), Moral Theory and Moral Judgments in Medical Ethics, 101–118.
© *1988 by Kluwer Academic Publishers.*

for constructing a coherent and reflective Marxist position. The key thesis of my interpretation is that Marx's vision of life in communist society serves as the ultimate normative source of whatever practical guidance his theory has to offer. The vision of life in communism is not by itself sufficient for practical guidance, of course, even if we assume, as Marx does, that life in communism is so superior that its desirability is beyond question, at least to anyone whose values are not distorted by ideology. Also needed are explanatory and descriptive elements: Marx's general theory of history (especially his account of the process that transforms capitalism into socialism and then communism), as well as more particular facts about existing institutions and power relations in a given society at a particular time.

In precisely what the superiority of life in communism is supposed to consist is a matter of some controversy among Marxists. This much, however, is clear. According to Marx, communism is a form of society in which the ideals of community, freedom, and the all-around development of the individual's capacities are finally actualized. Only in communism can humanity achieve harmonious, non-exploitive, bounteous production. All of this is made possible, according to Marx, through genuinely democratic control over the means of production, by which he apparently means that each has roughly equal power (at least in the long run) in decisions concerning the use of productive resources ([10], pp. 291–294).[1] Socialism, or as Marx himself called it, the lower stage of communism, though an improvement on capitalism, contains various flaws that will only be remedied by the transition to full-blown communism. The vision of life in communism provides the evaluative perspective from which Marx criticizes capitalism and judges that the tradition from capitalism to socialism, and ultimately, to communism will mark not only change but genuine progress in human history.

To say this is not to deny that Marx sees communism, not as a static condition, but rather as a kind of framework or matrix for new forms of human fulfillment. Nor is it to saddle him with the view that communism is a fully determinate goal during the period of revolutionary struggle. Even more importantly, the thesis that the vision of life in communism is the ultimate normative source of practical guidance in Marxism does not imply that Marx was guilty of the 'idealism' for which he criticized other socialists. Marx did not believe that significant social change would result from merely articulating a vision of the ideal society and then exhorting people to pursue it. Instead, he emphasized that the goal of communism was firmly rooted in the actual process of change revealed by his philosophy of history and that the masses were to be motivated to revolution chiefly through straightforward appeals to their self-interest.

What is most striking about Marx's evaluative perspective is what it does *not* include, namely, juridical concepts – concepts of justice and rights ([1], pp. 50–85; [14], pp. 50–85). Marx never says that the superiority of communism lies, even in part, in its being a just society or one which respects rights. Nor is his fundamental criticism of capitalism that it is unjust or that it violates rights. Juridical concepts also play no significant role in Marx's account of successful revolutionary motivation: he thinks it is quite unnecessary – and potentially confusing and divisive – to appeal to the workers' sense of justice or to urge them to stand up for their rights. Indeed, Marx appears to reject the juridical point of view entirely, charging that talk about justice is 'ideological nonsense' and 'outdated verbal rubbish' ([9], p. 24).

It is crucial not to underestimate the role which the vision of communism plays in Marx's theory. Marx criticizes capitalism for causing avoidable death, waste, hunger, mental and physical exhaustion, monotony, and loneliness. He believes that so long as capitalism exists these evils are unavoidable because they are necessary features of that system. It is only by comparison with communism that Marx is able to support his claim that capitalism causes unnecessary and avoidable death, hunger, etc. So, Marx's criticisms of capitalism are *essentially comparative*, and the ultimate standard of comparison is life in communism ([1], pp. 15–16).

However, the comparative criticism of capitalism has revolutionary implications for conduct only if communism is a *feasible* social order. Unless communism can at least be approximated in practice, the fact that it is superior to capitalism is no reason at all for abolishing capitalism and striving for communism. It follows that the practical guidance Marxism affords depends upon whether or not there are solid grounds for believing that virtues Marx ascribes to communism can actually coexist in one social order.

In particular, Marxism's success in providing practical guidance hangs upon whether we have good reason to believe that democratic control over the means of production can achieve great productive efficiency without exploitation or alienation. As I have argued elsewhere, this prediction about democratic control over the means of production can only be adequately supported by a *theory* of democratic social coordination [3]. Such a theory would have to overcome a number of well-known and potentially devastating objections purporting to show that democratic procedures are seriously inefficient and that the standard devices for remedying these inefficiencies succeed, if they succeed at all, only by abandoning the ideal of equal power which makes democracy attractive in the first place ([12], pp. 2–120).[2]

At present such a theory of democratic social coordination is lacking. We shall see shortly that this fact has profound implications for attempts to draw practical guidance from Marxism in coping with concrete moral problems.

There are two quite different ways in which a conception of the good society, in this case communism, can function as a source of evaluative judgments. On the one hand, the good society can be thought of as an attainable end, a goal toward which particular actions and social practices are to be directed. On this first view, all practical guidance provided by this conception of the good society is strictly instrumental. The guidance is compelling only if the end is not only desirable or morally attractive, but also feasible. On the other hand, a conception of the good society can serve as an *ideal*, as a standard for assessing current arrangements and as a source of practical guidance quite independently of any assumption that the ideal is attainable. The medieval Christian ideal of 'the imitation of Christ' was of this sort. Indeed, those who endeavored to shape their lives according to this ideal explicitly denied that the ideal was an attainable goal. Similarly, Kant seems to have regarded the notion of a Realm of Ends as an ideal that could function as standard of assessment and as a source of practical guidance without serving as a goal to be obtained.

One of the most distinctive features of Marx's view (and of orthodox Marxism) is the rejection of the second way in which a conception of the good society is to serve as a standard for assessment and a source of practical guidance. For Marx communism is the appropriate standard for assessing capitalism and, more importantly, for ascertaining what we ought to do, only insofar as it is an attainable goal. It is distinctive of Marx that he rejects ideals that are not attainable goals. For this reason it is more accurate to say that for Marx communism as a goal, not as an ideal, is the ultimate normative source of practical guidance.

II. THE STRUCTURE OF MARXISM AS A GUIDE TO ACTION

Granted my interpretation of Marx's evaluative perspective, it should come as no surprise that I understand Marxism to be consequentialist in structure. This general claim, however, requires qualification, since there are at least two quite different types of consequentialism: monistic and pluralistic. Utilitarianism is the most familiar and popular instance of the first type.

Utilitarianism maintains that there is ultimately a *single maximand*, utility, toward which all actions or practices ultimately ought to be directed. Though it can admit a plurality of goods, even of intrinsic goods, utilitarianism, as a monistic consequentialist view, maintains that they are all not only commensurate but aggregatable. Pluralist consequentialism, in contrast, while holding that actions and practices are to be evaluated solely according to their efficacy in producing a specified goal, denies that there is a single maximand. Instead, the goal is irreducibly complex, consisting of two or more goods to be realized. In the case of Marxism, the goods which comprise the goal are (roughly) freedom, self-actualization, and community as harmonious, cooperative productive activity.

Richard Miller has argued that Marx is not a utilitarian ([11], pp. 35–40). One of his arguments for this thesis supports the more general conclusion that if Marx was a consequentalist of any sort he was a pluralistic rather than a monistic consequentialist. Miller correctly notes passages which at least suggest that Marx rejected the view that all human goods can be reduced to a single good (call it 'utility' or what you will). And it is true that Marx himself never says anything to suggest that the goods which he believes will be attained in communism are commensurate with one another, much less that they can be aggregated into a single maximand.

The most obvious challenge to any pluralistic consequentialism is that it must provide some rational way of *ordering* the various goals when they conflict. In the case at hand, what is needed is a set of priority principles which rank the goals of community, individual development, and freedom. Marx himself never addresses this problem, and the fact that he does not supports the conclusion that he proposed no moral *theory*. It is my suspicion that he never took the priority problem seriously because he thought that such important human goods are in conflict only in societies whose modes of production are defective. If this was his position, then he believed that all good things would go together in communism, or at least that nothing so formal as a theory of value (much less a set of coercively backed principles of justice) would be needed to resolve value conflicts.

One more qualification is in order. Although Marx believes that the ultimate standard for evaluating institutions, practices, and actions, is their efficacy in bringing about the goods of communism, he also sometimes suggests that certain aspects of the activity of striving for communism can themselves have value independently of their contribution to that goal. The idea is that the goods of solidarity that revolutionaries can experience during the struggle provide a kind of preview of the fulfillments that will be available to all once the struggle succeeds ([1], pp. 92–93; [11], pp. 66–68). This qualification, however, does not contradict the thesis that Marx's normative position is consequentialist. There can be no doubt that for Marx the evaluation of practices and actions depends ultimately upon their conduciveness to the goal of revolution – the establishment of communism. If, for some reason, a case should arise in which pursuing the certain goods of solidarity in the process of revolution threatened to frustrate the attainment of the goal, then the former would have to be sacrificed to assure the successful pursuit of the latter.

III. THE LIABILITIES OF MARXISM AS A CONSEQUENTIALIST VIEW

The most obvious objection to Marxism interpreted in this way is a very general one that has often been levelled against utilitarianism: it reduces all moral issues to problems of selecting the best means to an end (in this case the establishment of communist society), recognizing no moral restrictions on how the end is to be attained. Indeed, as we have already seen, Marx explicitly rejects rights principles, which in common morality and most ethical theories have functioned as strong constraints on how goals may be pursued. This rejection of rights, when taken together with Marx's tendency to embrace revolutionary violence without moral qualms and his dictum that communists 'preach no morality', at least strongly suggests that Marx recognized no significant moral limitations on the pursuit of the revolutionary goal. To my knowledge he nowhere even considers the need for such constraints.

There is another, related problem which has led other consequentialists, especially utilitarians, to try to develop rules (whether those rules specify rights or not) to impose constraints on goal-directed behavior. Rule utilitarians have noted that the direct and unrestricted pursuit of utility can be self-defeating. One way in which this can occur is through lack of coordination. Individuals each trying to maximize utility in each particular decision they make will be unable to coordinate their behavior with another in mutually beneficial ways. Rules of coordination (for example, the rule of the road 'drive only on the right') can solve this problem.

Marx's emphasis on the role of the party elite can perhaps be developed to address the problem of coordinating revolutionary behavior if the party elite is seen as issuing *authoritative rules* that focus revolutionary activity, or at least constrain the range of activities in order to enhance coordination. On this interpretation, the party is to be obeyed not simply because it (allegedly) has a superior *knowledge* of tactics and strategy, but also because there is a need for an authoritative source of rules of coordination even if, as in the case of the rule of the road, which rule is chosen is not a matter of knowledge at all.

There is another way in which consequentialism can be self-defeating which applies with special force to Marxism and for which Marx offers no remedy. If there are no significant constraints on the ways in which the goal is pursued, the process of pursuing it may so corrupt the individuals participating in that process that the end cannot be achieved. This problem of the means tainting the end seems especially acute for Marxism, since the process as Marx describes it embraces violence, and deprivations of the rights of the workers' class enemies, without any of the constraints imposed by rights principles, or by any moral principles at all. And it is a sad truth that in real world revolutions, including Marxist ones, the brutal, authoritarian behavior that was first justified as a temporary necessity has often become a permanent feature of the post-revolutionary regime.

It is fair to say that the writings of Marx utterly fail to recognize the seriousness of this problem, much less to offer a coherent solution to it. This is not to deny that a sophisticated Marxist of the rule consequentialist sort could attempt to develop an account of constraints of revolutionary tactics and strategies designed to avoid corruption of the end by the means. However, it is important to emphasize that this route will be very hard going if the Marxist cleaves to what I take to be a central feature of Marx's theory: its rejection of juridical concepts. Marx jettisons the most powerful terms of constraint in the moral vocabulary while offering nothing to take their place.

Richard Miller has argued that Marx's abandonment of juridical concepts and the lack of any discussion of the need for moral constraints on revolutionary activity represents nothing less than a rejection of morality – all morality as such ([10], pp. 15–50). Miller's conclusion, however, rests on an implausibly narrow construal of what morality is. In fact, Miller's view of morality is so narrow that neither Aristotle's view, nor utilitarianism, nor Rawls's theory of justice as fairness, nor any position which permits destruction of an incorrigible criminal or of an evil enemy in a just war is a morality!

According to Miller, morality, at least so far as it applies to 'political decision', has three basic features, all of which Marx rejects. (1) Equality: 'People are to be shown equal concern or respect or afforded equal status.... everyone is to be treated as an equal'. (2) General norms: 'The right resolution of any major political issue would result from applying valid general norms to the case at hand. These rules are valid in all societies in which cooperation benefits almost everyone but... [there is scarcity]'. (3) Universality: 'Anyone who rationally reflects on relevant facts and arguments will accept these rules, if he or she has the normal range of emotions' ([10], [17]). Miller's contention is that Marx rejects all three of these tenets and that this shows that Marx abandons morality.

Ascription to the second and third tenets certainly cannot be assumed to be a necessary condition of having a morality. Many moral theorists, including most recently Rawls, have eschewed any attempt to offer a set of substantive general norms that are valid for all societies or even for all societies in the circumstances of justice ([12], pp. 223–51). Some, for example, Ronald Dworkin, may be read as offering some very general principles (in Dworkin's case the principle that all are entitled to equal concern and respect) which are supposed to apply across most or perhaps even all societies in the circumstances of justice [6]. But it would be uncharitable to saddle Dworkin and like-minded theorists with the hubristic view that these extremely general and abstract principles can by themselves achieve '... the right resolution of any major political issue...' in every particular society. For example, one might hold, as I believe both Dworkin and Rawls do, that certain very general moral principles will yield resolutions of most though not all moral issues, but only when supplemented by the results of appropriate democratic political procedures. This kind of view need not assume that democratic procedures will yield the same results in all societies. Contrary to Miller's unargued assumption, morality need not be universal morality in this absolutist sense, and a morality need not claim perfect decidability for all issues.

Miller's third requirement for morality is difficult to assess because of its vagueness, but it too seems overly restrictive. It is in fact a metaethical claim and one which some who offer normative moral theories reject. Miller has confused the issue of whether a view is compellingly rational to all who have the normal range of emotions with the question of whether something is a moral view at all. Anyone who denies that substantive moral principle need be universal in the absolutist, transhistorical sense specified in tenet (2), may also reject tenet (3).

It is tenet (1) to which Miller devotes the most attention. He notes Marx's belief that the interests of the bourgeoisie and their allies are not to be taken seriously. (He concedes, though, that Marx does hold that the fact that something would serve any person's interest is a reason in favor of it.) From the premise that Marx does not accord the proletariat's class enemies 'equal status', Miller concludes that Marx rejected the Equality Principle and that this is good evidence that he abandoned morality.

What is remarkable is that Miller fails to see that on this criterion, neither Rawls's view, nor Kant's, nor any view which subscribes to the priority of the right over the good qualifies as a moral view. For, as Rawls points out, it is a distinctive feature of deontological moral theories that they do not count all interests equally – indeed, some interests, namely those that run contrary to principles of justice, are to be given no weight at all.

It is true that such theories, at least if they are Kantian, nevertheless claim that all are to be treated with equal respect. But, of course, this is taken to be quite compatible with depriving the individual of all his liberties, and even his life, if he is sufficiently evil or if he is the enemy in a just war. Only the most radical pacificism would forbid infringements of property rights, abrogations of other basic civil and political liberties, and the use of force in *all* circumstances, including the most extreme. Therefore, it is fallacious for Miller to cite Marx's statements about the need for a dictatorship of the proletariat which will trample the rights of the bourgeoisie and disregard their interests, and then to conclude that Marx rejects the Equality Principle, a basic tenet of morality [5]. After all, Marx says that the class struggle is a fight to the finish, a war, and even goes so far as to say that the persistence of capitalism threatens the survival of the species ([8], p. 230).[3] (This latter extreme prediction is in fact echoed by those contemporary Marxists who claim that capitalism was responsible for the two most destructive wars the world has ever known and threatens to lead us to a nuclear Armageddon.)

The analogy with the morality of a just war warrants further scrutiny. According to perhaps the majority of what are undeniably moral theories and perhaps commonsense morality as well, depriving the enemy of his most basic rights and even of life is neither immoral nor even incompatible with treating him with equal respect – so long as it is indeed a just war, and so long as we use no more force than is required, avoid unnecessary suffering, etc.

I suggest that instead of assuming, as Miller does, that Marx rejected morality, we should consider the alternative hypothesis that his views about revolutionary violence are consistent with rather traditional moral views, if the latter are combined with a very extreme and questionable set of empirical assumptions about the way the world now is and how it can be in the future. Marx may have thought that capitalism is such a great evil, the alternative so grand, and the nature of the struggle so desperate – and so lacking in room for compromise – that revolutionaries are morally justified in regarding

ordinary moral obligations toward the enemy as being suspended for the
duration of the conflict. Similarly, a partisan fighting against the Nazi reign
of genocidal terror might conclude that the gravity of the struggle justified
relaxing some of the most basic moral constraints on his behavior toward
German soldiers, without in any sense adopting an anti-moral position.

However, regardless of whether Marx's advocacy of class war without
moral constraints was based upon a wholesale rejection of morality or upon
the assumption that the nature of the struggle warrants the suspension of
basic moral obligations toward the bourgeoisie and their allies, he is open to
weighty criticism.

Consider the first alternative: the proletariat's struggle against their class
enemies need recognize no moral constraints because no moral constraints of
any kind are valid. If this was Marx's view, then he failed to give us good
reasons for adopting it. It can, of course, be given a sort of Thrasymachan
defense, and some Marxists, including Engels, have suggested such a
position, contending that all morality is an illusion, an ideological
smokescreen for naked interest. To my knowledge Marxists who have held
this view have tended simply to assert it, rather than to argue for it in any
systematic way [10].

On the other hand, if the Marxist acknowledges that there is such a thing as
morality – and that morality includes constraints on how we may treat human
beings in pursuing our ends, even those whose ends are commendable – then
it is the Marxist who must show why the usual moral constraints are
suspended when it comes to the way proletarians behave toward their class
enemies.

Such a suspension of moral constraints would be warranted only if the
analogy of a just war for extremely high stakes were apt or, perhaps, if the
feasibility of a vastly superior life for all in communism were very firmly
grounded in an adequate theory of non-capitalist social coordination.
However, neither of these conditions is satisfied. Contrary to Marx's claim,
we are not typically confronted with a life and death struggle in which the
only alternatives are violent revolution and a capitalist order which increasingly 'immiserates' the vast majority, breaking them mentally and physically,
so that they must choose between starvation and 'wage slavery'. Marx's
Jeremiads notwithstanding, the crushing contradictions of capitalism – a
system which Marx says literally threatens civilization – have often given
way to the more tolerable tensions of the welfare state. No doubt there are
situations in which revolutionary workers are like soldiers fighting for a just
cause in mortal combat. For instance, if striking Chilean mineworkers are

attacked by government troops they may under certain circumstances fight back with lethal force. From this it does not follow, however, that *in general* the revolutionary struggle is subject to no serious moral constraints.

Even more importantly, the recent historical record of authoritarian Marxism regimes, taken together with the conspicuous absence of an adequate theory of social coordination in communism, undercuts Marx's prediction that the abolition of private property in the means of production will result in society that is radically better than what exists now. If the prediction of a vastly superior life after the destruction of the system of private property is not well grounded, and if the claim that class struggle is the moral equivalent of a just war to the finish is hyperbole, then it is hard to see how anyone who believes that morality is not illusory could plausibly ascribe to the Marxist view that the revolutionary's conduct toward those who oppose social revolution is not subject to serious moral constraints. Since Marxism, as I have interpreted it, recognizes no such constraints, it is morally defective as a practical guide.

Now that we have an interpretation of Marxism before us and some understanding of its peculiarities and weaknesses, we can examine attempts to apply it to three concrete moral problems.

IV. CASE 1: A CONFLICT BETWEEN FULFILLING SPECIAL OBLIGATIONS AND PARTICIPATING IN THE REVOLUTIONARY STRUGGLE

A young man, Peter, has just become the sole caretaker for his widowed, ailing mother. She now depends on him for physical as well as emotional support. Peter is a committed communist who until his mother's illness was actively involved in various revolutionary activities. He believes that significant participation in the struggle against capitalism is not compatible with giving his mother the attention she needs. What ought he to do? [Adapted from an example of Sartre's in *Existentialism is a Humanism*].

This case was chosen for two reasons. First, it concerns obligations, not to the class enemy, but to a member of one's own class. Second, it is a test case to ascertain whether Marxism has anything significant to say about questions of private morality.

If a traditional moral view can resolve the young man's dilemma at all, it will presumably do so by appeal to a hierarchy of obligations in which the strictness of duties of justice is decisive. For if the regime under attack by the revolutionaries is a seriously *unjust* one, then the duty to protect those whose rights are being violated may in at least some cases take precedence over one's special obligations to one's family. The moral imperative that grave unjustice ought to be resisted *regardless of the consequences*, 'even though the world perishes', may be hyperbolic, but it is fair to say that at least in the common morality of the Judaeo-Christian culture, what Rawls calls 'the natural duty of justice' is thought to rank very high in the hierarchy of duties. This same traditional morality also views the duty to resist grave injustice as being independent of consequences in another way. The natural duty of justice is thought of in a noncalculating or nonconsequentialist way. Although no one is required to throw his life away or to neglect his other obligations in clearly futile gestures of resistance, one's duty to resist grave injustice is not seen as being contingent on the knowledge that one's effort will make a decisive difference in the struggle. This, I believe, is just one instance of a much more general phenomenon: the appeal to rights is thought to provide reasons for acting that are largely independent of calculations of consequences.

Since Marxism eschews talk about rights and justice, it cannot even conceptualize Peter's dilemma as a conflict between a higher natural duty of justice and an obligation arising from a special relationship. Nor can an appeal to the rights of those oppressed by the current regime provide a reason for acting independent of calculations concerning the effectiveness of Peter's contribution to the revolution. In addition, as I have argued in another context, much of what Marx says about revolutionary motivation suggests what may be called a simple rational self-interest theory. According to this theory, what moves the masses to successful social revolution is not their sense of justice, nor any other moral sentiment, but rather the recognition that it is in their interest to overthrow the ruling order and create a new and better society. Indeed, Marx and later Marxists often suggest that the fact that it relies only on rational self-interest is a distinctive virtue of Marxism's account of social change.

If the proletarian's revolutionary motivation is simply rational self-interest, then a familiar problem arises which threatens to thwart successful collective revolutionary action. Given the simple rational self-interest model, collective revolutionary action is a public good for the proletariat as a class and as such is vulnerable to the free-rider problem. Each proletarian may reason as follows: 'Either enough others will contribute to the struggle to achieve success or they will not, regardless of what I do. Since my contributing is a cost to me (and in the case of Peter, to his mother to whom he is attached), and since I will be able to enjoy the fruits of revolution if it succeeds regardless of whether I contributed, the rational thing for me to do is not to contribute'. If enough proletarians reason thusly, collective action will not occur.

There are, it seems, two ways out of this difficulty that are consistent with the central tenets of Marx's view, in particular, with his rejection of any appeals to the sense of justice as a spring of revolutionary motivation. (1) The Marxist can emphasize very strongly something that Marx only suggests, namely, the motivating role of certain positive experiences that can occur in the process of revolution and that have value independently of whether the goal of the process is actually achieved. The good of solidarity with comrades in arms in the war against capitalism may move the worker to contribute. The difficulty here, of course, is that this appeal to 'in-process benefits' is more apt for explaining how collective action *continues* in the face of adversity than for showing how it gets *started* in the first place.

This problem is compounded for Marx, since he stresses that capitalism alienates the worker from his fellows, especially through the ruthless competition for jobs. Even if this account of how the free rider problem can be solved can be adequately developed, however, it does nothing to resolve Peter's moral dilemma, or even to explain why we should think it is a moral dilemma. In particular, it is not clear that Marxism can tell us why the prospects of enjoying the in-process benefits of revolutionary activity ought to override one's obligations to one's family, if one has no reason to think that one's contribution will be decisive to the success of the revolution.

The other, most promising strategy by which the Marxist can avoid the free rider problem is to emphasize the importance of developing a noncalculating attitude. If the workers can be led or can lead themselves simply to fix their aspirations on the vision of communism and to identify with its attainment, then they will not ask the fatal question, 'Will my contribution make a difference?' Their attitude will be noncalculating and to that extent nonrational. But it will be rational for the proletariat as a group to develop this noncalculating attitude if doing so is necessary to achieve that which is in their interests as a group. If this attitude is successfully developed, it will function as the sense of justice functions in traditional morality: the desire to achieve communism will override other concerns, including the desire to aid one's helpless mother, and this overriding will not be thought of as being contingent upon the assumption that one's contribution to the higher goal will be decisive.

The obvious difficulty with this way of handling Case One – and more generally, of avoiding failures of collective action – is that the rationality of developing the noncalculating attitude itself depends on a calculation of a different sort. Whether it is rational to develop the noncalculating attitude – let us call it 'loyalty to the revolutionary ideal' – depends upon whether there is sufficient reason to believe that the struggle against capitalism is a fight to the finish against an evil enemy, or at least that communism as a society that is greatly superior to capitalism is in fact feasible. Without good evidence for at least one of these assumptions, it would be irrational to develop the noncalculating attitude of uncritical loyalty to the revolutionary ideal, and insofar as this attitude would override one's moral commitments to others, it would be morally irresponsible as well. Yet, as I have already noted, Marxism fails to provide a theory of democratic, nonmarket social coordination powerful enough to show that communism as Marx envisions it is feasible. Marxism is also mistaken in its assumption that the struggle against capitalism is analogous to a just war to the finish. These central defects of Marxism undercut its ability to provide adequate practical guidance in situations like Case One.

V. CASE TWO: POLICY DECISIONS CONCERNING INSTITUTIONS IN THE HEALTH CARE SYSTEM

Many analysts have noted that the U.S. health care system is currently undergoing rapid and profound changes, in particular, that the era of the independent private practitioner is waning and that medicine is becoming 'corporatized' through rapid growth of HMO's (Health Maintenance Organizations), large for-profit hospital chains, and other forms of corporate group practice. A heated debate has developed over whether corporatization and the fostering of a more *competitive* environment in health care will ease or exacerbate two related problems: the dramatically rising costs of health care and the lack of access to health care for the poor. Many have also expressed concern that corporatization and competition are undermining the fiduciary relationship between physician and patient. What can Marxism tell us, as members of the general public and voters, or as persons in positions of power able to exert influence on public policy, about how we ought to respond to these institutional changes in health care? More specifically, ought a Marxist to take a stand on the issue of competition versus regulation and how should he or she view the increasing corporatization of health care?

This case was chosen for two reasons. First, it poses the kind of problem for which Marxism ought to be best equipped to provide practical guidance –

a political issue, not one of private morality or of a conflict between social commitment and private obligation. Second, this case is of interest because, as we shall see, it illustrates the interplay between Marxism as a theory to *explain* institutional change and Marxism as a source of practical guidance.

The initial response to this case is straightforward, or at least so it would seem. A Marxist should oppose the 'commercialization' of medicine, the move toward creating a genuine competitive market in health care, not simply because this development may worsen the problem of access to care for those who lack private insurance and are ineligible for publicly subsidized care, but also because Marxism condemns the 'marketization of human relations' in general. For the Marxist the purely instrumental interpersonal relations of the market are dehumanizing and alienating, and nowhere is this more apparent than in the provision of a good as important as health care. The Marxist should resist these developments in health care for the same reasons that he opposes capitalism in general.

It can be argued, however, that this initial reaction does not represent the most coherent and reflective Marxist response to the growth of commercialization and competition in health care, because it overlooks the way in which the Marxist theory of history should shape Marxist responses to issues of public policy. Drawing on Marx's historical writings about the transition from feudalism to capitalism, the Marxist could argue that the 'corporatization' of medicine and the abandonment of the ideal of the private physician as an independent professional (rather than as an employee in a competing firm) is an outmoded historical vestige that must be swept away before the transition to socialism can be achieved. According to this Marxist analysis, independent physicians are the twentieth-century medical analogs of the dwindling class of nineteenth-century 'independent craftsmen' who still owned their own means of production and vainly attempted to avoid being assimilated into the class of wage-workers. These craftsmen, like many independent physicians, viewed themselves as professionals dedicated to a skillful service and contrasted themselves sharply with those who merely sell their services as a means of making a living. Nevertheless, Marx viewed all attempts to preserve the independence of the small craftsmen as a futile, romantic distraction from the revolutionary struggle. In his view, the temporary persistence of a small class of individuals who own their own means of production and maintain a degree of independence can only foster the illusion that 'petty capitalism' is a viable alternative, not just for the few, but for many. This in turn can be an obstacle to the masses becoming genuine revolutionaries. Marx even suggests at times that the revolution is not likely

to come until the process of 'proletarianization' has run its full course and the
independent craftsmen have fallen into the class of dependent wage-workers.

Similarly, a contemporary Marxist might view the current trend toward
'corporatization' and 'commercialization' in health care as a progressive step
toward socialism, not just in medicine, but throughout society. If this were
the case, then the fact that these developments represent the further encroach-
ment of market relations into a central area of human relations would not be a
sufficient reason for the Marxist to oppose them, even if they also resulted in
an exacerbation of the problem of access to care. Instead of opposing the
'commercialization' of health care, the sophisticated Marxist might in fact
support it.

This seemingly paradoxical Marxist response depends, once again, on an
assumption about the predictive power of Marxist theory. Tolerating or even
encouraging the 'commercialization' of health care as a necessary evil –
along, with its potentially deleterious effects on access – is only acceptable if
the Marxist has good reason to believe that a new system will emerge whose
virtues will compensate for the current evils of a system that treats life and
health as commodities to be bought and sold. If, as I have argued, this sort of
prediction is the Achilles heel of Marxism, then supporting the growth of
competition in health care may be both irrational and morally irresponsible.
Thus, what answer Marxism provides to the problem in Case Two – or
whether it provides any answer at all – depends upon whether predictions of
the feasibility of a significantly better noncapitalist system can be given
adequate support.

VI. CASE THREE: CAPITAL PUNISHMENT

In a brief but provocative newspaper article attacking the practice of capital
punishment, Marx states that the only adequate moral justification for capital
punishment is retributivist. However, he then suggests that in the sort of
society in which there is a need for an institution of criminal justice, certain
conditions necessary for an adequate retributivist justification for capital
punishment – namely, voluntariness and fair terms of social cooperation – do
not obtain. Taking Marx's views here as a guide, what position should a
Marxist take on capital punishment, and more generally, on the punishment
of criminals?

As in Case Three, the correct Marxist response here at first may seem
obvious. If capitalism produces, or at least encourages, criminal behavior to

such an extent that the only plausible moral justification for punishment does not apply, then surely such punishment ought to be opposed. Yet this conclusion does not follow. For Marx also believed that the capitalists are products of the social system, that in a sense they are not responsible for what they do, but that this fact in no way should deter revolutionaries from depriving them of their property, their liberty, and even their lives. So, even though a Marxist should strive to abolish the social system which (he believes) produces criminals, it does not follow that he should oppose executions or other forms of punishment while the system persists. If criminals are in fact sufficiently dangerous and if, as Marxist theory suggests, they are largely immune to rehabilitative efforts so long as they live in a society that encourages them to be criminal, then rational prudence may dictate that they be incarcerated at the very least. So, while Marxism urges us to eliminate the conditions that spawn the need to punish, it does not tell us that we ought not to punish.

VII. CONCLUSION

I have argued that Marx's theory, as a source of practical guidance, is thoroughly consequentialist. Further, I have shown that it is vulnerable, not only to standard objections to consequentialist views in general, but also to the charge that it is a morally irresponsible utopianism which prescribes a wholesale suspension of moral constraints in the pursuit of a goal which it has not shown to be attainable.

At the outset I noted that the conception of communism which Marx sees strictly as an attainable *goal* might instead be thought of as an *ideal*. As an ideal, Marx's conception of life in communism has much to recommend it. Whether or not it is a fully coherent ideal, and whether it is uniquely preferable among competing ideals, are not questions that were ever systemically addressed by Marx, partly because he was convinced that his ideal was an attainable goal and thought that the range of feasible types of society was at this point in history quite narrowly constrained. And among what Marx thought to be the feasible alternatives, communism was, perhaps, uniquely preferable.

If, as I have argued, Marxism as a strictly consequentialist source of practical guidance is seriously defective, then the task for those who are attracted to Marx's vision of life in communism is to develop the communist ideal more fully, to demonstrate its superiority over competing ideals, and to show that it can serve as a fruitful source of practical guidance. Whether or not the successful completion of this task would properly be called a Marxist *moral* theory is an interesting question, but one that cannot be answered in advance.

NOTES

[1] This is one of the few places in which Marx does anything to elaborate on the claim that communism will be a democratic form of social coordination. For an examination of these passages, see [1], pp. 171–175.

[2] For a more selective discussion, see [2] and [4].

[3] In [7], p. 261, Marx writes of '...the depopulation of the human race by capitalism'.

BIBLIOGRAPHY

[1] Buchanan, A.: 1982, *Marx and Justice: The Radical Critique of Liberalism*, Rowman and Littlefield, Totowa, New Jersey.

[2] Buchanan, A.: 1983a, 'Marx on Democracy and the Obsolescence of Rights', *South African Journal of Philosophy* 2, 130–135.

[3] Buchanan, A.: 1983b, review of A. Wood, *Karl Marx*, in *The Journal of Philosophy* 80, 43–433.

[4] Buchanan, A.: 1984, *Ethics, Efficiency, and the Market*, Rowman and Littlefield, Totowa, New Jersey.

[5] Buchanan, A.: forthcoming, review article of R. Miller, *Analyzing Marx*, in *Philosophical Studies*.

[6] Dworkin, R.: 1977, *Taking Rights Seriously*, Harvard University Press, Cambridge.

[7] Marx, K.: 1967, *Capital*, Volume 1, International Publishers, New York.

[8] Marx, K.: 1977a, 'The Communist Manifesto', *Karl Marx: Selected Writings*, D. McLellan (ed.), Oxford University Press, Oxford.

[9] Marx, K.: 1977b, 'Critique of the Gotha Program', *Karl Marx: Selected Writings*, D. McLellan (ed.), Oxford University Press, Oxford.

[10] Marx, K. and Engels, F.: 1972, Karl Marx and Frederick Engels, *Selected Works: The Civil War in France*, International Publishers, New York.

[11] Miller, R.: 1984, *Analyzing Marx*, Princeton University Press, Princeton.

[12] Mueller, D.: 1979, *Public Choice*, Cambridge University Press, Cambridge.

[13] Rawls, J.: 1985, *Philosophy and Public Affairs* 14, 223–251.

[14] Wood, A.: 1981, *Karl Marx*, Routledge and Kegan Paul, London.

University of Arizona
Tucson, Arizona

MARY B. MAHOWALD

MARX, MORAL JUDGMENT, AND MEDICAL ETHICS: COMMENTARY ON BUCHANAN

Marx, Marxism, and Marxists are distinct sources of possible guidance for resolving moral problems. Karl Marx is the German political philosopher who lived and wrote during the nineteenth century. Marxism refers to various interpretations of Marx's thoughts and writings by others. Marxists are those who practically align themselves with one of these interpretations through their actions, through their own writings, or both. Exegetes of Marx elaborate different, sometimes conflicting versions of Marxism, and Marxists differ in their practical interpretation of Marx's views. Marxism may, of course, be understood and explained by individuals who are not Marxists, and even by those who oppose Marx or Marxism. Allen Buchanan exemplifies the exegete who is not a Marxist, and who in fact is critical of Marx's views [2, 3, 4].

This commentary will exhibit a more sympathetic and constructive view, yet one which is also critical of Marx. It may thus be considered a Marxist version of Marxism. The critical component involves both agreement and disagreement with different aspects of Buchanan's interpretation of Marx. The sympathetic and constructive component emphasizes two fundamental concepts that thread through Marx's writings, neither of which is developed by Buchanan, equality and community. After explaining these features of an alternative interpretation of Marx, I will apply the resultant view to the cases described by Buchanan, extending these to further applications in medical ethics.

I. CRITICAL CORRELATIONS

Marx's evaluative perspective, according to Buchanan, rests on a 'vision of life' as 'a form of society in which the ideals of community, freedom, and the all-around development of the individual's capacities are finally actualized'([4], p. 102). That vision is the criterion by which social and political practices may be evaluated. To the extent that a given practice promotes these ideals, it is justified or justifiable, and may even be obligatory. Buchanan avoids the term 'moral' in describing the kind of justification or obligation thus provided. True, Marx rejected both 'morality' and 'moralism', and is not

119

Baruch A. Brody (ed.), Moral Theory and Moral Judgments in Medical Ethics, 119–131.
© 1988 by Kluwer Academic Publishers.

himself a moral philosopher in the usual sense of the term. However, his critique of moral philosophy is comparable to his critique of philosophy in general, as expressed in the eleventh thesis on Feuerbach: philosophy has been empty theorizing ([15], p. 109). His rejection of 'morality' stems from its construal as empty ideology. As Kai Nielsen puts it:

morality in his (Marx's) society… is a collection of disguised bourgeois prejudices masking and rationalizing bourgeois domination in a class society. The thing to do, according to Marx, is to strip morality of all the mystification created by moralizing and to see morality for what it is, namely as an ideology in which the class interests of the dominant class are, through mystification, insinuated as being in the interests of the society as a whole ([12], p. 6).

Although Buchanan apparently disagrees, the vision of life in communist society does serve as a moral criterion if we construe 'moral' as political, or at least as embracing the meaning of 'political'. This construal is legitimate if we look beyond the above criticisms to what Marx and Engels actually said and did: 'their readiness, throughout their lives in their pamphleteering, in their theoretical work and in their private correspondence, to quite unselfconsciously make moral judgments and moral assessments which they gave no sign at all of regarding as ideology, as class biases or as subjective' (*ibid.*).

Marx appeals neither to a concept of individual rights, nor to a sense of justice as motivation for promoting these ideals. Again, however, Marx's rejection of these juridical concepts stems from his view that they represent bourgeois egoism and abstract philosophizing that impede the development of human beings as *Gattungswesen* or 'species-beings', i.e., free, conscious, social, productive individuals [8]. According to Buchanan, Marx mainly appeals to the self-interest of the masses as grounds for overthrowing the capitalist society that exploits them. But self-interest need not be understood as conflicting with the interests of others or of all of society. Buchanan fails to give sufficient weight to Marx's concept of transformation of consciousness through which he expects these interests to converge gradually. Not only is it true that the communist ideal represents a unity between the interests of the one and the many, progress towards that ideal is itself a unifying process. Marx acknowledges the defects of the dictatorship of the proletariat, the first phase of communist society, but regards it as democratic in comparison with the preceding dehumanizing stage of capitalism. Throughout the transition to the second stage, the consciousness of the bourgeoisie is to be democratized so as to allow for a truly classless society.

Marx further maintains that the ideal of communism is achievable. As Buchanan puts it, 'communism as a goal, not as an ideal, is the ultimate normative source of practical guidance' ([4], p. 102). Neither Marx nor history, however, has demonstrated the feasibility of achieving the second phase of communism. This leaves Marx open to the charge of utopianism, which he so abhorred in other political ideologies. His expectation that the second phase of communism can be actualized suggests a radically different concept of human nature than that which underlies the theory of capitalism. Marx views human beings as capable of merging self-interest with societal interest, and views such development as progress in humanization. Capitalist society, in contrast, views human beings as essentially competitive in their self-interest. The contrast gives rise to significantly different concepts of equality, which I will consider subsequently.

In delineating the liabilities of Marx's 'thoroughly consequentialist' theory, Buchanan refers to the usual criticism of utilitarianism: 'it reduces all moral issues to problems of selecting the best means to an end, recognizing no moral restrictions on how the end is to be attained' ([4], p. 106). This represents a serious moral problem unless constraints are introduced under the aegis of a rule consequentialism, as Buchanan himself suggests. The constraints would be designed to thwart the self-defeating feature of un-restricted pursuit of a laudable end, e.g., through lack of coordination, or corruption of revolutionaries pursuing the end. Buchanan thinks such constraints would be difficult to develop without the juridical concepts of rights and justice which Marx rejects; I believe they can be developed through use of other fundamental concepts which I will now address.

II. CRUCIAL CONCEPTS: COMMUNITY AND EQUALITY

The German language supplies Marx with several different expressions for the single English term *community*. Among these are *Gemeinwesen*, *Gemeinde, Gemeindewesen*, and *Gemeinschaft*. At least two meanings may legitimately be attributed to these terms for 'community' as used in Marx [8]. The first meaning is that of a presently existing social group or communal reality; the second, a not-yet existing communal goal or ideal. If and when the goal is achieved, the two meanings will coincide.

Community as *Gemeinwesen* is the underlying reality in human beings which accounts for their basic tendency to associate with one another through the formation of society. It refers to the essence of human beings as social, a presently human and humanizing feature which explains their being (*wesen*) together (*Gemein*). This is the term for community which is used by Marx most frequently.

The terms *Gemeinde* and *Gemeindewesen* are used occasionally to designate either a previously existent or a presently existing communal being rather than an unrealized communal ideal. We read, for example, in the *Pre-Capitalist Economic Formations*, of communities that were extant during the second phase of ownership, the ancient stage of society:

the community [*Gemeinde*] – as a state – is, on the one hand, the relationship of these free and private proprietors to each other, their combination against the outside world – and at the same time their safeguard. The community [*Gemeindewesen*] is based on the fact that its members consist of working owners of land, small peasant cultivators... ([7], p. 72; [9], p. 379).

Gemeinschaft as the German expression for community occurs very seldom in the texts of Marx. It is used in passages that suggest the ideal of communism, rather than an existant communal reality. For example, in the first part of the *German Ideology* he describes what he means by *Gemeinschaft*. After recalling the inevitable limitedness of the human individual as such, and the particular defects of previously and presently existing forms of society, Marx calls for a radically new form of worldwide social intercourse. Only in such a community, he claims,

has each individual the means of cultivating his talents in all directions. Only in a community [*Gemeinschaft*] therefore is personal freedom possible. In the previous substitutes for community, in the state, etc., personal freedom existed only for those individuals who grew up in the ruling class and only in so far as they were members of this class. The illusory community in which, up to the present, individuals have combined, always acquired an independent existence apart from them, and since it was a union of one class against another it represented for the dominated class not only a completely illusory community but also a new shackle. In a real community [*Gemeinschaft*] individuals gain their freedom in and through their association ([1], pp. 247–248; [11], p. 74).

The different meanings of community in Marx posit a value to be pursued and suggest a means through which to pursue the ideal fulfillment of that value, as well as a criterion by which to measure progress (or regress) towards (from) fulfillment. Whether or not Marx calls the value of community 'moral', we may do so. It is as moral a value as autonomy or justice, but I will not argue for that here. Like those terms, its meaning remains problematic, and it may be used to describe values that are not moral. Nonetheless, community represents a positive human good, a non-empirical but real value. For Marx, human beings, through their essentially communal nature (*Gemeinwesen*), build communities (*Gemeinde, Gemeindewesen*) which bring them closer to the communal ideal (*Gemeinschaft*) which is only achievable in the second stage of communism. Buchanan and I disagree with Marx that the ideal is fully achievable, but this does not deny the moral worthwhileness of its partial achievement. The moral judgments of presently existing communal entities, whether these be institutions or individuals, may thus be morally assessed on the basis of their approximation to the ideal of *Gemeinschaft* [15]. Although Marx's concept of community does not amount to a moral theory, its elements can provide practical guidance for moral dilemmas such as those described by Buchanan.

In some ways the term 'equality' (*Gleichheit*) is a more elusive concept than 'community', even though the original German is consistent in its use of the same term and its cognates (*gleiche, ungleiche, Ungleichheit*) ([10], [15]). The adjectival form is used more often than the noun, as in 'equal right' (*gleiche Recht*), and there is no doubt that Marx rejects the concept of equal rights, as Buchanan and others recognize. Nonetheless, Marx's use of the term equality and its cognates has both favorable and unfavorable meanings for Marx. Both meanings are evident in a passage from the *Critique of the Gotha Programa* where he acknowledges that the equal rights that emerge after the overthrow of capitalism are 'bourgeois rights'. While Marx views the situation as an improvement over the 'crude equality' of capitalism, he criticizes the temporary dictatorship of the proletariat because 'equality consists in the fact that measurement is made with an *equal standard*: labour' ([15], p. 387). He thus notes the inadequacy of that standard

But one man is superior to another physically or mentally and so supplies more labour in the same time, or can labour for a longer time, and labour, to serve as a measure, must be defined by its duration or intensity, otherwise it ceases to be a standard of measurement. This *equal* right is an unequal right for unequal labour. It recognizes no class differences, because everyone is only a worker like everyone else, but it tacitly recognizes unequal individual endowment and thus productive capacity as natural privileges. *It is, therefore, a right of inequality, in its content, like every right*. Right by its very nature can consist only in the application of an equal standard; but unequal individuals (and they would not be different individuals if they were not unequal) are measureable only by an equal standard in so far as they are brought under an equal point of view, are taken from one *definite* side only, for instance, in the present case, are regarded *only as workers* and nothing more is seen in them, everything else being ignored... Thus, with an equal performance of labour, and hence an equal share in the social consumption fund, one will in fact receive more than another, one will be richer than another, and so on. To avoid all these defects, right instead of being equal would have to be unequal ([15], p. 387–388).

Clearly, Marx's condemnation of rights is tied to a negative concept of equality, one which is at odds with the ideal of distributing 'to each according to need' and 'from each according to ability'. But this very critique is based on a positive concept of 'genuine equality', a situation where the differences among individuals form the baseline against which distribution is determined. As Jeffrey Reiman has noted, Marx is really quite clear that 'one and only one defect results from 'equal right', and that defect is *inequality*' ([14]).

This account of equality in Marx raises the question of its relationship with the juridical concept of justice, which he repudiated. Is it possible for Marx to endorse equality as morally desirable, while also referring to talk of 'just distribution' as 'obsolete verbal rubbish' ([3], p. 282)? Buchanan gives a hint that this is possible in discussing Richard Miller's claim that Marx's theory fails to include a concept of equality as one of the essential features of morality. 'It is fallacious', he claims,

for Miller to cite Marx's statements about the need for a dictatorship of the proletariat which will trample the rights of the bourgeoisie and disregard their interests and then conclude that Marx rejects the Equality Principle ([14], p. 109).

As evidence of Miller's fallacious reasoning, Buchanan cites Marx's advocacy of the class struggle as a 'fight to the finish', presumably in quest of equality.

Whether Buchanan construes Marx's overall position as retaining a concept of equality while rejecting that of justice remains unclear. However, it is difficult to separate the two, either conceptually or practically, especially if the justice referred to is distributive justice. Thus, for example, Michael Walzer subtitles his book *Spheres of Justice*, 'A Defense of Pluralism and Equality', and spends most of the chapter entitled 'Complex Equality' on the topic of distributive justice [16]. Ronald Dworkin in his two-part article 'What Is Equality?' discusses ' distributional equality', and contrasts his theory of equality with '*other*' theories of justice [5]. And both of John Rawls's principles of justice entail a reference to equality, i.e., the equal liberty principle, and the difference principle which reduces social inequalities [13]. Unless Buchanan explicitly separates the two concepts, he must either jettison the concept of equality along with that of justice, or accept the concept of justice back into Marx's theory, to join that of equality. The latter alternative is apparently unacceptable to Buchanan; this leaves him with a task which may well be conceptually impossible.

Reiman, on the other hand, explicitly conjoins the two concepts, relating Marx's theory to Rawls's second principle of justice. The 'socialist' principle of Marx, 'to each according to his time labored', applies to the time which spans the overturning of capitalism to the overcoming of scarcity. The 'communist' principle, 'from each according to his ability, to each according to his needs', applies to the period which follows. Reiman describes the first

principle as 'one of equality in the sense that each person derives a share of
the social product equal to his input measured objectively by time worked (or
effort expended)' ([14], pp. 320–321). He then relates the principle to
Rawls's view:

This is precisely what the difference principle would require once it was no longer thought
necessary or appropriate to provide differential incentives to those of greater talents... This
principle would, as Marx observes, still countenance inequality, because any attempt to measure
all individuals by an objective standard allows the natural differences between peoples' abilities
to meet that standard to function in effect as grounds for unequal treatment ([14], p. 321).

Accordingly, Marx· 'criticizes the first principle because of its in-
egalitarianism and moves to the second principle because it is more perfectly
egalitarian' ([14], *ibid.*). Reiman concludes that the actual historical sequence
of principles of justice includes progress from Rawls's two principles, to
Marx's principle for socialism (under conditions of scarcity), to his principle
for communism (under conditions of abundance). This represents, he
maintains, 'the actual tendency to limit the amount of permissible inequality
to the least amount necessary to maximize the standard of living of the least
advantaged as the material conditions of doing this develop' ([14], p. 322).

Marx's unfavorable view of equality thus embraces both the situation in
which the concept masks inequality, as in capitalist society's concept of
'equal rights', and the situation where a degree of inequality remains
inevitable because the ideal of communism has not yet been achieved. His
favorable view is reflected in those features of the dictatorship of the
proletariat which represent a reduction of inequalities or a greater degree of
equality, e.g., through the fact that it is the proletariat rather than the bourgeoisie that controls society. When transformation of bourgeois consciousness occurs to the degree that a classless society is possible, then equality in
its fullest and most favorable sense can be actualized. At this point the
concepts of community and equality both describe Marx's social ideal.

III. APPLICATIONS

To the extent that these concepts remain present in Marx's theory, they shed
light on the cases described by Buchanan regardless of Marx's rejection of
the juridical concepts of rights and justice.

Buchanan maintains that the 'central defects of Marxism undercut its
ability to provide adequate practical guidance in situations like Case One',

i.e., the case involving conflict between fulfillment of personal obligation and participation in the revolutionary struggle. Marxism, he says, "cannot even conceptualize Peter's dilemma as a conflict between a higher natural duty of justice and an obligation arising from a special relationship" ([4], p. 112). According to Buchanan, this defect occurs because Marx eschews "talk about rights and justice" ([4], p. 112). But clearly such 'talk' refers to the juridical concept of justice, and this is not necessarily coincident with a 'higher natural duty of justice'. A higher natural duty, whether or not it is called 'justice', is coincident with Marx's egalitarian, communal ideal. As 'higher' it suggests a criterion for resolving the dilemma in favor of support for the revolutionary struggle, which is more important for Marx than one's obligation to a single individual. In its construal of the ideal of equality and community, Marx's theory also permits the view that such a decision would be a virtuous act rather than one that is morally obligatory. No doubt Peter would be aware that his desire to stay with his mother is partly motivated by self-interest. Such self-interest is not immoral, and in fact, as Buchanan observes, Marx himself suggests that "rational self-interest is a distinctive virtue of Marxism's account of social change" ([4], p. 112). Nonetheless, through the transformation of consciousness of which human beings are capable, self-interest is wedded to interest in others. Since such transformation constitutes moral progress for individuals and society, this suggests a criterion for determining whether a specific course of action is moral, viz., its likelihood of promoting the communal interests of all of us. Ultimately, Marxism does not tolerate a dichotomy between the needs of oneself or one's parent, and the needs of others.

Short of achieving the ultimate communal, egalitarian ideal, however, the morality of present decisions can be measured by the degree to which they reduce inequalities and alienation. These constitute morally relevant features of a decision to care for one's ailing, lonely mother, whose individual needs ought to be addressed according to the ability of each respondent. Thus there is a Marxist rationale for a decision postponing participation in the revolution in order to care for one's mother; the rationale is not based on Peter's relationship to his mother but upon the fact that he is the one who might best tender that care. While it is more moral or virtuous to act in the interests of all rather than one, Marx's theory also provides guidance for promoting equality and community in one-to-one relationships. My main disagreement with Buchanan, therefore, is that he fails to recognize the usefulness of an ideal that cannot be wholly realized. Marx himself recognized approximation to that ideal as genuine improvement.

Although the dilemma described by Case One is not specific to medical ethics, a comparable conflict would arise in that context if Peter were a physician and either (a) his 'ailing mother' were instead an ailing patient, or (b) the 'revolutionary struggle' were instead his professional commitment to patients. What Buchanan has omitted from his description of Peter is a feature that clearly complicates real-life ethical dilemmas even more, i.e., one's professional obligations. I think, however, that Marx's theory provides practical guidance here as well.

The conflicts between personal and professional obligations which physicians often face are heightened by the fact that the values promoted by medicine, e.g., health, life, and alleviation of human suffering, are so fundamental that they may be viewed as more important than other human values, e.g., individual liberty, or maintenance of close family ties. The socialization process undergone by medical students promotes the sense that medicine is a very special profession, demanding a deeper commitment than other professions. Peter, having experienced that socialization and agreeing that the values of medicine are generally 'higher' than those of other professions (at least for him), would be further reinforced by Marx's theory to place the interests of patients ahead of his mother so long as their needs were greater than hers, and his own professional ability was crucial in responding to those needs. However, that same reasoning, with a similar proviso, would apply to the question of whether he might leave medicine in order to participate in the revolutionary struggle. So long as social needs are greater than those he might respond to as a physician, and so long as his participation would make a practical difference, then the more moral or virtuous path for Peter to pursue is the route to revolution.

Marx's theory would have Peter ask: How can I, with my own set of talents, relationship, and limitations, best promote equality and community in today's society? Neither his *role* as son, nor his *role* as a professional are in themselves critical to his response. But what he can do as who he *totally* is, i.e., son, physician, citizen, human being, *is* critical. The route to social change which Peter thus chooses is unlikely to mean that he will march off to war with his comrades. He is more likely to seek political appointments or public offices from which he can have greater impact on society's health, or involve himself in lobbying efforts to fund the health care needs of the poor and/or to forestall a possible nuclear holocaust. An increasing number of today's physicians have practically implemented decisions along these lines. Their moral motive is consistent with Marx's theory, whether or not acknowledged as such.

Buchanan believes that Case Two is a particularly apt context for Marx's theory because it raises a political issue rather than a question of private morality. For Marx, political and moral responsibility are the same, which is why points made with regard to Case One apply here also. For Buchanan, Marxist theory is again unhelpful because of the unfeasibility of Marx's ideal. It is irrational, he claims, to support an ideal which, by virtue of its unrealizability, constitutes the 'Achilles heel' of Marx's theory.

As with Case One, however, the ideal of community and equality provides practical guidance for answering the question: 'Ought a Marxist to take a stand on the issue of competition versus regulation, and how should he or she view the increasing corporatization of health care?' Clearly the Marxist should take a stand because the issue calls for a statement of ideological commitment. But what should that stand be? Buchanan apparently thinks a simplistic version of Marxism opposes corporatization, while a more sophisticated version may see it as a necessary step on the way to communism. I believe Marx would reject commercialization of health care because competition opposes community by causing alienation among competitors, and increases inequalities by giving free rein to the different abilities of different competitors. Once the profit motive is the controlling influence, health care is no longer a profession but a business.

The more sophisticated Marxist is not sophisticated enough if he or she fails to recognize that capitalist society has developed and maintained those physicians who function as the twentieth-century remnant of 'independent craftsmen', still owning their own means of production and vainly attempting to avoid assimilation into the class of wage-workers. While such individuals are craftsmen in a certain sense, they are surely part of the capitalist elite, who set their own fees and increase their capital while wages paid to other health care workers remain fixed by others. Corporatization of health care simply exacerbates the inequalities between these classes, as well as between physicians and the wage-earning public, negating the humanitarian orientation which is the hallmark of medicine as a profession. The overthrow of capitalism is morally and politically justified now, but if corporatization of health care becomes the dominant mode of health care provision, it will be even more necessary.

Buchanan discusses Case Three, the issue of capital punishment, on the basis of a brief article published by Marx in the New York *Daily Tribune*. Marx rejects both the utilitarian argument that capital punishment serves as a deterrent, and the Kantian and Hegelian argument that punishment is the right of the criminal. His main point in the article, however, is that the brutality of capital punishment reflects the brutality of the bourgeois system which causes the crimes thus punished. His article calls for reflection 'upon an alteration of the system that breeds these crimes, instead of glorifying the hangman who executes a lot of criminals to make room only for the supply of new ones' ([6], p. 489).

As with the preceding cases, Buchanan thinks Marx's theory is unhelpful, and I disagree. The argument, according to Buchanan, is as follows:

Even though a Marxist should strive to abolish the social system which (he believes) produces criminals, it does not follow that he should oppose executions or other forms of punishment while the system persists.... So while Marxism urges us to eliminate the conditions that spawn the need to punish, it does not tell us that we ought not to punish ([4], p. 117).

If, as Marx suggests, the overcoming of capitalism would yield (at least in the second phase of communism) a society in which capital punishment is no longer necessary, then the ideal features of that society function as a political/moral guide for the present situation. As Buchanan suggests, there is an important distinction in Marx between capitalists as individuals and the capitalist system that produces them. Punishment of individuals for crimes resulting from the system is inconsistent with this distinction and with Marx's emphasis on equality and community. However, capital punishment is justified in particular cases to the extent that it brings society closer to that ideal. In other words, Marx's consequentialism is the context in which the permissibility of capital punishment may be established in certain cases. Under capitalism, this would not occur if its endorsement serves to reinforce the capitalist system, as Marx suggests it does. During the first phase of communism, capital punishment is only permissible as a means of promoting the second phase, and not if it only prolongs the dictatorship of the proletariat.

Although Case Three does not illustrate a dilemma specific to medical ethics, we might append questions that would place it in that context. We might ask, for example, (a) whether physicians as such should oppose capital punishment, or (b) whether it is morally permissible for a physician to serve as executioner in a situation where capital punishment has been legally sanctioned. Regarding (a), Marx's rejection of class distinctions argues against the 'specialness' of physicians as a class, insofar as that might entail an inequitable distribution of prestige, power, or income. Physicians and non-physicians alike should generally oppose capital punishment. But if physicians constitute a greater leverage in promoting its elimination, that represents a different practical scenario, in which doctors have a responsibility for using their influence to effect that end.

Regarding (b), again because of Marx's rejection of class distinctions, it is as morally permissible for a physician to serve as executioner as for a non-physician. Although it is difficult to think of a situation in which capital punishment would in fact promote greater equality and community, *if* that were to occur, it would be appropriate for whoever might best accomplish the task to do so. If the mode of execution were lethal injection, a physician's expertise might be more appropriate than a hangman's. Capital punishment might allow the physician to contribute to society according to ability, but it would hardly provide for the criminal according to his or her need.

For each of the three cases described, specific details are lacking. While this is inevitable to some extent, it is particularly significant for using those cases as a test of whether Marx's theory provides practical guidance. For example, in Case One we do not know whether Peter could postpone his participation in the revolution, or whether his mother is also committed to the revolutionary ideal or goal. The issue relevant to Case Two might apply to corporate organization of physicians, hospitals, or nurses, or all of these, or simply to one group of individuals whose circumstances are unique. Case Three is not specified as applicable to any particular crime, group or individual, yet these circumstances might well alter the manner in which Marxist theory would apply. The consequences crucial to Marx's reasoning would differ importantly for each specific case. The unknown features of Buchanan's examples thus make it impossible to provide final answers to the moral questions raised. This does not represent a flaw in Marx, but a flaw in our intellectual and linguistic ability to capture the particularity of real situations. The same problem would occur in considering applications of other moral theories.

The history of philosophy amply illustrates flaws in those other moral theories, except perhaps in the minds of their originators. This does not imply their inability to provide moral guidance, however. Marx's theory, particularly through the concepts of equality and community which are crucial to his social ideal and to progress towards that ideal, provides guidance in confronting moral dilemmas, both personal and political, in health care and in life. Guidance does not mean answers. Although Marx's theory is flawed, several of its fundamental principles serve as practical guides to moral judgment.

BIBLIOGRAPHY

[1] Bottomore, T. B. (trans.): 1956, *Karl Marx, Selected Writings in Sociology and Social Philosophy*, McGraw-Hill, New York.
[2] Buchanan, A. E.: 1982, *Marx and Justice: The Radical Critique of Liberalism*, Rowman and Littlefield, Totowa, New Jersey.
[3] Buchanan, A. E.: 1981, 'The Marxian Critique of Justice and Rights', *Marx and Morality, Canadian Journal of Philosophy*, Supplementary Vol. 7, 269–306.
[4] Buchanan, A. E.: 1988, 'Marxism and Moral Judgment', in this volume, pp. 101–18.
[5] Dworkin, R.: 1981, 'What is Equality?', *Philosophy and Public Affairs*, 185–246, 283–345.
[6] Feuer, L. S. (ed.): 1959, *Marx and Engels. Basic Writings on Politics and Philosophy*, Doubleday, Garden City, New York.
[7] Hobsbawm, E. J. (ed.): 1965, *Karl Marx. Pre-Capitalist Economic Formations*, International Publishers, New York.
[8] Mahowald, M. B.: 1973, 'Marx's *Gemeinschaft*. Another Interpretation', *Philosophy and Phenomenological Research* 33, 472–488.
[9] Marx, K.: 1953, *Grundrisse der Kritik der politischen Ökonomie*, Dietz Verlag, Berlin.
[10] Marx, K.: 1960, *Kritik des Gothaer Programmas, Politische Schriften, Zweiter Band*, Cotta-Verlag, Stuttgart, pp. 1014–1038.
[11] Marx, K. and Engels, F.: 1962, *Die Deutsche Ideologie Werke*, Band 3, Dietz Verlag, Berlin, pp. 9–530.
[12] Nielsen, K. (ed.): 1981, 'Introduction', *Marx and Morality, Canadian Journal of Philosophy*, Supplementary Vol. 7, 1–17.
[13] Rawls, J.: 1971, *A Theory of Justice*, Harvard Belknap Press, Cambridge.
[14] Reiman, J. H.: 1981, 'The Possibility of a Marxian Theory of Justice', *Marx and Morality, Canadian Journal of Philosophy*, Supplementary Vol. 7, 307–322.
[15] Tucker, R. (ed.): 1972, *The Marx-Engels Reader*, W. W. Norton, New York.
[16] Walzer, M.: 1983, *Spheres of Justice. A Defense of Pluralism and Equality*, Basic Books, New York.

Case Western Reserve School of Medicine
Cleveland, Ohio

SECTION IV

CHRISTIAN CASUISTRY

RECONCILING THE PRACTICE OF REASON: CASUISTRY IN A CHRISTIAN CONTEXT

I. ON REPRESENTING THEOLOGICAL ETHICS

My assignment is to address the relation between moral theory and concrete moral judgments from 'the perspective of theological ethics. This would seem to be a straightforward enough task, so that I can get down to business rather quickly. But unfortunately, I must tell you that, before I can begin to analyze the 'case' I have provided, I need to make clear the status of the perspective from which I am working.

I suspect it is already clear to most of you in that terms of the other approaches represented in this volume – i.e., utilitarianism, Kantianism, contractarianism, and Marxist – theological ethics is different in kind. Each of the others is a theory about morality represented by distinct thinkers and developed through refined discourse and argument. In contrast, theological ethics certainly is not a theory, and it is no easy matter to identify those thinkers who would be considered representative of it as a peculiar genre of moral reflection. To put the matter differently, none of the other approaches, with the possible exception of Marxism, has a body of sacred literature to which the thinker must relate. Christian theologians do not have a theory of moral rationality, since they have something better or worse depending on your point of view – namely, a Bible and a church to which they are accountable.

For the theologian, therefore, some of the questions before this conference do not have the same immediacy. For example, we were asked to discuss whether our concrete moral judgments can be derived from our moral theory without reliance on 'extra assumptions'. To which I can reply only, 'What theory?' Or we were asked to consider whether there are better alternatives to this deductive approach, when I am even unsure if a religious tradition's way of dealing with moral decisions is deductive. Most religious communities do not start with a theory and then try to determine if x or y is permissible; rather, they begin with a sense that assumes x or y is or is not to be done given the nature of their community. All of which makes it seem that theologians begin with a disadvantage in considering these questions, since

135

Baruch A. Brody (ed.), Moral Theory and Moral Judgments in Medical Ethics, 135–155.
© *1988 by Kluwer Academic Publishers.*

we do not begin with a theory of what makes ethics or a theory of moral rationality.

Of course, I am not suggesting that theological thinkers do not represent options that may more or less be characterized in terms of familiar philosophical alternatives. Joseph Fletcher is well known for espousing utilitarianism as the most appropriate form of Christian love. Paul Ramsey is equally well known for arguing that what Christians mean by love is best expressed deontologically. It would be tempting to try to assess the basis of such a difference and how it could be adjudicated, but in the process I would avoid dealing with the question of how theological ethics does or should function.

For I suspect the issue that the inclusion of the theologian amid the philosophers is meant to raise is not how our moral theory makes a difference for moral judgments but how God might make a difference. Therefore, the question is whether belief in God does or can make a difference for moral decisions and their justification. Any constructive response to this question seems doomed, moreover, since most philosophers assume no logical entailment can be demonstrated between belief in God and our moral principles and judgments. Matters are no better, however, if I try to take refuge in theology, since many theologians argue it is a theological mistake to try to speak on behalf of God in matters having to do with ethics.

For example, Karl Barth argues that when a moralist tries to deduce the good or evil in human conduct as if it were the command of God, he is trying to

set himself on God's throne, to distinguish good and evil and always to judge things as the one or the other, not only in relation to others but also to himself. He makes himself lord, king and judge at the place where only God can be this. He does so by claiming that in a *summa* of ethical statements compiled by him and his like from the Bible, natural law and tradition, he can know the command of God, see through and past it, and thus master and handle it, i.e., apply it to himself and others, so that armed with this instrument he may speak as law ([1], p. 10).

Of course, it is possible to argue, as I would, that Barth is wrong in denying the value of casuistry. But that does not settle the difficulty, for if Barth is wrong, he is so because he fails to appreciate how religious communities have always generated informal, as well as extremely sophisticated, modes of moral reflection which can only be called casuistry. They have done so not in an attempt to preempt God's judgment, but in order to be more faithful to God. Indeed, in this respect theological ethics is really much better off than the philosopher's, as there exists a rich literature dealing with concrete moral issues for informing the conscience of the faithful.

Yet the matter cannot be solved so easily, for I cannot pretend to speak for all religious traditions. Casuistry among Jews is not the same as casuistry in the Roman Catholic tradition, and they are both different from Protestant traditions. Judaism has a long tradition of reflection derived from the rabbis that is not easily characterized in terms of contemporary philosophical options; Catholicism's casuistical tradition is closely tied to the sacrament of penance and is at least alleged to be based on a version of natural law; Protestants have not developed such an explicit tradition of moral reflection but have generally appealed to Scripture as the ultimate touchstone for their concrete moral judgments. Of course, all of this is made even more complex by the diversity within each of these traditions.

As a result, I feel a bit like the Protestant during Brotherhood Week in the local school district who was asked, along with a rabbi and a Catholic priest, to give his religious views on some issue. The rabbi began by developing the history of rabbinical reflection over the centuries on the topic and noted what seemed to be the general consensus; the priest appealed to the magisterial office of the Church and the best wisdom of the majority of moral theologians; and the Protestant began by saying, 'It seems to me'. Which is a way of saying that what you are going to get from me is not a report about how casuistry is done by theologians in general, but rather an exposition of how I think practical reason should work for Christians. I will do this by directing our attention to the way the Mennonite tradition has handled the questions of Christian use of the courts.

II. ON REPRESENTING MYSELF

Representing myself is no easy matter. I am one of the persons who has argued that modern ethics has distorted the character of the moral life because of its undue attention to decisions and their justification. Following Iris Murdock I have argued that decisions are what we do when everything else has been lost. Prior to the question of the kind of choices we must make is the question of the kind of person we should be. Therefore, virtue is prior to decision, character to choice.

Put more accurately, I have argued that situations are not like mud puddles that we cannot avoid, but the fact that you confront a mud puddle depends on the kind of person you are. Casuistry is a necessary activity of any moral position, but the status and way it is done depends on prior communal presuppositions about the kind of people we should be. Elsewhere I have suggested that casuistry is the attempt through analogical comparison to discipline our descriptions of what we do and do not do in the hopes that we can live more truthful lives. So understood, casuistry is not so much an attempt to determine and/or justify our decisions in terms of universally agreed-on rules or principles as it is the way a community explores the implications of its convictions.

From this perspective, as important as the decisions we make are the matters we never bring to decision; or, if the matter is brought to decision, it is understood to be an exception that requires carefully stated reasons why it is even being considered. Thus, for Roman Catholics the question of whether marriage can be dissolved by divorce is not open to discussion. When you marry you do so for a lifetime. That annulments can be considered is not a way to 'get around' this commitment, but rather a way of discovering what such a commitment entails.

My difficulty with 'quandary ethics' is not only with its concentration on decisions, but that it too often fails adequately to attend to the problem of the description of the 'problem'. Those who conceive of ethics primarily in terms of resolutions of quandaries tend too readily to accept conventional assumptions about how the 'quandary' is to be described. By failing to attend to where we get certain descriptions or how they are to be used, we ignore the significance of a community maintaining the practices that make the description truthful. Indeed, it seems to me that one of the difficulties of theoretical accounts of morality, such as utilitarianism or Kantianism, is that their casuistical judgments only make sense because they continue to trade on descriptions which they cannot justify from within their methodological constraints.

When religious traditions attempt to display their casuistry in terms of contemporary philosophical alternatives, they cannot help but leave out an important element of their story. For it appears that they must express their moral reflection in terms of adherence to certain fundamental principles by which a range of behavior is approved or disapproved and decisions can be justified. Moreover, certain theological traditions of moral reflection, particularly some Roman Catholic manuals of moral theology, look as if they exemplify this model. However, I would argue that this correspondence is misleading, since the casuistry of religious communities, and in particular the Catholic community, only makes sense against the background of a community's practices and convictions.

This is true not only for the Catholic community but for any substantial account of moral rationality. For if, as I have suggested, casuistry is the ongoing attempt of a community to understand itself through analogical comparison, such comparison requires the location of central paradigmatic examples. Such examples are not arbitrarily chosen; rather, they are determined through the experience of a community as developed in a tradition. Some examples become central because they serve to remind that community of what it is about across generations.

As a community develops over time, new and unanticipated problems arise that require reconsideration of those paradigms, their relation to one another, as well as what we thought their implications to be. The testing of the analogies and disanalogies at once may confirm as well as change assumptions about the meaning of the examples. The crucial point, however, is that the rationality of their process is finally determined by how well the community understands the analogical comparisons that serve to draw out the implications of those examples.

Even though I cannot pretend to represent more than myself in what follows, at the same time I want to claim that the perspective I develop illumines the casuistical traditions of religious communities. It does so, I think, because it makes clear that moral reflection draws upon and reflects the moral virtues and convictions of those communities. Moreover, by focusing on the community I can show that the dichotomies between reason and revelation, individual autonomy and communal authority, Scripture and rationality, are false alternatives when religious convictions are rightly forming practical wisdom.

It is my hope, however, that the constructive account I develop of how I think casuistry should work in the Christian community will also illumine how moral reason should work for any community. It is my contention that there is not, nor can there be, any tradition-free account of practical reason. There are certainly different traditions whose material content will make a difference for the kind of questions discussed, but each tradition in its own way will reflect the community that makes the activity of moral reflection intelligible. Indeed, from my perspective the deductive character of much of contemporary moral philosophy is but the mirror image of Protestant fundamentalism. Both assume that moral questions can be decided on the basis of a few principles without any community acting to mediate those principles in terms of the goods of that community.

III. ON REPRESENTING JOHN HOWARD YODER

Before developing these contentions through discussion of my 'case', I think it will be useful to attend to John Howard Yoder's recent account of practical reason in the Protestant tradition. In a chapter of his *The Priestly Kingdom*, called 'The Hermeneutics of Peoplehood', Yoder notes that there is no reason to think that the designation 'Protestant' is a 'necessary and sufficient determinant of one distinctive style of practical moral reason' ([10], p. 21). Therefore, he proposes to offer an account of practical reason that is clearly his own, but which, he hopes, draws out the implicit assumptions about such matters common to the origins of Protestantism.

He begins by noting that the Reformers called the church back to the Catholic principle that all decisions of the church must be determined by an open process. In terms of questions of moral discernment, church order, and matters of teaching on morality, the reformers followed the admonition of I Corinthians 14:26, that 'at all your meetings, let everyone be ready with a Psalm or a sermon or a revelation'. Yoder notes that this emphasis was later interpreted, critically by Roman Catholics and complementarily by later Enlightenment figures, as recommending an individualistic interpretation of Scripture and morality. But at least at the beginning, the Protestant insistence on both the perspicuity of Scripture and the priesthood of all believers was an attempt to avoid the alternative of collectivism and individualism for theological and moral reflection.

Such alternatives could be avoided because it was assumed that the church must be a voluntary community which affirmed individual dignity (the uncoerced adherence of the member) without enshrining individualism. 'The alternative to arbitrary individualism is not established authority in which the individual participates and to which he or she consents. The alternative to authoritarianism is not anarchy but freedom of confession' ([10], pp. 24–25). Yoder suggests that the struggle in the West between collectivism and individualism is at least partly the result of the failure of the mainstream of the Reformation to challenge the principle of the establishment of the church. As a result, the church continued to underwrite those moral judgments that were thought necessary to maintain the wider social order. The moral resources for moral rationality made possible by a voluntary commitment to a community distinct from total society were therefore largely lost.

A further implication of the Protestant Reformation, according to Yoder, is that practical reason as developed in congregational settings should be shaped by the assumption that it must serve the process of reconciliation. Practical moral reasoning is a conversation of a community that can risk judgment because of its willingness to forgive. Moral judgments are not deductive applications of universally valid rules, but the confrontation of one person by another on matters that matter for the whole community. Private wrongs in fact are public matters since the very nature of the community, and its moral discourse, depends on calling sin sin with the hope of reconciliation. As Yoder notes, most discussions of practical moral reasoning do not concretize decisions about issues in terms of a conversation between people who differ on an issue. Even less do discussions of practical moral reason see that conversation surrounded by a church (i.e., a locally gathered body) which will ratify either the reconciliation or its impossibility. As a result, we seem to have no alternatives, both philosophically and theologically, to individualistic intuitionism and complete objective rigidity.

Yoder's characterization of how practical reason should work to inform Christian conscience directs our attention to questions of how our community works rather than concentrating on how ideas or principles work. Practical reason is not a disembodied process based on abstract principles, but the process of a community in which every member has a role to play. Such a process does not disdain the importance of logical rigor for aiding in their deliberation, but logic cannot be a substitute for the actual process of discernment.

The conversation made possible by such a community draws from people of different gifts and virtues. For example, certain people have the charisma of prophecy, whose primary focus is neither prediction nor moral guidance, but stating and reinforcing the vision of the place of the believing community in history in which any moral reasoning gains intelligibility. Equally important are what Yoder calls 'agents of memory', those who do not pretend to speak on their own but as servants of communal memory. These 'scribes' are practical moral reasoners who do not judge or decide anything, but remember 'expertly, charismatically, the store of memorable, identity-confirming acts of faithfulness praised and of failure repented' ([10], p. 30). Scripture is crucial for moral reflection, as texts inform the community's memory through the 'charismatic aptness of the scribe's selectivity' ([10], p. 31). Such selectivity, however, must be informed as well as critically related to the tradition which is essential to the church's interpretation of Scripture.

The community of practical discourse also depends on what Yoder calls 'agents of linguistic self-consciousness'. These are those teachers who are charged with the steering of the community with the rudder of language. Such people, realizing at once the power and danger of language, will be attentive to the temptations to use verbal distinctions and/or purely verbal solutions to 'solve' substantial problems. Also crucial are 'agents of order and due process' who have the task to oversee and lead the community. Their task is to insure that everyone is heard and that conclusions reached are genuinely consensual.

That such agents are required in the Christian community is but a reminder that the existence of such a people is not determined by a series of decisions, but rather requires the development of virtues and the wisdom gained from those who have attempted to follow Jesus in the past as well as the present. This entails that practical reason of Christians may be distinctive and particularistic. Yoder, however, does not discount the importance of public comprehensibility or appeal to outside audiences, but rather questions whether those who first seek a 'natural', 'public', or 'universal' ground for practical reason can sustain their assumption that such a position can stand alone. From Yoder's perspective such 'universal' starting points cannot help but reflect the provincialism of the status-quo, which the practical moral reasoning of Christians must always be expected at some point to subvert.

So runs Yoder's account of practical reason, to which in the main I subscribe. I hope it is now clear that the alternative I offer is not just a report on how I think Christians should think about concrete moral matters, but also a critique of accounts of practical reason that isolate reasoning from any concrete group of people or tradition. Such accounts of practical reason always end up underwriting our assumption that the way things are is the way they ought or have to be; but our task, through the power of practical reason, is to change the way things are by changing ourselves.

IV. ON REPRESENTING OLIN TEAGUE

It is now time to try to make this account of practical reason concrete by considering the case of Olin Teague. Olin's story goes like this:

Olin Teague farms land, which he inherited from his family, that lies midway between Middlebury and Shipshewana, Indiana. He is now in his late fifties. While not wealthy, he makes a modest living raising corn, pigs, and a few milk cows. The latter primarily provides the milk used to make the cheddar cheese his family has made for generations. He has four children, three grown and married, his youngest finishing Goshen College and planning to go to medical school. Olin has promised to help pay her expenses, since she is planning to be a medical missionary for the Mennonite Central Committee. Olin is not particularly pious, but he and his family have long been members of the local Mennonite church.

As a way to make extra money to help pay his daughter's medical expenses, Olin agreed to let Jim Burkholder, the owner of the Wagon Wheel Cafe in downtown Shipshewana, buy his cheese to sell at his cafe. Because of the large Amish population in the surrounding county, Jim reasoned that tourists would be eager to buy 'authentic' farm-made cheese. Olin and Jim agreed on a price for the cheese, with the understanding that Jim would pay Olin once a year at the end of the tourist season. At the end of the first year Jim owed Olin $3,000. However, Jim told Olin that he could not pay, for even though the cheese has sold well, the cafe had failed to make a profit. He made clear to Olin that it would be some time, and perhaps never, before he could pay at all. Olin was quite upset at this turn of events, but it never crossed his mind to do anything other than talking to Jim about how he might put his finances in order. Olin's daughter, however, had to delay her plans to go to medical school at the University of Indiana.

Most of us, I suspect, have the same response on reading this case – namely, why did it not occur to Olin to sue. After all, these kinds of situations are a dime a dozen in the business world, and such suits are thought to be normal business practice. Indeed, for most of us taking Burkholder to court would not even raise moral issues. In such matters that is simply the way you proceed. Then why did it not occur to Olin to sue?

If you asked Olin himself, the answer you got might prove quite unsatisfactory for illuminating the nature of practical reason. For Olin's most probable answer would be, 'I am a Mennonite'. That is Olin's reason for not suing. From Olin's perspective to ask him why he does not sue Jim is about as dumb as asking a Texan why he likes Mexican food: they just go together. That does not mean we are prevented from inquiring further into what 'being a Mennonite' means to Olin, but our search for further moral rationale should not imply that there is something wrong with Olin's reason for not suing Jim.

Of course, 'I am a Mennonite' suggests that there is quite a story to tell in order to explain Olin's behavior. The background of the story begins in the history of Israel, where procedures were provided for the total community to share the burden of those who had gotten themselves so deeply into debt that their own and their family's future seemed forever mortgaged. Though there is debate about the extent to which the jubilee legislation requiring the forgiveness of debt (Leviticus 25) was institutionalized in Israel, the very fact that Israel preserved such legislation testifies to the concern to limit the destructive debt of those who made up the people of Israel. Those who follow God simply do not condemn one another to live in perpetual economic dependence.

Of equal, if not more importance, is the extent to which Mennonite life has been shaped by I Corinthians 6:1-11. There Paul admonishes the Corinthians by rhetorically asking

When one of you has a grievance against a brother, does he dare go to law before the unrighteous instead of the saints? Do you not know that the saints will judge the world? And if the world is to be judged by you, are you incompetent to try trivial cases? Do you not know that we are to judge angels? How much more, matters pertaining to this life! If then you have such cases, why do you lay them before those who are least esteemed by the church? I say this to your shame. Can it be that there is no man among you wise enough to decide between members of the brotherhood, but brother goes to law against brother, and that before unbelievers? To have lawsuits at all with one another is defeat for you. Why not rather suffer wrong? Why not rather be defrauded? But you yourselves wrong and defraud, and that even your own brethren. Do you not know that the unrighteous will not inherit the kingdom of God? Do not be deceived; neither the immoral, nor idolaters, nor adulterers, nor homosexuals, nor thieves, nor the greedy, nor drunkards, nor revilers, nor robbers will inherit the kingdom of God. And such were some of you. But you were washed, you were sancified, you were justified in the name of the Lord Jesus Christ and in the Spirit of our God.

For our purposes there is no need to provide an extended historical analysis of this passage. No doubt it would be of interest to know what the courts were like to which Paul refers, or what kinds of disputes were actually brought before them. But such issues cannot determine the meaning of the text for the moral guidance of the Christian community – at least as far as Mennonites are concerned. For them what is interesting is the kind of community Christians are meant to be in order to hear and live according to this text. For they assume that because of the kind of sanctified people Christians have become, these early Christians were right to make the question of appearing in court prismatic for determining the nature of their community.

The admonition not to take one another to court, therefore, is placed against the background of their being a particular kind of people with a distinct set of virtues. Therefore, unlike most Christians, who have tried to turn such passages into a legal-like regulation so you can start to find exceptions to it, Mennonites understand the admonition to be but a logical extension of their commitment to be a people of peace. Their reading of this text and the significance they give it is not because they think every command of the Bible should be followed to the letter, but rather reflects their understanding that the fundamental ministry of Christians in the world is reconciliation.

So their reading of the text and the behavior it prohibits is informed by their understanding of the virtues necessary to be Christian. But it is important to note that they have no 'individualistic' conception of virtues, but rather their conception is communal. Reconciliation is a central virtue because it denotes the communal reality that joins Mennonites in a common story and tradition. No doubt, at times in their history the prohibition against litigation may have become law-like for some Mennonites, but even as such it stands as a reminder of the kind of people they are to be.

Because Mennonites read this text as but an extension of their general commitment to peacekeeping, they extend its significance beyond the bare requirements of the text. The text says that they are not to take one another to court. Note that is not because they do not make any moral judgments about what is right or wrong. Obviously, Paul is more than willing to make such judgments, and in rather harsh terms at that. This is no easy ethic of tolerance. Indeed, Paul even suggests that Christians are ultimately to judge the world rather than vice versa. So, not going to court has little to do with overlooking wrong, but rather has to do with discovering a way that Christians can respond to wrong in a way that builds up rather than destroys community.

As Guy Hershberger, a contemporary Mennonite theologian suggests, the reason Christians are prohibited from settling their differences in a court of law is that such settlements violate the Christian adherence to love and non-resistance as a basic form of human relatedness. Therefore, he argues, not only should Christians not sue one another, they should not engage in aggressive litigation against any person, whether he or she be Christian or non-Christian.

The Christian is commanded to beware of covetousness and to love his neighbor as himself, yes even his enemy if there is such. The Christian must exercise a ministry of reconciliation, bearing witness to the way of the cross in order that the neighbor, even one who may have wronged him, may be won for Christ and brought into the kingdom. Aggressive suits at law are in every sense a violation of this mission, for how can a Christian win a man to Christ when he is suing him at law? It is equally clear that the Christian may not evade his responsibilities so as to be the cause for a just legal action to be brought against him. He who willfully evades the payment of his bills, for example, so as to invite legal action against him is even more in the wrong than the aggressor. According to the teaching of Matthew 18 the one falls under the disciplining of the church as much as the other([5], p. 318).

Some in the Christian tradition have argued that the reason Christians should avoid litigation is the abhorrence of publicity as well as in general trying to get along with the use of government. On such grounds they are not as insistent as Hershberger that all coercive litigation is to be avoided. If the only issue is publicity, then it may be possible to go to court without violating Paul's admonition. Hershberger, however, is not concerned with such legalistic readings of the text, since for him the negative prohibition is less important than the positive commitment to find means of reconciliation. Litigation, resting as it does on ultimate appeal to governmental coercion, is (when used in just self-defense) morally the equivalent of the direct appeal to the services of the police. Whether the force is overt or covert is not of deep moral significance as long as the sanctions are coercive in character. The rejection of self-defense by litigation is therefore a part of the general 'other-cheek' attitude of the Christian toward evil.[3]

Obviously, this Pauline text is not self-interpreting but depends on further theological construals for its concrete significance to be understood. For example, since Hershberger argues that the basic issue involved in Paul's admonition to avoid the courts is the coercive intent, he does not assume that state machinery is bad in and of itself. On the contrary, it is argued that

> since the law exists for the promotion of justice and the protection of human rights, the Christian must stand on the side of law. To be sure lawmakers can go astray, and when they do so the Christian also has the obligation to prophesy against that which is wrong. But he may never stand in the way of the law's pursuit of its rightful purpose. In the payment of taxes and in the honest reporting of business affairs relating thereto, in faithful compliance with laws designed to protect the health, safety, and welfare of the people, and in cheerful cooperation with the state in the furtherance of these ends, there should be no question as to the Christian's obligations. This includes laws for the regulation of working conditions, including such matters as wages, length of the working day, and overtime rates. The Christian's business affairs should be in legal order, and legal counsel should be freely employed to make sure that they are so. All of this is using the law as a means for the doing of justice to the brother and the neighbor, while evasion of the law would be to deal with him unjustly([5], p. 317).

Such is an example of Mennonite casuistry. Moreover, it is not just a position of an individual, but it has been confirmed by the Mennonite Church General Assembly in 1981. After a lengthy process they approved a 'Summary Statement' called *The Use of the Law* to clarify the Mennonite position on the place of the law [8].[4] They note that such a statement is necessary because of the rapid increase in lawsuits in our society, particularly where liability insurance makes it likely that a high level of monetary compensation may be forthcoming. They suggest that this is a subtle temptation, as such a use of the law might be to satisfy selfish desires rather than to assure justice in human relationships. They note that Mennonites, in spite of their traditional hesitancy to bring suit, have become more involved in legal proceedings, and therefore, that some guidance is needed.

They begin by affirming the

> positive role of law in human society and encouragement for the professional practice of law. It is the role of law to maintain order, to clarify and interpret law and statute, and to determine what justice requires in the light of society's values. The adversarial system, with its rules of evidence, presumption of innocence, and other customs, is designed to find justice on an objective and fair basis. Christians should use the positive provision of the civil law with adequate legal counsel in order to fulfill the intention of law. Carefully drawn contracts and other instruments written according to the provisions of the law, are an obligation of Christian integrity [*ibid.*]

There is no reason why Christians are excluded from using the courts to settle a point of law, secure the interpretation of a contrast, establish good zoning laws, etc.

They note in particular that many Mennonites serve poor people who suffer from basic inequities rooted in economic, social, legal, and religious structures that sometimes can be addressed through litigation. While not prohibiting such action, they advise that

Church persons engaged in such mission should have their proposals for litigation on behalf of others monitored by a church resource so that reconciliation and peace concerns are not overlooked [*ibid.*]

By this they mean that no such action should be undertaken without having their views tested by concrete congregation of people. For, they note

the teachings of Jesus and the apostles, the nature of the Scripture, the complexity of our situation, and the conflict between selfishness and altruism within each Christian combine to create a specific need for the involvement of a Christian community or congregation to interpret and apply the Scriptures and discern the will of God in a given situation. While congregational involvement does not guarantee faithfulness in every respect, there is a greater possibility of openness to the renewing Spirit of God than a traditional literalism, individualism, or authoritarian leadership [*ibid.*]

In short, moral discernment is the responsibility of the whole community.[5]

When individual Christians face a legal dispute, they must accordingly commit themselves to work with appropriate persons or committees of the congregation. Such counselors should seek to help the believer discern how concerns for justice and love apply, to give support needed to overcome greed or self-justification in order to maintain a reconciling stance, and when and if it is necessary for the Christian to accept loss, the church should share the loss if possible. While such counsel does not replace the need for legal advice, Christians should inform their lawyers of their faith and commitment.[6] In particular, Christians should not permit lawyers to make moral choices for them simply on the basis of accepted practices of law. It is the Christian's responsibility to look for alternatives that will avoid the coercive effect of the law in these instances. The 'report' goes into some detail about what such alternatives might involve – e.g., mediation, etc.

Particularly interesting is the commitment of the whole church to absorb some of the loss the refusal to go to court might entail. Usually moral reason works to show what we have to do given the limits of the situation, but here moral reason expands those 'limits', making possible a different alternative. Thus, it has been the practice of Mennonites to aid those who may have been the innocent victim of an accident but who could not receive damages because of their unwillingness to go to court. However, there is no suggestion that if such mutual aid is not forthcoming they are any less obligated to live in a non-resistant and reconciling way.

However, it is certainly the case that this form of mutual aid has not been as forthcoming as it was in the past. Indeed, it is hard to know which began to occur first – the loss of mutual support or Mennonites more willing to go to court to redress grievances. No doubt, *The Use of the Law* is partly an attempt to renew and give rationale to the Mennonite refusal to use courts as they become subject to the same forces that make most of us so litigious. That such is the case but reinforces the general point, that how we reason about concrete cases is determined by the habits and practices of particular communities.

In particular, we see that the casuistry of the Mennonites surrounding the use of law to settle disputes draws on profound assumptions about what constitutes a good community that encourages the flourishing of good people. Their refusal to resort to legal remedies not only between themselves, but between themselves and non-Mennonites, is not the result of a literalistic application of Scripture. Rather, they take the Scripture seriously for forming their moral reflection about the use of courts because that issue illumines their general sense of what it means to be a reconciled and reconciling people. The virtues of the community make the question of whether they should take one another to court moot. Because that alternative is ruled out does not mean, however, that decisions do not remain to be made. But now they may involve more the necessity of setting up forms of helping the improvident through credit, counseling and/or refinancing services.

To take such an approach, moreover, suggests that even though this peculiar 'moral problem' is relative to the Mennonites' particular set of commitments, that does not mean they are only interested in their own. For if they are inventive in developing social techniques for themselves, they may also help pioneer social inventions for wider society. Schools, hospitals, factories, and social services were all originally social inventions created by Christian moral commitments that forced Christians to find reasonable responses. So it may be that the Mennonite commitment to the personal resolution of disputes can help us find means to avoid the depersonalization of our legal system.

I am not suggesting that Olin has thought through all this when he responds to Jim's inability to pay what he owes. He may not even know what I Corinthians 6 says. He may not know how the Mennonite refusal to go to court fits with the pacifist assumptions of the Mennonites. But that is only important if you assume 'know' is to be restricted to 'being aware'. In a perfectly straightforward sense Olin's habits as a Mennonite made him know what the practical wisdom of the community required of him. He did not have to decide whether he should or should not sue Jim, because that simply was not one of the descriptive possibilities, given Olin's habits. The 'decision' he made to talk with Jim about how better to arrange his finances is but correlative to the descriptive possibilities created by the habits and convictions that make Olin Olin.

Before concluding, there are two objections to my presentation of Olin that should be considered, even though I cannot adequately respond to them. First, some may object that I have equated Mennonite with Christian in a manner that cannot be justified. That is certainly descriptively true, as most Christians do not share the Mennonite hesitancy to go to court. Normatively, however, I think they should, and insofar as all Christians assume the centrality of God's reconciling work in Jesus as central to their faith, Mennonites at least have the basis to carry on the argument.

Such an argument would need to attend to historical developments, as well as to more strictly theological considerations about the nature of the church. For even among those Christian traditions that have abandoned the admonition for Christians not to go to court, there remain institutions that at least suggest that such a concern is not unimportant – e.g., the continuing presence of ecclesiastical courts. So, to observe that many Christians do not conform to the practice of the Mennonites is not the end of the matter, just the beginning.

The second objection is that my presentation of Olin as a representative of Mennonite practice is all well and good, but irrelevant to the 'real world'. For most people do not share Olin's community, and therefore quite a different way of resolving disputes must be sought. Fairness, not reconciliation, must be the hallmark of all relations, as well as practical reason. Again, I have no stake in denying the descriptive power of this objection, but I see no reason why I should let it determine the presentation of how I think Christians should reason practically.

Instead, I think much might be made of how the alternative I have presented might make a difference for how some of our current moral practice could be changed. For example, the current difficulty of the relation between patients and physicians might appear quite differently if there were some alternative to the adversary manner of resolving error in medicine. I am not suggesting that patients should forgive and forget physician error, but that too often patient and physician alike are caught in an adversary position which is ruled by the ethos of fairness that distorts the complexity of medical care. There is no way that medicine can be practiced without error – i.e., often in trying to help, physicians hurt patients. Our tendency is to try to deny that such mistakes are intrinsic to patient care. In the process we distort the moral nature of medicine by robbing the patient of participation in the process.

The truthful practice of medicine necessarily requires reconciliation, as physicians must be able to acknowledge their errors in a manner that heals rather than destroys community. Such acknowledgment, moreover, is crucial for the care of patients, as we learn only by the public exposure of our mistakes. The current extent of malpractice may seem to make such a suggestion a form of foolish idealism, but in fact I think it is the hardest realism. In fact, such reconciliation is common in medicine, but it is not noticed because of the dominant paradigm of moral rationality.

V. ON REPRESENTING GOD

I began by disavowing my ability to represent adequately theological ethics particularly, if that designation is meant to represent all ethics associated with religious traditions. Different religious traditions will generate different conceptions of practical reason. Instead, I have tried to present an account of how practical reason should work within a Christian community. In particular, I have stressed that rationality is a communal process that involves Scripture and virtues, as well as judgments about particular practices and their implications for other aspects of our lives. Rationality in a Christian context therefore both shapes and is shaped by the fundamental commitment of that community to be a community of the reconciled as well as of the reconciling. The 'case' I chose to analyze, while clearly not a significant moral issue from some perspectives, hopefully has helped to illumine these general contentions.

I am aware that this presentation must appear exceedingly strange to philosophers. Formal considerations of the nature of rationality qua rationality have been ignored. No attempt has been made to characterize the prohibition against litigation in the Mennonite community in terms of deontological or teleological alternatives. That does not mean, however, that the process of reasoning about litigation among Mennonites is devoid of logical features. Rather, the logic serves their material commitments rather than vice versa. Thus, questions of when litigation can be used are carefully considered in terms of the reason for prohibiting litigation between Christians in the first place. Thus, if the reconciling intent is not abrogated by the process itself, they reason analogically that certain kinds of litigation may be permitted.

Even though such a procedure may strike philosophers as unphilosophical, I should think it is not without philosophical interest. For example, in *Ethics and the Limits of Philosophy* Bernard Williams makes the interesting observation that, though virtue affects how one deliberates, it often is not clear in what way the virtues actually affect deliberation. Someone who has a particular virtue does actions because they fall under certain descriptions, but Williams contends that it 'is rarely the case that the description that applies to the agent and to the action is the same as that in terms of which the agent chooses the action. A courageous person does not typically choose acts as being courageous, and it is a notorious truth that a modest person does not act under the title of modesty' ([9], p. 10). It should, therefore, be of considerable interest how Mennonites understand, as well as how the early Christians seem to have understood, the relation of the virtue of reconciliation to litigious activity. In particular, it strikes me that the role of community for understanding such a relation is one aspect often overlooked in philosophical accounts of practical reason.[7]

Yet, it is not my place to tell philosophers what they may or may not find of philosophical interest in what I have done. However, I cannot pretend that matters between theologians and philosophers can be left so independent and peaceful. For, obviously involved in the very manner I have presented my case is a philosophical point, or perhaps better, a critique of the contemporary philosophical passion to reduce practical rationality to a single pattern. It seems to me that Williams is right to see this drive toward a 'rationalistic conception of rationality' not as a requirement of philosophical discourse in itself, but rather as coming 'from the social features of the modern world, which impose on personal deliberation and on the idea of practical reason itself a model drawn from a particular understanding of public rationality. This understanding requires in principle every decision to be based on grounds that can be discursively explained. This requirement is not in fact met, and it probably does little for the aim that authority should be genuinely answerable. But it is an influential ideal and by a reversal of the order of causes, it can look as if it were the result of applying to the public world an independent ideal of rationality' ([9], p. 18).[8]

I hope it is clear from my presentation that there is nothing about the community specific account of rationality I have provided that denies the importance of giving reasons for our actions. The issue is not whether it is important to give reasons, but is the kind of reasons we need to give and the purpose they are to serve. Mennonites are no less committed than Kantians to work toward a society in which moral conflict can be resolved short of violence. The difference is that Mennonites do not think such resolutions occur by trying to take a shortcut around the necessity of the process of reconciliation through the positing of a disembodied 'rationality'.

Philosophers have a terrible hunger for the universal. That they do so is admirable, since that hunger is charged by the moral commitment of a peaceful community. Yet their search for the universal too often looks to the development of general theories of rationality devoid as much as possible of distinctive content. In contrast, I am arguing that the way forward is through the appreciation of particular communities that are committed to finding as much shared understanding as possible on particular issues (cf. [9], p. 117). If such communities do not in fact exist, then no amount of philosophical reflection on practical reason will be of much use.

But finally, what does all this have to do with God? One might well agree with all or at least some of what I have done and still think God is largely irrelevant. Reconciliation is a good idea for most communities. The fact that the Christians have a set of peculiar views about Scripture is their problem. Moreover, as I noted, most Christians do not believe that appeals to Scripture are sufficient to settle moral issues. So, there is nothing about my account that would entail the necessary belief in God, or that God shapes morality through particular commandments.

I shall not try to respond to these kind of observations directly. Instead I will tell you a story. It is a true story, unlike the one I made up about Olin and Jim. A few years ago between Middlebury and Shipshewana an Amish family was taking a ride in their buggy. A group of high school boys from LaGrange, Indiana, was out in the country driving fast and generally raising hell. Passing this family's buggy, they threw a stone into it, unintentionally killing a young child. They were subsequently apprehended, but the county prosecutor could not try them for the actual crime, because the Amish family would not testify at the trial. As a result they were convicted on a much less severe crime. During their time in prison, the Amish family sought them out in order to effect a reconciliation.

I do not tell this story because I think it proves that God exists. Rather, I tell it because I think the behavior of this Amish family, and of the community that supports them, would be unintelligible without their belief in a God who refused to let our sin determine his relation to us. Even more strongly, I believe that the behavior of the Amish in this case can easily be construed as decidedly immoral if such a God neither exists or, more importantly, lacks the characteristics they attribute to him. Only when the question of God's existence is raised in terms such as this do I suspect it is even a question worth considering.

NOTES

[1] In particular, see my 'Casuistry as a Narrative Art' (Chapter Seven) in Hauerwas ([4], pp. 116–134). Even though analogy is at the heart of the practice of practical reason, it would be a mistake to conclude thereby that what is needed is a 'theory of analogy'. Rather, as David Burrell maintains, what is needed is a series of reminders about the way we can and do negotiate analogous expressions. 'We must not look for a theory, but are rather invited to look to our own usage and sharpen our consciousness of its actual conditions. Rather than demand criteria *tout court*, we are reminded that many such criteria are already operative in our reasoning, and asked to scrutinize the ways we *use* the ones we do rely upon' ([2], p. 44). See also J.F. Ross ([7]).

[2] One of the reasons that the issue of description has been so overlooked in contemporary moral philosophy may be that the assumption of the distinction between fact and value is written into the very nature of moral language. In contrast, Bernard Williams argues that the fact-value distinction has largely been brought to our language rather than found there. When we actually look at moral language, according to Williams, we find that moral notions are 'thicker', since they presume a union of fact and value – e.g., treachery, promise, brutality, and courage. Williams goes on to suggest that 'the way these notions are applied is determined by what the world is like (for instance, by how someone has behaved), and yet, at the same time, their application usually involves a certain valuation of the situation, of persons or actions. Moreover, they usually (though not necessarily directly) provide reasons for action' ([9], pp. 129–130). Julius Kovesi's work ([6]) continues to be unfairly ignored for consideration of these questions.

[3] I owe this way of putting the matter to John Howard Yoder's informal paper 'Possible New Procedures For Use in Areas Where Existing Legal Procedures are Not Compatible With Scriptural Principles'. This was prepared for use in helping reformulate the Mennonite stance toward litigation. I am indebted to Yoder for directing me to the background documents of this debate among Mennonites.

[4] This is the printed statement that was adopted by the Mennonite Church General Assembly in Bowling Green, Ohio, August 11–16, 1981. The document is introduced by Ivan Kauffmann by noting that the Christian use of the law has been an issue since the early 1950s. Many Mennonites felt the need for such a statement, as often they found themselves in business positions that involved litigation. In response, the Mennonite Auto Aid sponsored a study of litigation from 1959 to 1965. That study, along with a conference on the issue, drew no conclusions. A task force appointed by the general board in 1976 drew up the 1981 statement. I have purposely drawn on a church-related document rather than the reflection of a single individual, since too often we associate rationality with the work of individuals. The traditional anonymity of Catholic moral theologians is a morally significant sign that their task was fundamentally communally determined.

The Use of the Law is not paginated, but since it is only twelve pages long I think no one would have trouble finding my references.

[5] For an interesting contrast see James Gustafson's recent work ([3], pp. 333ff). Many of Gustafson's analyses of the elements of discernment, such as evaluative description of circumstance, the significance of space and time, and intuition, are compatible with the process the Mennonites use. What is missing, however, is any sense of the importance of actual exchange of views within a concrete congregation.

[6] *The Use of Law* notes that 'when members are part of large or corporate entities involved in litigation, the local congregation might not be an adequate source for counsel. In such instances the individual member and the congregation may well seek help from the conference to identify counsel and help in the situation, which would usually include business and professional peers in the church. Managers or business enterprises generally have not had the benefit of direct church support. Effort should be made in the various areas of the church to see that adequate counsel is available to all who desire such counsel'.

[7] I suspect one of the reasons for this is the philosopher's concern to avoid relativism. For example, Williams notes that 'the trouble with casuistry, if it is seen as the basic process of ethical thought, is not so much its misuse as the obvious fact that the repertory of substantive ethical concepts differs between cultures, changes over time, and is open to criticism. If casuistry, applied to a given local set of concepts, is to be the central process of ethical thought, it needs more explanation. It has to claim that there are preferred ethical categories that are not purely local. They may be said to come from a theory of human nature; they may be said to be given by divine command or revelation; in this form, if it is not combined with the grounding in human nature, the explanation will not lead us anywhere except into what Spinoza called "the asylum of ignorance". An exponent of the casuistical method could perhaps fall back simply on the idea that the categories we prefer are the ones we have inherited. This has the merit of facing an important truth, but it will not be able to face it in truth unless more is said about ways in which those categories might be criticized' ([9], pp. 96–97). I hope that the analysis I have provided of a community committed to reconciliation necessarily generates such criticism.

[8] Elsewhere Williams rightly suggests that 'the dispositions help to form the character of an agent who has them, and they will do the job the theory has given them only if the agent does not see his character purely instrumentally, but sees the world from the point of view of that character. Moreover, the dispositions require the agent to see other things in a noninstrumental way. They are dispositions not simply of action, but of feeling and judgment, and they are expressed precisely in ascribing intrinsic and not instrumental value to such things as truthtelling, loyalty, and so on' ([9], p. 108).

BIBLIOGRAPHY

[1] Barth, K.: 1961, *Church Dogmatics*, vol. III/4, T. and T. Clark, Edinburgh.
[2] Burrell, D.: 1982, 'Argument in Theology: Analogy and Narrative', in C. Raschke (ed.), *New Dimensions in Philosophical Theology*, Scholars Press, Chico, Ca., pp. 37–52.
[3] Gustafson, J.: 1981, *Ethics from a Theocentric Perspective*, University of Chicago Press, Chicago.
[4] Hauerwas, S.: 1983, *The Peaceable Kingdom: A Primer in Christian Ethics*, University of Notre Dame Press, Notre Dame.
[5] Hershberger, G.: 1958, *The Way of the Cross in Human Relations*, Herald Press, Scottdale, Pa.

[6] Kovesi, J.: 1967, *Moral Notions*, Routledge and Kegan Paul, London.
[7] Ross, J. F.: 1981, *Portraying Analogy*, Cambridge University Press, Cambridge.
[8] *The Use of the Law: A Summary Statement*, 1982, Scottdale, Pa.
[9] Williams, B.: 1985, *Ethics and the Limits of Philosophy*, Harvard University Press, Cambridge.
[10] Yoder, J. H.: 1984, *The Priestly Kingdom: Social Ethics as Gospel*, University of Notre Dame Press, Note Dame.

Duke Divinity School
Durham, North Carolina

LAURENCE THOMAS

CHRISTIANITY IN A SOCIAL CONTEXT:
PRACTICAL REASONING AND FORGIVENESS

Practical Reasoning is not a matter of descending from the Olympian heights of impartial, objective, faceless rationality into the sobering valley of reality via the particularities of our lives. The points of departure for practical reasoning are our lived experiences; and the backdrop against which we have all such experiences is a community. Thus, what we take for granted and what we consider to be either reasonable or plausible is determined not in the abstract but in the context of a community. This is so even when community standards themselves are being rejected. For if nothing else, rejected standards serve as the baseline for what is deemed unacceptable. On this much Professor Hauerwas and I are in complete agreement.

So, we agree that impartialist moral theories are unsatisfactory insofar as they attempt to define a perspective from which moral behavior is to be assessed which is independent of any form of community life. The view from nowhere (to appropriate a turn of phrase on [5]) is not to be had; and that is why impartialist theories, with their insistence finding it, invariably miss the mark.

But, now, 'Reconciling the Practice of Reason: Casuistry in a Christian Context'([4]), all parenthetical page references unaccompanied by a bracketed reference will be to this article) is not just a plea for community, but a plea for a certain kind of community, namely a Christian one. I imagine that the thesis which Hauerwas would like to maintain is this: The nature of the Christian community (properly conceived) is such that the forms of practical reasoning which flow from it are superior to the forms of practical reasoning which flow from moral but otherwise non-Christian communities. That is to say, members of the Christian community reason about moral issues in a morally superior way because Christianity defines or embodies a morally superior vantage point from which to do so. In commenting on the practice of Mennonites not to take one another to court, Hauerwas writes: 'So not going to court has little to with overlooking wrong, but rather has to do with discovering a way that Christians can respond to wrong in a way that builds up rather than destroys community' (p. 145). I take the distinguishing feature of Christianity to which Hauerwas is drawing our attention to be the doctrine's admonishment to forgive those who trespass against one.

157

Baruch A. Brody (ed.), Moral Theory and Moral Judgments in Medical Ethics, 157–168.
© 1988 by Kluwer Academic Publishers.

I shall challenge Hauerwas's position on three accounts: (1) The Mennonite community is a closed community and it may very well be that the practice of forgiving would flourish in any such community (Section I, Part I). (2) The Christian community at large is a non-closed community: and the practice of forgiving would not flourish in any non-closed community (Section I, Part II). (3) There are many moral issues the focal point of which is not that of moral wrongs; and there is no reason to think that, with respect to these issues, the practical reasoning of the Christian community will be superior to the practical reasoning of secular moralities. Thus, even if it can be shown that Christianity makes a difference in practical reasoning about moral matters, it will turn out that the scope of that difference is not as far-reaching as perhaps Hauerwas supposes it to be. I shall draw on examples in medical ethics to illustrate this point (Section II).

To meet the challenge of (1) and (2), Hauerwas must argue, respectively, that either (a) there is nothing about a closed community, as such, which makes it conducive to the virtue of forgiveness flourishing among its members, or (b) if individuals are Christians, then the virtue of forgiveness is favored to flourish in their lives regardless of the social circumstances of their lives.[1] If they can be established, (a) would show that being a Christian is a necessary condition for the flourishing of this virtue, and (b) would show that being a Christian plays a most causally efficacious role in the flourishing of this virtue. To meet the challenge of (3), Hauerwas must show that the difference which forgiveness makes comes to more than just making it possible for moral debate to take place in a less hostile environment, allowing for the sake of argument that forgiveness does make this difference.

I. FORGIVENESS AND COMMUNITY

Then came Peter to him and said, Lord how oft shall my brother sin against me, and I forgive him? till seven times? Jesus saith unto him, I say *not* unto thee, Until seven times: but Until seventy times seven (Matthew 18:21-22, emphasis added).

Christianity makes forgiveness a virtue. It is this distinguishing feature of Christianity to which Hauerwas draws our attention. Forgiveness is not a virtue of any secular moral theory. To be sure, no secular moral theory makes forgiveness a wrong, provided that one's doing so is not indicative of a lack of self-respect. Still, no such moral theory has it as an integral part of its theoretical structure that a mark of its adherents is their willingness to forgive those who have wronged them. Not even utilitarianism is an exception to this point. At best, forgiveness has derivative value on a utilitarian account of things, even though the theory may very well require that we identify considerably with the good of others, as Sidgwick observed.

Christianity assumes that human beings are morally fallible; indeed, that all are is a part of its theoretical structure (Matthew 6:15; Romans 3:23; 1 John 1:8), it being understood that morally wrong actions and sin come to pretty much the same thing from the Christian perspective. The admonishment to forgive thus embodies this conception of human beings. We are not entitled to demand perfection of others if we cannot rightly demand it of ourselves – and, as the account goes, we can't, seeing that we are all sinners who have fallen short of the glory of God.

Of course, no moral theory assumes that human beings are morally infallible. It is just that whereas Christianity claims to atone for one's infallibility, and so to blot it out, through an act of faith, secular moral theories lack the theoretical framework to deal similarly with the moral failings of their adherents. Whereas in the secular world, making restitution is generally the only way in which a person can make up for his wrong-doing (hence, the insistence on it is, for that very reason, understandable) Christianity radically alters the role which restitution plays in human interaction by, in general, turning the issue of making up for one's wrong-doing into a non-issue. In fact, the doctrine makes it embarrassing not to forgive: If, after all, a wholly righteous and just God is willing to forgive a person for his wrong–doing, it becomes rather difficult for a Christian who is neither wholly righteous nor just to explain her not being willing to do so.

It is all too obvious, I imagine, that in a community which makes forgiveness a virtue, practical reasoning about some important moral matters will have a much different focus than what it would have in a community which does not make forgiveness a virtue. This is because an unyielding insistence on restitution (or otherwise making up for one's wrong-doing) is incompatible with the virtue of forgiveness; accordingly, a community of individuals who widely embrace this virtue would attach far less importance to restitution than a community of individuals who do not. This would be true only where the virtue of forgiveness is among the centerpieces of a community's moral framework; and it would seem that only a moral framework which has a deity at its basis can accord such standing to this virtue. So, to the question 'whether belief in God does or can make a difference for moral decisions and their justification' (p. 136), the answer is this: Believing in a Christian God has to make a tremendous difference in terms of how a

community of individuals reasons about moral matters, *if* so believing entails
that forgiveness is widely embraced as a virtue, and *if* this virtue would not
be otherwise embraced. Hauerwas wants to say that it does; I am not
convinced that he has made his case.

A.

I turn now to the story of Olin Teague, the Mennonite Christian. At the outset
it should be observed that Mennonite communities are relatively closed
communities (to be contrasted with a non-closed community, which I shall
explain in Part II of this section).[2] That is, the set of members remains rather
constant; in particular, aside from the offspring of their members, there are
very few additions to Mennonite communities. These individuals exhibit the
characteristic features of a closed community: In addition to having a
common set of beliefs, they live in comparatively close proximity to one
another, interact frequently, and identify with the lived lives of one another –
and not just each other's beliefs, specifically religious beliefs in this instance.

Now all by itself, that is, in the absence of widely shared Christian values,
a closed community constitutes quite fertile soil for the virtue of forgiveness
to flourish as a practice, due to the bond of trust that is generally characteristic of closed communities. Moreover, the disposition to forgive is reinforced
when we can count on those forgiven to measure up in the future, and so
when we can have the projected counterfactual belief [8] that were we to
forgive others they would nonetheless measure up in the future.[3] In a closed
community this disposition and its concomitant belief is underwritten by the
fact that it generally pays for each member of a closed community to
cooperate with one another, lest she or he should fall into disfavor with the
others, thereby losing the benefits which come with being a favorably
regarded member of the community. For the admonishment to forgive is not
tantamount to an admonishment to let oneself be mistreated and used by
others. Thus, it is of the utmost importance for members of a closed community who wish to remain a part of that community, though they have erred
in their ways, to communicate their firm intention to do right in the future, as
well as to show their deep sorrow for having gone astray.[4]

Also, in a closed community, the tremendous familiarity brought about as a
result of frequent interaction tends to give rise to a heightened sense of
accountability on the part of the members of the community to one another.
That is, there is a community or, in any case, a significant set of individuals

in that community to whom one feels accountable for one's words and deeds. And this is another mechanism of social interaction which reinforces the disposition to forgive, since the belief that the person will rightly behave in the future is thereby rendered more credible.

Finally, it is not unreasonable to suppose that the willingness to forgive receives reinforcement from the conviction that one's act of forgiving will yield a positive return in that the person forgiven will be better off for it. The very nature of a closed community, in addition to constituting a network of social forces which contribute to a person's bringing and keeping his behavior in line, also makes it relatively easy for individuals to gauge the rehabilitative effects of their efforts. Being virtuous may very well be its own reward. But this truth, if it be such, is quite compatible with its being even more rewarding to see one's virtuous behavior bear fruit.

I have endeavored to show that a very strong case can be made for the view that the practice of forgiving will flourish in a closed community simply in virtue of its being such, and so without reference to Christian beliefs concerning the importance of forgiving one another. In view of the aims of Hauerwas's essay, a question of great importance is this: If a closed community is a Christian one, such as a Mennonite community, will the practice of forgiveness flourish even more so or in morally superior ways?

I shall make no attempt to answer this question. But it will be recalled that what is at issue is whether Christian morality is superior to secular morality on the grounds that when a community embraces the former it responds to the wrongs of its members in a way that builds rather than destroys the community. It is clear, I trust, that unless Hauerwas can answer affirmatively the question which I have raised, then his thesis is far less compelling than no doubt he would like it to be.

B.

Now, Hauerwas may want to concede that between a Christian closed community and secular closed one the difference with respect to the issue at hand is sufficiently negligible. If Christianity makes a difference in a much broader social context, that is good enough, surely. The broader social context I have in mind is non-closed communities.

Among the characteristic features of a non-closed community are the following: There is a fair amount of anonymity among the members; that is, most are unfamiliar with who the other members of the community are. And,

in any case, individuals do not strongly identify with the good of one another
– at least, not simply in virtue of persons being members of the community.
Non–closed communities tend to lose and gain (new) members continually.
Examples of non-closed communities are academic institutions (especially
large ones), large apartment complexes (as in New York high-rises), and, of
course, cities and parts of cities. Insofar as the set of individuals called
Christians constitutes a community – the Christian community at large, let us
say – it is a non-closed community. Indeed, even some churches can be non-
closed communities. (In any community, closed or non-closed, there can be
especially strong ties between various individuals.)

Now, it goes without saying that a closed Christian community, such as a
Mennonite community, is a non-identical subset of the Christian community
at large. In his writing Hauerwas gives the distinct impression that he is using
the closed Christian community of Mennonites to bring out what the virtues
are or, at any rate, could be in the Christian community at large, the idea
being, I suppose, that the Mennonites display most vividly what the Christian
community at large could be like. In responding to someone who might
object that the world of Olin Teague is not the world of most people,
Hauerwas writes:

... I have no stake in denying the descriptive power of this objection, but see no reason why I
should let it determine the presentation of how I think Christians should reason practically.

Instead, I think much might be made of how the alternative I have presented might make a
difference for how some of our current moral practice could be changed. For example, the
current difficulty of the relation between patients and physicians might appear quite differently if
there were some alternative to the adversary manner of resolving error in medicine (p. 149).

I seriously doubt whether the Christian community at large or, *a fortiori*,
the world (which is also a non-closed community: it gains and loses [new]
members continually) could be like the Mennonite community with respect to
the practice of forgiveness. This is because similar forces of social interaction
are not at work in a non-closed community, even if it is a Christian one.
Specifically, there are no social mechanisms in place which would warrant
the belief that a stranger to one, and most others, will not exploit the fact that
his anonymity enables him to get away with wrong–doing; accordingly, a
non-closed community is not conducive to its members having the belief that
the person forgiven will be determined to do the right thing in the future,
since in most cases the individual to be forgiven will be a stranger to the one
who has been wronged. Or, at any rate, the life of the transgressor will be
sufficiently unfamiliar to the individual who has been wronged; nor, for that
very reason, will the former much identify with the good of the latter.

I have not argued against the view that the moral virtues of Christianity are superior to those of secular moral theories. My point, rather, is that the furtherance of Christian virtues is not independent of the social conditions under which persons live. Altruistic motivations [1], of which the disposition to forgive is an instance, will be operative in our lives only if they are reinforced from time; such reinforcement is not independent of the beliefs that we have about how others will behave; and how others behave is very much tied to the nature of their environment.

For all anyone knows, it may be that belief in a Christian God undergirds a person's altruistic motivations, so much so that they will be operative in a person's life regardless of the social conditions in which she lives. If true, this is an exceedingly powerful aspect of Christianity which renders irrelevant the claims of this essay, in particular, the distinction between closed and non-closed communities. However, I do not see that Hauerwas has advanced this claim, at least not explicitly; though, since he is a Christian, I imagine that it is precisely this claim that lies behind the claims that he does explicitly make.

On any reading of the New Testament, there can be no doubt that Christians are presented as flourishing to varying degrees. Judging from the epistles written by the Apostle Paul, the Corinthians had their problems, and the Galatians theirs. Moreover, each of the seven churches presented in the book of Revelation (Chs. 2, 3) had different problems for which they were chastised. Love for God is as central to Christianity as anything might conceivably be; yet the Church of Ephesus was criticized for having lost its love for God.[5] So, if love for God need not flourish among Christians, I see no reason to suppose that forgiveness must do so. In other words, if one central Christian virtue can fail to flourish among Christians, then in the absence of independent reasons for thinking otherwise it is reasonable to suppose that others may also fail to flourish. The virtue of forgiveness may be the exception here, but Hauerwas has not advanced any reasons for thinking that.

II. PRACTICAL REASONING AND CHRISTIANITY

As I observed in Part I of the previous section, a society in which the virtue of forgiveness flourished would surely be a less litigious society. More generally, such a society would, as Hauerwas observes, have a significantly less adversarial character to it. And there can be no doubt that such a society would be a better one. For example, there would not be the pandemonium that seems to have set in among physicians who for fear of malpractice suits are either refusing to perform certain operations or perform then only at extraordinary costs stemming from additional tests designed to block the charge of carelessness.

But many of the issues in medical ethics have little or nothing to do with the adversary character of society. The issues of abortion, euthanasia, the allocation of scarce medical resources (euthanasia's neighboring issue), and medical paternalism come quickly to mind. The first vividly forces us to wrestle with the concept of a person; the second pertains to the claims that issue from a right to life; the third pertains to how competing claims can be met in a world of scarce resources; and the fourth has to do with when people are justified in acting on behalf of others without their permission and to what extent, if any, people are justified in withholding relevant information from those whose well-being they affect by their actions.

Now, to be sure, there are Christian communities (or better: sects) which no doubt have settled views about these matters, just as there are all sorts of groups of individuals with settled views about these matters. However, having a settled view about a moral issue is not the same thing as reasoning in a superior way about a moral issue. Settled views can be morally horrendous, as is presumably the case with the settled, but nonetheless racist and anti-Semitic, views of dyed-in-the-wool neo-Nazi members. I am unable to see that the members of a society would reason better about any of the issues in medical ethics mentioned in the preceding paragraph if the Christian virtue of forgiveness were manifested in the basic structure of that society. And this is for a conceptual reason perhaps.

Forgiving presupposes a conception of the moral landscape with respect to what is wrong or, in any event, the wrong being forgiven; it in no way speaks to how the boundaries between right and wrong should be drawn. Accordingly, we should not expect the virtue of forgiveness to inform our understanding concerning the morality of many of the issues in medical ethics, any more than we should expect the virtue of patience (also extolled by Christianity) to do so.

There can be no doubt that a world where people are disposed to forgive will be a much better world in which to live. This is so if for no other reason than that it would make for a more harmonious society as we endeavor to understand how the boundaries of right and wrong should be drawn with respect to pressing moral issues. And this backdrop of harmony becomes increasingly more important as medical technology outstrips our traditional moral concepts. I conclude with a concrete example to illustrate this point.

I take it to be just a matter of time before the issue of abortion as we now know it will no longer exist. At the moment it is rather difficult to remove a fetus from the womb without killing it. But it is just a matter of time, whether we like it or not, before we shall be able to remove harmlessly a fetus from its mother's womb and place it in an artificial womb until the ninth month. Given such medical technology, what should the practice of society be? No side to the abortion debate has really taken this issue seriously. Anti-abortionists have only argued that the fetus has a right to life and that, therefore, abortion is wrong. Those of the pro-choice persuasion have maintained some version of a woman has a right (variously defeasible) to do with her body as she pleases.

If medical technology develops along the lines suggested, then, the concerns of both parties will have been spoken to, since it will be possible to remove the fetus from the womb without killing it. Anti-abortionist arguments will hardly show that the fetus should not be removed from the womb and placed in an artificial one; and pro-choice arguments will hardly show that the fetus should not be allowed to live after it has been safely removed from the womb. As one can see, although the concerns of both parties to the abortion debate will have been spoken to, the question of how the fetus morally ought to be handled will have been anything but settled. An adversary society, where virtually by conceptual fiat to concede anything is to concede too much, is hardly the setting which will make for an easy resolution of the moral quandary I have raised.[6]

And from these considerations it may be thought to follow that a society in which the virtue of forgiveness flourishes will be one in which people will reason better about moral issues. But notice that if this is true, it will not be because, as Hauerwas suggests, such a society will thereby be one in which individuals reason in a morally superior way about moral matters, but because such a society will provide a morally superior atmosphere in which to reason about moral matters which, in turn, may enhance the quality of moral reasoning itself. However, one may very well question the assumption that the quality of moral reasoning is enhanced in a less adversary environment. I shall not do so.

It is simply worth noting that the claim that (i) a Christian society provides a morally superior atmosphere, because of its non-adversary nature, in which to reason about moral matters is not the same as, nor does it entail, the very strong claim that (ii) simply in virtue of being a Christian a person will reason better about moral matters. For (ii), but not (i), entails that, *if* a person stands in a certain relationship to God, the quality of her moral reasoning *thereby* improves. No further features are appealed to. By contrast, (i) does appeal to a further feature, namely, a non-adversarial environment. Christianity may very well foster such an environment, but for all we know, we may be able to come by it in other ways. And even if we cannot, as surely Hauerwas would like to say, we are still left with a weaker claim, since a further feature is appealed to in any case. Claim (i) is quite compatible with a person's being a Christian and not reasoning in a better way about moral matters, since it is quite possible to be a Christian and yet find oneself in an environment that is far from non–adversary in its character. Claim (ii) is not compatible with a person's being a Christian and, at the same time, not thereby reasoning better about moral matters.

Against all of this, it might be objected: what difference does it make, between the two alternatives under consideration, as to how people come to reason better about moral matters, so long as the end result is the same, namely, that people are reasoning better about moral matters? The answer is this. What is at stake is a view about the efficacy and significance of Christian salvation in the lives of individuals. Things are exactly parallel to the issue of the virtue of forgiveness. It is one thing to say that, on account of being a Christian, a person will be disposed to forgive regardless of what she takes others to be disposed to do; it is quite another, surely, to say that a Christian will be disposed to forgive insofar as she perceives that others in her community are so disposed.

In either case the question is about what it takes for a certain quality to flourish in a person's life, given that she is a Christian. The very strong claim is that it *suffices* that a person bears a certain relationship to God. A weaker claim is that, in addition to bearing such a relationship to God, other things must be true about the person's environment. The weaker claim makes God just one amongst other variables, the stronger one does not. I take Hauerwas to have been arguing for the stronger claim. I have been arguing that he has not made a satisfactory case for that claim.

Matters can be summed up succinctly as follows. I have been supposing all along that on Hauerwas's view God suffices to make *the* difference. And, in effect, my argument has been that this view of God is incompatible with a view which attaches the kind of importance that Hauerwas does to community. At any rate, there is a tension here that needs to be resolved.

NOTES

* This essay is a response to Stanley Hauerwas's essay 'Reconciling the Practice of Reason: Casuistry in a Christian Context', which was delivered at the NEH Conference on Moral Theory and Moral Judgments. I am grateful to the Earhart Foundation whose funds supported, in part, both my work on this paper and my attendance at the conference. Baruch Brody commented helpfully on the penultimate draft of this essay.

[1] While a guarantee would surely be preferable, in its absence, there is nothing at all insignificant about the fact that one outcome is favored over another, as being the favorite in a game or race makes abundantly clear. I see no point in insisting on a guarantee here when moral philosophy in general would not seem to admit of this sort of thing. I have exploited the importance of an outcome's being favored in [9].

[2] My thinking about the dynamics of a closed community owes much to Trivers ([3], p. 193).

[3] The notion of a projected counterfactual belief is a technical term which I have developed [8] and is to be contrasted with an exemplified counterfactual belief. If X believes that Y (a friend) would do such-and-such (e.g., care for her children were she to die), where the basis for this belief is *not* that Y has treated her that way in the past, then X has a projected counterfactual belief in this regard. By contrast, if X believes that Y (who is caring for her children) will prepare them dinner should she return home later than usual, where the basis for this belief is that he had done so in the past, then her belief in this regard is an exemplified counterfactual belief.

[4] My remarks here follow Trivers' account of the psychological system underlying human altruism ([3], pp. 211–223).

[5] 'Nevertheless I have somewhat against thee, because thou has left thy first love' (Revelation 2:4).

[6] For some sense of the perils of an adversary society, see [2] and [6]. In East Cleveland the premiums for insurance for playgrounds went from approximately $200,000 a year in 1985 to $800,000 in 1986. The result is that the face of playgrounds is changing rapidly, as swings, monkey bars, and so on are being removed. A child, Dan Wiedl, is quoted as saying: 'Well, they'd have to change the name. You couldn't call it a playground if there was nothing to play on. That sure wouldn't be right' ([6], p. 6). A city official is quoted as saying: 'It's really ironic. You end up denying those services that make a community worth living in to save the community itself' ([6], p. 1).

BIBLIOGRAPHY

[1]   Blum, Lawrence: 1981, *Friendschip, Altruism, and Morality*, Routledge and Kegan Paul, Boston.

[2]   Brody, Michael: 1986, 'When Products Turn Into Liabilities', *Fortune Magazine* **113** March 3, 20–24.

[3]   Clutton-Brock, T. H. and Harvey, Paul (eds.): 1978, *Readings in Sociobiology*, W. H. Freeman and Company, San Francisco.

[4]   Hauerwas, Stanley: 1988, 'Reconciling the Practice of Reason: Casuistry in a Christian Context', in this volume, pp. 135–55.

[5]   Nagel, Thomas: 1986, *The View From No Where*, Oxford University Press, New York.

[6]   *Plain Dealer*: 1986, 'Summer's here, heat's on: Insurance woes burn kids' fun at parks',

June 23, 1, 6.

[7]   Trivers, Robert L.: 1971, 'The Evolution of Reciprocal Altruism', *The Quarterly Review of Biology* 46, 35–57. (All parenthetical references will be to its reprinting in [3].)

[8]   Thomas, Laurence: 1985, 'Beliefs and the Motivation to be Just', *American Philosophical Quarterly* 22, 347–352.

[9]   Thomas, Laurence: 1986, 'Justice, Happiness, and Self-Knowledge', *Canadian Journal of Philosophy* 16, 63–82.

Oberlin College
Oberlin, Ohio

SECTION V

FROM THEORY TO PRAXIS

ALAN DONAGAN

THE RELATION OF MORAL THEORY TO MORAL JUDGMENTS:
A KANTIAN REVIEW

"My sympathies are all in the wrong place, and I don't like it [said Wimsey]. I know all about not doing evil that good may come. It's doing good that evil may come that's so embarrassing".

"My dear boy", said the Rector, "it does not do for us to take too much thought for the morrow. It is better to follow the truth and leave the result in the hand of God. He can foresee where we cannot..." Dorothy L. Sayers, *The Nine Tailors*

My object in this paper is to show how moralists working in the Kantian tradition go from their general moral principles to judgments in individual cases; and to do so by examining how they would proceed in an exemplary individual case. In an earlier paper [5] I attempted to exhibit the contemporary doctrine of informed consent in medical practice as an example of how moral precepts are arrived at in the Kantian tradition. In now attempting to explain how moral principles are applied in that same tradition, I have chosen an example that is more revealing than any I know of in medicine: President Truman's decision to drop atomic bombs on Hiroshima and Nagasaki. However, its application is universal.

In claiming that the moral theory I am about to discuss was Kant's, I offer few scholarly credentials. More may be found in my paper, 'The Structure of Kant's Metaphysics of Morals' [6]. Yet I hope that Kant's own writings,[1] together with those of philosophers other than myself who are developing Kantian moral theory for our day, will suffice for you to recognize the theory I present as his.

I. KANT'S DEONTOLOGY AND THE REASONS FOR IT

Morality, according to Kant, is a deontology: a system of absolute or categorical requirements on our conduct imposed by practical reason. To the extent that those requirements come to be normally accepted in a society, their validity will appear intuitively obvious to its members. Yet such intuitions are fallible, and morality does not depend for its binding force on anybody's having them. Kantian moral theory is not intuitionist.

By abjuring intuitionism, Kant puzzles philosophers today. His deontology

Baruch A. Brody (ed.), Moral Theory and Moral Judgments in Medical Ethics, 171–192.
© *1988 by Kluwer Academic Publishers.*

is expressly a version of traditional Judaeo-Christian morality, which notoriously forbids conduct of certain kinds even when conduct of those kinds maximizes good. Most non-intuitionist moral theorists today find this hard to understand. For they begin by assuming, first, that the fundamental concept of ethics is that of goodness, and secondly, that a good is something that can be brought into being or destroyed by action. Having made these assumptions, they cannot well escape concluding that morality is consequentialist: that actions are morally right if and only if the amount of good that results from them is not less than that which would have resulted from any alternative, and morally wrong if it is. And if that were so, then Kant's attempt to work out a non-intuitionist rational deontology could not have succeeded. Yet, unfortunately for them, many non-intuitionists have not freed themselves from intuitions that owe something to the Judaeo-Christian moral tradition: with half of their minds they want somebody to do what with the other half they believe to be impossible.

Samuel Scheffler, for example, concludes his well-known book, *The Rejection of Consequentialism*, 'by acknowledging that an adequate rationale for agent-centred restrictions [that is, restrictions on an agent's duty to maximize the goods his tradition recognizes] still eludes us, by insisting that the elusiveness of that rationale is deeply troubling, and by expressing the hope that the genuine intuitive appeal of such restrictions will not blind us to the need to understand and explain them better...' ([25], p. 129). True, Scheffler was writing about contemporary philosophy, and Kant's name appears neither in the index of his book, nor, as far as I have noticed, in its text. However, in a short paper, 'Agent-Centred Restrictions, Rationality and the Virtues' [24], he appears to extend to Kant the censure he earlier passed on his contemporaries.

I freely acknowledge that there are reasons for doubting whether any rationale for traditional Judaeo-Christian deontology is adequate. What I cannot understand is why philosophers who profess to want such a rationale reject Kant's without making strenuous efforts to find out what it is. He is not, after all, a minor philosopher. Yet those of us who accept the rationale for traditional deontology that can be found in his writings continue to find that their principal task is not to defend it, but to make it known. If the expositions of that rationale in the writings of those who reject it were as accurate as those of intuitionism in the writings of anti-intuitionists, I doubt whether Kantians would be under much polemical pressure.

Kant's fundamental working idea in moral theory was that reason is practical as well as theoretical. This is apt to make philosophers nowadays knit their brows. What is reason? It is sometimes maintained that no practical principles are dictated by reason except those of means-end rationality, or efficiency. And although the objections to confining practical reason to efficiency are becoming well known, the usual response is to seek a stipulative definition that may hope to command some measure of acceptance, and then be pressed into service in moral theory.[2]

That is wrong-headed. Reason is a highly complex capacity most human beings have. You have it if what you say and do is such that you can be credited with beliefs and other propositional attitudes at all. You exercise it in distinguishing those of your beliefs that are fundamental from those that are not, and in regarding them as relatively immune to objections. You also exercise it in responding to reasoned criticism of your beliefs with acceptance or reasoned counter-argument, which may take the form of an appeal to authority. When most of us find ourselves challenged on points about the general theory of relativity or quantum mechanics, we refer to encyclopaedias or standard texts.

It follows that the concept of reason and its relatives, the concepts of rationality and irrationality, are dialectical. When anybody claims that some principle of logic, or physics, or cosmology, or morals is a fundamental requirement of reason, he ought to be prepared to say why: to exhibit the place it has in the body of his beliefs, and to defend that body of beliefs by argument. There are no beliefs it is improper to question, not even the principles of logic, although there are some (the principle of contradiction in logic, and the practical principle of means-end rationality are examples) in which move and countermove are familiar enough for them to be considered practically unchallengeable.

Fundamental moral principles are not, however, reducible to principles of logic. A fundamental moral principle that most moralists judge quite certain is the principle of impartiality: that it is contrary to reason for A to treat B in a manner in which it would be impermissible for B to treat A, 'merely on the ground that they are two different individuals, and without there being any difference between the natures or the circumstances of the two which can be stated as a reasonable ground for difference of treatment.'[3] Yet if all actions were permissible, and it has not been shown that any principle of logic would be violated if they were, then this principle would be false. Moralists rightly do not worry. The idea that reason cannot be practical unless its practical principles are reducible to those of logic is fantastic.

A practical principle may be put forward as required by practical reason provided that reasons are given for doing so, and that objections to doing so are shown to have less weight. In moral theory as in other fields of intellectual inquiry (mathematics, for example) there will often be disagreement about whether or not this condition has been met. And, as in other fields, the fact of disagreement does not show that it has not been.[4] Of course, anybody who finds what he puts forward as a practical principle to be generally rejected will do well to think again, if it really is rejected as lacking weight, and not merely as failing to satisfy some arbitrary 'philosophical' test.

Let us now look at the grounds on which Kant held that action for the sake of producing the best consequences overall must be limited. They are neither unfamiliar nor evidently mistaken.

The idea behind them is that the beings that make up the world are of two kinds: those such that a non-derivative good reason for doing something is that it is for their sake – he calls them 'ends in themselves'; and those such that a non-derivative good reason for using, and if necessary destroying them, is that it is necessary for the sake of ends in themselves. No being can be of both kinds. That any beings are ends in themselves in this sense is of course disputable.

Kant's position is that only if some beings can be identified as ends in themselves can a theory of goodness be constructed. And he not implausibly maintains that adequate reasons can be given for identifying rational agents, or persons, as ends in themselves, and only them. The supreme good of such ends is that they choose to act according to reason: that is, that their wills be good. Their natural good is that they exercise their natural capacities, according to reason, throughout their lives. Beings that are not ends in themselves, mere things, are good to the extent that they are fitted to subserve the natural good of things in themselves. Kant therefore proposes that we think of the world, as we sometimes speak of it, as divided into persons and things: the former are ends in themselves, and the latter are beings whose good is instrumental.

This fundamental idea generates a teleology different in kind from consequentialist ones in which ends are goods to be brought about. The very notion of maximizing ends in themselves is nonsensical. They exist independently of what is done for them. (Bringing ends in themselves into existence is not an end in itself.) Ends in themselves give rise to ends for action in two ways.

The first is as limits or, in Nozick's useful term, 'side-constraints'. It is logically impossible that a thing be both an end in itself, and also something to be used for the sake of other beings, and if need be harmed or destroyed, whether or not those other beings are ends in themselves. Hence no action is practically reasonable if it involves using (and if need be harming) an end in itself *solely on the ground* that it would be good for some other being or beings.

The second is by generating requirements to do good that are intrinsically restricted. Producing more rather than less good for ends in themselves is a *secondary* rational end: that is, one it would be inconsistent for anybody who recognizes that there are ends in themselves not to have. An end in itself is a being for whose sake it is rational to do things, and doing what it is rational to do for such a being is doing or producing what is good for it. Hence refraining from doing or producing something good for an end in itself is contrary to practical reason, *except* when doing or producing that good would either (i) treat some other end in itself as a mere disposable means, or (ii) would make it impossible to do some other proportionate good. In the former case, doing or producing that good would not be required by practical reason, but contrary to it; and in the latter, it would be permissible but not required.

Kant's answer to Scheffler's question, 'What is the rationale of restricting what agents may do for the sake of maximizing the good of agents overall?' is therefore: (1) that each and every agent is an end in itself, and as such is prior to the secondary end of producing more rather than less good for agents overall; and (2) that without the concept of such an end, not only would the concept of good be unintelligible, but, *a fortiori*, also that of maximizing it.[5]

The fact that Kant's deontology rests on a teleology of ends in themselves, and not on dialectical manoeuvres involving universalization, is sufficiently unfamiliar for it to be worth pointing out that Kant explicitly asserts it in the *Grundlegung*, in what I am tempted to think its most important sentence.

[W]ithout beings whose *Dasein* is itself an end ... nothing of absolute worth could be found, and if all worth is conditional and thus contingent, no supreme practical principle for reason could be found anywhere (*G*, 65–66/428).

In other words, unless some beings are ends in themselves, all worth would be relative; and if all worth were relative, there could be no such thing as morality.

The shape of the deontology that results from Kant's teleology is familiar. Various kinds of action, whether of commission or omission, are forbidden because by them some person would be treated as a *mere* means to be used for the sake of some end other than himself – as a being whose nature does not constitute him an ultimate end. Refraining from such actions is a 'perfect' duty, no matter what the cost to oneself. A second kind of duty, called by Kant[6] 'imperfect', is that each free rational agent act according to rational plans for cultivating his capacities and exercising them, and for doing what he reasonably can to promote the good of others. Kant took normal human beings to be self-supporting members of human societies. Hence he conceived duties of beneficence as duties to others who also belong to societies, not necessarily one's own, the normal members of which are self-supporting. And so he treated beneficence to others as limited by one's duties to oneself.

Even granting the distinction between ends in themselves and beings that are not ends in themselves, it is not obvious what treating something as an end in itself is. For example, it is tempting to suppose that it is not using it. In a recent paper, Nancy Davis has taken it for granted that Kant and the philosophers today who accept his formula that rational beings are to be treated always as ends and never as means only have as the background of their work, and sometimes as its framework, 'the conviction that there is something wrong with using persons' ([3], p. 387). Others have interpreted Kant as sometimes taking it to imply that no action of which any harm to a rational being is a possible outcome is permissible (for example, in his objections to suicide), and as at other times inconsistently allowing exceptions to be made by voluntary agreement (for example, in his treatment of the duties of servants to masters).[6] The most economical way of showing that these interpretations are mistaken is to examine the principle on which much of Kant's treatment of war depends, the principle he called 'the universal law of *Recht*'.[7] For it shows not only how Kant understood what treating something as an end in itself is, but also why he so understood it.

He formulated the universal law of *Recht* as follows:

Act externally in such a way that the free use of your will is compatible with the freedom of everyone according to a universal law (*MdS*, I, 34/231).

First of all, this law reminds us that ends in themselves are beings possessed of practical reason, and as such freely choose their ways of life subject only to its constraints. One needs very little acquaintance with the conditions of human life to perceive that happiness, the natural goal of every human being, is unthinkable without engaging in enterprises involving risk and uncertainty. And if treating oneself as an end is compatible with accepting risks of loss, injury and even death, treating others as ends is compatible with accepting that they too will incur such risks. Well, what risks is it reasonable to incur? In one's own case, those inseparable from whatever rational plan of life one adopts. And in the case of others, those inseparable from whatever rational plans of life they adopt. And what plans are rational? Even between competent judges, some questions will remain unsettled; but others (for example, the question whether a plan for a life as a heroin addict can be rational) will not. To the extent that they can be settled, free uses of the will that are in themselves rationally permissible can be distinguished from those that are not.

Unfortunately, it is conceivable that each of us may have a project for attaining our own happiness that is not in itself contrary to practical reason, and yet it be impossible, given the way the world is, for all our projects to be carried out. Projects that are unobjectionable in themselves may be in conflict with one another. For example, two persons may wish to obtain a piece of property that belongs to a third, who is willing to part with it. Both projects are permissible, but both cannot succeed. Does practical reason provide some way of deciding which, if either, succeeds? Of course it does. Even if the competing parties do not belong to political societies, which establish laws for deciding such questions, judicial bodies for settling disputes about what the law is in a particular case, and executive bodies for enforcing their judgments, there are rules on which they could agree by which neither would be reduced to a mere means to the others' good.

Given that all parties to the potential conflict in the above example are not disadvantaged by prior wrongs in which the others have participated, the obvious rule is that the owner may part with his property on whatever terms he will; and that if he chooses to part with it to whoever offers him the return he judges best, neither he nor the one who offers that return should be molested by the party who offers less. In short, in situations in which not everybody can accomplish purposes in themselves permissible and practicable, there are procedures formulable as sets of rules applying to all equally – that is, as universal laws – for determining which purposes are to be accomplished. The universal law of *Recht* therefore amounts to this: that when you are in a situation in which you and others cannot all accomplish purposes in themselves unobjectionable, you are to agree on a rule that will not reduce any of you to mere means to the good of the others.

In laying down how free rational agents are to conduct themselves, the universal law of *Recht* both implies a permission and limits it. As long as your actions do not infringe the freedom of everyone according to applicable universal law, nobody is entitled to interfere with them. But if they do not, you are accorded no such immunity.

[I]f a certain use of freedom is itself a hindrance to freedom according to universal laws (that is, is *unrecht*) then the use of coercion to counteract it, inasmuch as it is the prevention of a hindrance to freedom, is consistent with freedom according to universal laws; in other words, this use of freedom is *recht* (*MdS* I, 35/231).

Hence, the very possibility of *Recht* 'can be held to consist immediately in the conjunction of universal reciprocal coercion with the freedom of everybody' (*MdS* I, 36/232).

There are decisive reasons for not being content with private agreements about what is *recht*. Even with good will, which is often absent, individuals will differ about who is entitled to what. And even if everybody is prudent in resorting to force to obtain what he considers his due, *Recht* will be continuously violated. What is needed is an accepted public authority to define *Recht*, to decide how what is defined applies to disputed cases, and to enforce its decisions. Such a public authority would be a political society. Hence, persons living outside a political society, so far as they care about *Recht*, must work for the establishment of one; and, when it is established, must obey its laws, even though they will almost certainly be defective.

We can now illustrate Kant's rationale for restricting action directed to maximizing good overall. The driver of a vehicle bringing medical supplies to the scene of an accident may not break whatever universal law may be in force forbidding dangerous driving, even though every minute gained will save lives, and few are likely to be hurt by breaking that law. What law is in force will vary from society to society. In most U.S. jurisdictions the law of dangerous driving for ambulances is different from that for physicians driving private vehicles. But the rationale for the different restrictions adopted by different societies is the same in all cases. There are *some* ways of using the streets that endanger the lawful use of them by others, and so impair their freedom as ends in themselves. Differences of opinion about what those ways may be are settled for better or worse by the legislative processes of each society. The uses of the streets thus declared wrong are wrong, no matter what good to others may result.

II. KANTIAN MORALITY AND WAR: (A) PRINCIPLES

The implications of the universal law of *Recht* for life outside a political society differ from those for life within one. The fundamental principle is the same: *Recht* is to be upheld, and when it is violated, the violators are to be coerced *just so far as may be necessary to restore the violated state*, and no further. However, since it is contrary to reason for those outside a political society not to do what they can to establish one, the rule of private enforcement of *Recht* is: coerce those who violate *Recht* to restore it, but in such a way as not to hinder the establishment of a political society. In other words:

as far as you can, treat those you coerce as potential fellow-citizens.

In a political society, by contrast, the enforcement of *Recht* is for the most part committed to the public authorities. And their task, unlike that of private enforcers, is not merely to rectify violations of *Recht*, but to suppress violent resistance to their authority, even in petty matters. Hence, public authorities have a duty which private ones do not. In putting down forcible resistance, they have no licence to employ more force than is necessary; but if it is necessary, they have a duty to employ lethal force.

Kant believed that the political system by which eighteenth century Europe was divided into sovereign states defectively but genuinely established systems of public law by which the freedom of each to pursue his own happiness in his own way could be reconciled with the freedom of everybody else to do likewise. And I do not see how he could have taken a much different view of the twentieth century state system (with the exception of Nazi Germany and possibly of Stalin's empire). The laws of states as they were in his day and as they are in ours therefore morally bind those within their jurisdictions, although only to the extent that they do not directly conflict with morality itself, for example, by establishing systems of slavery. Hence it follows that it is contrary to the universal law of *Recht* for one state to violate the integrity of another that is doing no wrong; for that would prevent the citizens of that other state from exercising their freedom compatibly with the freedom of their fellows according to a rationally established system of public law.

The part of the moral law that applies to warfare (and in particular, the part of the division of it that Kant called *Recht*) follows directly from these considerations. Kant's treatment (it may be found in the second section, 'Das Völkerrecht' of Part II of the *Rechtslehre*, 'Das öffentliche Recht') is deeply traditional in content: it restates the classical sixteenth-century theory of the just war. Yet he does so in a radically new setting: namely, that of utterly rejecting the traditional assumption that war is an evil that cannot be eliminated from the human condition. (This was too much for the self-proclaimed moderns, Hegel and Nietzsche.) On the European states of the 1790s, each 'violat[ing] the rights of another who is just as lawlessly disposed towards [it]', he remarked with savage indignation that 'whatever *happens* to them as they destroy themselves is entirely *recht*' (*Perpetual Peace*, 380). But, not foreseeing that atomic weapons would shorten the time allowed to humanity for gaining wisdom, he cherished a distant hope that the 'game' of mutual wrong would one day bring itself to an end.

[E]nough of their race will always survive so that this game will not cease, even into the remotest age, and they can serve as a warning to later generations. In this manner, the course of world events justifies providence. For the moral principle in man never dies out, and with the continuous progress of culture, reason, which is able pragmatically to apply the ideas of *Recht* in accordance with the moral principle, grows through its persistence in doing so, and guilt for transgressions grows concomitantly (*ibid.*).

Political societies, like individuals, will pass from a state in which there is no public *Recht* into one of public *Recht* only when they unify themselves into a *rechtlich* world commonwealth, and do it by morally permissible means.

III. KANTIAN MORALITY AND WAR: (B) CONDITIONS OF A JUST WAR

Most wars are between states whose policies are acquisitive without regard to *Recht*, and who would attack their neighbors if they believed they would gain power by it. Hence even states that have a just cause for making war seldom make it justly; for they seldom make it for that reason. Yet it is possible that a state should make war justly. According to the principles laid down in the preceding sections, a just war must satisfy the following conditions. First, it must be defensive: 'a state is permitted to employ violent measures to secure redress when it believes that it has been injured by another state, inasmuch as, in the state of nature, this cannot be accomplished by a judicial process' (*MdS* I, 250/346). Threats, as well as actual violence, are injuries; and Kant was prepared to consider 'the mere menacing increase of power' as a threat. His reasoning, evidently sound in my opinion, was that between states as between individual persons you are not in a state of lawful freedom if you are credibly threatened with violence.

Kant does not go into detail about what 'to secure redress' implies. Traditional just war theory,[8] as G. E. M. Anscombe expounded it in a fine paper she wrote as an undergraduate, lays down four conditions that must be satisfied:

(i)   that securing redress must really be intended, and not some further unjust end, such as to annex the enemy's territory;

(ii)   that employing violence must be the only possible means of securing redress;

(iii)   that there must be a reasonable hope of victory; and

(iv)   that securing redress must be a good that outweighs the probable evil effects of the war.

I take the reasons for these conditions to be fairly plain.

The first and second are not so much specific conditions as emphatic restatements of the sole ground on which a war can be just at all: namely, that it be to redress a wrong done. Redress cannot be a state's sole intention in making war if it will not stop until it has gained something else, or if it insists on making it when it can obtain redress without it. If the injurer is willing to redress the injury, *Recht* has not yet broken down, and it is hypocrisy to claim that war is necessary to restore it.

The third condition depends on the point that, if an agent does not believe the action he proposes has a reasonable hope of accomplishing a certain end, then his intention in doing what he proposes cannot be to bring that end about. Of course the bounds of reasonable hope are not precise. As Davidson has pointed out,

in writing heavily on this page I may be intending to produce ten legible carbon copies. I do not know, or believe with any confidence, that I am succeeding. But if I am producing ten legible carbon copies, I am certainly doing it intentionally [4], p. 92.

However, if in writing heavily on this page I claim that I intend to produce thirty legible carbon copies, I am certainly lying.

The fourth condition turns on the fact that the duty to compel others to redress wrongs (as distinct from that to redress wrongs you yourself have committed) is a duty of self-cultivation (where the wrong is to you directly) or of beneficence: and as such it is a duty to form and act on a rational policy, not a duty to redress every wrong in sight. It is not a rational policy either of self-cultivation or of beneficence to redress one wrong at the cost either of leaving worse wrongs unredressed or of suffering worse harms than those caused by the wrong you are redressing. It is irrational to seek to regain the worse of two pairs of shoes stolen from me at the cost of not regaining the better pair, or of losing a leg.

IV. KANTIAN MORALITY AND WAR: (C) WAGING A JUST WAR JUSTLY

Even if there is an injustice that a state may rationally judge to be so grave that making war to redress it would be *recht*, there are restrictions on how a war that is *recht* may be waged. What are they?

Kant's answer to this question presupposes that the means by which a state may permissibly pursue the redress of wrongs done to it by another state are analogous to those by which a private individual may permissibly pursue the redress of wrongs done to him by another private individual in the absence of an established system of public law. By violating what is owed to another, the wrongdoer forfeits the immunity to violence and deception that is owed to anybody who is innocent. If somebody robs me of what is mine, and forcibly resists me when I try to repossess it, I am entitled to employ violence to overcome his resistance, but how? Kant's answer, as we have seen, is that we may not employ violence in such a way as to hinder our becoming fellow-citizens. This presupposes that his violation of *Recht* has not already been such as to exclude that possibility.

Warfare between states, like private restorations of *Recht*, must, according to Kant, be 'conducted according to such principles as will not preclude the possibility of abandoning the state of nature existing among states (in their internal relations) and of entering into one that is *rechtlich*' (*MdS* I, 251/347). And that possibility would be precluded if a state were to pursue the defensive objects of a just war (redressing wrongs is defensive, according to the universal law of *Recht*) by measures that would make its subjects unfit to be citizens. 'For if it were to employ such measures, it would thereby make itself unfit to be considered a person in relation to other states in the eyes of the Law of Nations (and as such to participate in equal rights with the other states)' (*MdS* I, 252/347).

The equivalent restrictions on what a state may do in waging war are that it may not attempt to secure redress by inflicting or threatening to inflict on its enemy a worse harm than that which it seeks to redress, and that it may neither do violence to non-combatants (who are offering no resistance) nor threaten it. In his eighteenth-century innocence, Kant did not foresee terrorist attacks on civilian populations to break the will of their governments, but he did censure the eighteenth-century practice of plundering non-combatant civilians.

During a war, although it is permissible to impose exactions and contributions on a vanquished enemy, it is still not permissible to plunder the people, that is, to seize forcibly the belongings of individuals (for that would be robbery, inasmuch as it was not the conquered people themselves who waged the war, but the state to which they were subject and which waged the war through them) (*MdS* I, 253/347–48).

Since Kant wrote, a distinction with which he was presumably familiar, but which he did not choose to mention, has become of much greater practical importance. If a state justly wages war to redress some wrong done to it, it is entitled to attack the combatant services of its enemy, including its supply services, although not its military hospitals. And it is entitled to do this even if non-combatant bystanders will be injured. It is an unjust belligerent's duty to make peace; and, if it does not, it is its derivative duty to see that no innocent is harmed by its unjust belligerence. Its failure to discharge this duty does not deprive the just belligerent of the right to attack its combatant services.

The application of this principle is simple in theory, but difficult in practice. A just belligerent is entitled to bombard a fortress of the unjust one with artillery, even though some shells will fall on the territory around it. That non-combatants in that territory will suffer if the fortress is bombarded does not make it wrong to bombard the fortress: they should not be there. On the other hand, it would be wrong to bombard them in order to impede the military operations of the unjust belligerent, for example, by causing a panic. While they cannot make permissible military measures impermissible by getting in the way of them, what may be permissibly done to them when they get in the way may not permissibly be done when they do not. But how inaccurate may a bombardment be and count as a bombardment of the fortress and not as an impermissible attack on non-combatants living near it? As Anscombe has said, 'unscrupulousness in considering the possibilities turns [a legitimate attack on a military target] into murder' ([1], p. 66).

Her example of such unscrupulousness, from a correspondent, merits repetition.

[D]o you know that in the war the English bombed the dykes of our province Zeeland, an island where nobody could escape anywhere to. Where the whole population was drowned, children, women, farmers working in the field, all the cattle, everything, hundreds and hundreds, and we were your allies (*ibid.*)!

And her dry comment says all that needs saying:

That was to trap some fleeing German military. I think my correspondent has something (*ibid.*).

The most familiar example is the difference between the bombing policies developed before World War II in Europe and the U.S.

In Europe it was concluded that modern anti-aircraft defenses would make accurate bombing of military targets, which would only be possible by daylight, impossible. At the same time, it was believed that heavy attacks by night on industrial centers of population would break the will of the power so attacked to continue fighting. Britain both developed the policy further than its enemy, Germany, and pursued it more thoroughly. Despite a horrifying slaughter of non-combatant civilians and aircrews, if was ineffective. C. P. Snow has argued that, with better scientific advice, this would have been foreseen. On the other hand, its supporters maintain to this day that it would have been effective if it had been more thorough.

The U.S., by contrast, developed accurate daylight bombing techniques, and ultimately manufactured long-range fighters to protect the bombers. The combination proved to be effective; and by the end of the war in Europe, even the R.A.F., despite the protests of its bomber command, was largely being used against military targets.

There is a double lesson here. First of all, although the pre-war bombing policy of the U.S. was morally acceptable, and that of the European powers who planned for indiscriminate night attacks on civilian population centers was not, both policies appear to have been adopted on practical grounds, without reference to moral considerations. As Kant savagely remarked,

The practical politician tends to look down with great smugness on the political theorist, regarding him as an academic whose empty ideas cannot endanger the state, since the state must proceed on empirical principles (*Perpetual Peace*, 343).

Hence the second lesson. The practical politician's empirical principles are seldom free from error. The moral abominations that are sanctioned in the name of practicality are often about as practical as the typhus experiments carried out by the Nazis in the concentration camps. And the political morality that results from the empirical attitude has been unforgettably condensed by Anscombe into what might be called the Principle of Justification by Stupidity: 'Every fool can be as much of a knave as suits him' ([1], 65). Neglect of the moralist's empty non-empirical ideas commonly goes with accepting empirical calculations, many of which are improbable, and none of which is certain. And that was why Kant (see his comments on counsels of prudence) denied that morality could be grounded on empirical principles.

V. FROM SPECIFIC MORAL THEORY TO JUDGMENT: HIROSHIMA AND NAGASAKI

Given a general moral theory, and a general understanding of the varieties of human wars and the conditions under which they are fought, it is possible to derive a specific theory both of the conditions under which it is just to resort to war, and of those under which it can be justly waged. Judgments about individual cases, however, call for historical information. No judgment about the bombing of Hiroshima and Nagasaki can be justified if it rests on false historical premises. Now it is notorious that historians are divided about both the information possessed by those who ordered the bombing, and about their intentions. Since it is beyond both my competence and the scope of this paper to resolve these historical disputes, I shall try to show how Kantian moralists use historical information in making judgments about individual cases by considering in turn two different historical accounts of the bombing. My conclusions will be entirely conditional. Their form will be: *if* such and such an historical account is true, then such and such a moral conclusion follows. Every judgment of whether an individual action is right or wrong in an actual case depends on accepting an account of what it is, and in what situation it is done.

Besides the question whether a given individual action is right or wrong, a second question can be asked: namely, whether its doer's will is good or bad in doing it. Kant held that virtue demands not only that we do what is right, but that we do it with a right intention. And he also held that it is possible, owing to inculpable ignorance, to have a morally good will and yet to do what is in fact wrong. Answering questions of this second kind calls for information, not about what was done and in what situation, but about what the doer believed he was doing and in what situation, and about whether those beliefs were culpably arrived at or not. In this paper the only questions to be considered are of the first kind: whether, on either of two accounts of what they did and in what situation, President Truman and his advisers acted rightly or wrongly; and not whether their wills were good or bad in doing so. I assume that they were good, but I have no information about it.

Here a personal recollection may not be out of place. At the time, although just under what was then voting age, I had no doubt at all that President Truman acted rightly. He plainly represented the moral position of everybody I knew; and I believe that he represented that of most ordinary people in the Allied countries at the time. Few in his position would have decided otherwise than he did.

A. The Bombing of Hiroshima and Nagasaki: The Historical Account Accepted by Anscombe

The first historical account of the situation in which President Truman acted is that on which G. E. M. Anscombe founded her conclusion that he acted wrongly. I quote her own statement of it.

In 1945, at the Potsdam conference in July, Stalin informed the American and British statesmen that he had received two requests from the Japanese to act as a mediator with a view to ending the war. He had refused. The Allies agreed on the 'general principle' – marvellous phrase! – of using the new type of weapon that America now possessed. The Japanese were given a chance in the form of the Potsdam Declaration, calling for unconditional surrender in face of overwhelming force soon to be arrayed against them. The historian of the Survey of International Affairs considers that this phrase was rendered meaningless by the statements of a series of terms; but of these the ones incorporating the Allies' demands were mostly of so vague and sweeping a nature as to be rather a declaration of what unconditional surrender would be like than to constitute conditions. It seems to be generally agreed that the Japanese were desperate enough to have accepted the Declaration but for their loyalty to their Emperor: the 'terms' would certainly have permitted the Allies to get rid of him if they chose. The Japanese refused the Declaration. In consequence, the bombs were dropped on Hiroshima and Nagasaki ([1], p. 63–64).

Although both Hiroshima and Nagasaki contained military targets of great importance, Anscombe dismisses, on the following grounds, the defense that the targets of the bombings were military, and that, from the Allied point of view, non-combatants were killed and maimed incidentally and with regret.

In the bombing of these cities it was certainly decided to kill the innocent as a means to an end. And a very large number of them were killed, all at once, without the interstices of escape or the chance to take shelter, which existed even in the 'area bombings' of the German cities (*ibid.*, p. 64).

In short, the bombing of Hiroshima and Nagasaki was a successful attempt to end, by unjust means, a war that itself had ceased to be just because its aim had ceased to be to redress specific wrongs.

Given the account of the historical facts which she reasonably accepted, I do not see how it can be denied that Anscombe's conclusion follows from the principles of traditional just war theory, which in turn follow from the principles of Kant's theory of *Recht*.

B. *The Bombing of Hiroshima and Nagasaki: Its History According to Harper*

What has been most effectively questioned in the account of the historical facts which Anscombe accepted is whether 'the Japanese were desperate enough to have accepted the [Potsdam] Declaration but for their loyalty to the Emperor'. Even if the Emperor's position had been safe-guarded as it ultimately was (indeed, but for the Emperor's authority, there would not have been a surrender), it is contended that the Japanese would not have surrendered without the bombing. This is the position taken by Stephen Harper in his recent *The Miracle of Deliverance* ([8]). I quote, from the *Times Literary Supplement* [9], Michael Howard's summary of Harper's account of the situation confronting the Allies:

The Allies did indeed know that the civilians in the Japanese government were seeking a way of escape; but they also knew that the military colleagues of those statesmen were determined to prevent it. The Potsdam Declaration with its modified surrender terms was issued precisely to strengthen the hand of the Japanese peace party, but the military were strong enough to secure its rejection. The military leadership of Japan still planned an inch-by-inch defence of the Japanese home islands – to say nothing of the regions of South-East Asia which they still held with over half a million fighting troops. In the event of an allied landing they planned a massacre of their prisoners both in South-East Asia and in Japan. The quality of their defence of Okinawa, where they had inflicted 50,000 casualties and themselves lost 110,000 dead, made American estimates of probable casualties in an invasion of the home islands – half a million Americans out of an invasion force of five million, and ten million Japanese from the combined effects of battle, bombing and starvation – seem all too plausible. Only after the second bomb did their spokesmen in the Cabinet fall silent. Even then, a group of fanatical young officers attempted a coup, to sabotage the Imperial order to surrender (p. 869).

From a Kantian point of view, what moral difference does this different account of the historical facts make?

Plainly, it makes the decision more reasonable. For it comes to this: the Allies did not intend to impose outrageous terms on the Japanese; but they correctly believed that, except for the bombing, no satisfactory terms would have been accepted. If that is true, was the bombing legitimate according to Kantian moral theory?

Unfortunately it was not. Let us go back to the very first condition for engaging in war at all: that it be to redress specific wrongs. That condition obliged the Allies to inform the Japanese authorities what wrongs the Allies demanded that they redress, and what safeguards they demanded for that redress (disarmament, military occupation until a peace treaty was ratified, changes of constitution, and the like), and invite them to protest any conditions they found unreasonable. It also obliged them to consider in good faith whatever protests the Japanese made, and to accommodate them so far as was consistent with securing redress. Harper acknowledges that the modified surrender terms of the Potsdam Declaration were designed to strengthen the peace party; but he does not deny Anscombe's objection that they were too vague and sweeping to constitute genuine conditions. And her moral point was not that the Japanese would have accepted the Potsdam terms if the Allies had agreed to negotiate, but that those terms were such that it was morally wrong for a just belligerent confident of victory to try to impose them.

There is a second objection. The Allies' failure to state the aims on which it would have been legitimate for them to make war undermines Harper's historical case for concluding that the bombing was the one step that would have brought the war to an immediate acceptable end. It is an historical fact that the war party in the Japanese cabinet was strong enough to prevail in the actual situation – in which they were confronted with the Potsdam version of the demand for unconditional surrender. But that it would have been strong enough in the possible situation in which the Allies at Potsdam offered just terms is at best a probable inference; and it is an even less probable inference if they had been offered just terms from the beginning. Hence Harper has failed to establish the crucial historical premise that Anscombe denies: that the bombing was *the one step* that would have brought the war to an immediate acceptable end.

As Kant recognized, it is easy to become satirical about claims by impractical moralists that this or that was a practical possibility. 'Does Anscombe imagine that she could have done better than President Truman at Potsdam?' Yet Anscombe neither made nor needed to make any such claim. It was enough to point out that, after not even considering offering the Japanese peace terms that could be justified by traditional morality, practical politicians cannot justifiably claim in their memoirs that they *know* that the Japanese would have rejected such terms. Only if there was evidence that ways of ending the war justly without the mass killing of non-combatants by nuclear bombing were sought and not found, would there be a case for her to answer. For if it is even possible that there were such ways, it is hard to imagine a morality that would not require that they be sought before resorting to such killing. Howard furnishes no such evidence.[9]

Hence, even on Harper's account of the situation, Anscombe's conclusion stands. But it would be irresponsible philosophically to leave it at that. Consider the following situation, which, if Harper is right about the actual facts, would have been historically possible.

Suppose that the Allies had offered the most generous terms compatible with redressing the wrongs done by Japan, and with ensuring that those wrongs would not be repeated. In extreme cases (among which he would certainly have numbered the aggressions of Nazi Germany and Tojo's Japan) Kant explicitly recognized that the states justly resisting those aggressions are called on to 'take away from the malefactor[s] the power of committing [them]', and even to require that 'they adopt a new constitution that in its nature will be unfavourable to the passion for war' (*MdS* I, 256/349). And I do not think that Anscombe would disagree. Suppose further, that after the Allies had offered to negotiate on such terms, and to give the Japanese reasonable safeguards consistent with them, the Japanese had either refused to negotiate or, having negotiated, had rejected the terms offered. Would the Allies then have been entitled to bomb Hiroshima and Nagasaki as they did?

Not if the bombs could have been used to procure a surrender without attacking non-combatants. Various possibilities have been proposed. It is unnecessary for us to go into them. What matters is that there is no evidence worth the name that those who made the decision sought such a permissible alternative.

VI. FORESEEABILITY AND KANTIAN MORAL JUDGMENTS

At this point moralists in the Kantian tradition brace themselves for the consequentialists' ultimate weapon: the demand that they give a judgment on a situation in which *ex hypothesi* the only alternatives are an enormous calamity (hundreds of thousands of Allied lives lost, millions of Japanese) on one hand, and an impermissible attack on non-combatants on the other. Instead of bracing themselves, they should point out that the weapon is a fake, which can harm them only by bluffing them into forgetting how moral reasoning proceeds.

Morality, as Kantians understand it, is a matter of practical reasoning about how to conduct oneself in the actual world; and possible cases are of interest only so far as they can arise, for all we know, in the actual world. The case Kantians are now called on to judge is one in which a state that has observed strict justice in declaring war and waging it should find itself in a situation in which it could foresee that, despite being in the same overwhelming military position as the Allies had in relation to Japan in July 1945, and despite possessing equivalents of the Hiroshima and Nagasaki bombs and the capacity to make more, millions of lives would be lost unless the two bombs were used as they were at Hiroshima and Nagasaki. I see no reason to believe that such a situation could arise in the world as we know it.

My disbelief is reinforced by some of Harper's arguments, which presuppose not only the doubtful proposition that no permissible military use of the bombs would have had the same effect as their impermissible use against non-combatants, but also the certainly false one that the Allies' timetables for the various invasions they planned (in some cases, such as that of Malaya, incompetently) were as unchangeable as laws of nature. The case, in short, is really an appeal to the Principle of Justification by Stupidity: every fool can be as much of a knave as suits him.

R. M. Hare has acknowledged that the philosophical attention that is lavished on logically possible but fantastic cases, commonly to the neglect of actual ones, is dangerous in moral education, because it undermines confidence in the reliability of moral rules which often should be acted on unhesitatingly.[10] For all that, he is confident that moral rules are not absolute, and that there are cases in which a moral sage must break them. As a prisoner of the Japanese in 1945, it may be that he judges the bombing of Hiroshima and Nagasaki to be such a case.

My point is different. It is that the practice of considering fantastic cases muddles us in judging real ones, and tempts people of good will to mistake stupidity for intelligent realism, and timidity for foresight. If the European powers in the thirties had refused on moral grounds to consider the evil strategic bombing policies they adopted, they would have been saved from the consequences of their own stupidity. And I think this is so in all such cases. Except for those of wrongs cancelling wrongs, I know of no reason to believe that a large good (along with a large evil) has ever been brought about by a wrong action which could not have been brought about innocently. Hence I do not believe that counterparts of the fantastic cases with which traditional moral doctrines are commonly assailed can occur at all in the world we inhabit.[11]

NOTES

[1] Three works of Kant are referred to by the following abbreviations:

G	= *Grundlegung der Metaphysik der Sitten* [12];
KpV	= *Kritik der praktischen Vernunft* [16];
MdS	= *Metaphysik der Sitten* [17].

In the edition of Kant's *Gesammelte Schriften* published by the Berlin Academy G appears in vol. 4, *KpV* in vol. 5, and *MdS* in vol. 6. Two page references are given for each quotation or citation: the first to the original edition, the second to that of the Berlin Academy. One or the other will be found in most available German texts, and in most translations. For G and *KpV* I chiefly follow L. W. Beck's translations [13] and for *MdS* chiefly John Ladd's translation of vol. 1 [14] and James Ellington's of vol. 2 [15]. I have also used Ted Humphrey's vigorous translation of *Perpetual Peace* [18], although I occasionally depart from it. I refer to by the page numbers of Vol. 8 of the Berlin Academy edition, which appear in most translations. I regret that I have not had access to a text containing the pagination of the second German edition (Königsberg: F. Nicolovius, 1796).

[2] Analyses of rationality and irrationality have multiplied recently. A representative sample is provided by the symposium, 'Rationality and Morality' [23], with contributions by Kurt Baier, Brian Barry, Stephen Darwall, Jon Elster, David Gauthier, Allan Gibbard, James Griffin, John Harsanyi, Donald Regan, and Nicholas Sturgeon.

[3] The form of the principle of impartiality here given is owed to Henry Sidgwick, *The Methods of Ethics*, [26], p. 380.

[4] Alasdair MacIntyre criticizes what he calls the 'enlightenment project' on the twofold ground that what rationalist moral philosophers disagree about cannot be a principle of practical reason,

and that what is not 'analytic' cannot be. See [19], pp. 21, 66. On dissent in a natural science, see [2].

[5] I have not gone into Scheffler's objection that Kantian morality is practically inconsistent because, having imposed certain absolute restrictions on conduct, it proceeds to impose further restrictions on the observance of those restrictions. This objection rests on the false assumption that it cannot be a duty to observe a certain restriction unless it is also a duty to minimize total overall violations of that restriction. Cf. [24] and [25].

[6] What I say about the problem of risk-taking in Kantian ethics is especially indebted to remarks by Dan Brock.

[7] I have left Kant's word *Recht* and its cognates untranslated, because it has no English equivalent, and because its sense is sufficiently clear in context.

[8] For an accessible recent American exposition of traditional just war theory, see Joseph C. McKenna, 'Ethics and War: a Catholic View', [21]. It has been much reprinted, e.g., in [22]. Michael Walzer, *Just and Unjust Wars* [27] is a contemporary attempt 'to recapture the just war for moral and political theory' (cf. p. xiv).

[9] Nor does Howard's practical argument from the shortage of time bear inspection.

> In 1944–45, allied war leaders had in fact little time to speculate about post-war possibilities. Their attention was necessarily focused on the immediate task of destroying enemies whom they saw, with good reason, as powerful, desperate and overwhelmingly evil ([9], p. 869).

Why was the task 'immediate'?

> The Americans were planning an invasion of Kyushu in November 1945 (Operation OLYMPIC, with 750,000 men) to be followed in March 1946 by a landing in the Tokyo region (Operation CORONET, with 1.8 million men) (*ibid.*).

Perhaps negotiations, once opened, would not have been over by November (it seems unlikely). But why treat the date for Operation OLYMPIC as unchangeable? Of course, if you treat your military plans as unalterable facts of nature you will have practical problems. One is reminded of Germany in 1914 impudently declaring that, unless Belgium violated her treaty obligations, and allowed the passage of the German army through its territory to attack France, 'Germany would be obliged, to her regret, to regard the Kingdom [of Belgium] as her enemy' ([21], p. 52). In such cases, it is difficult to determine the proportion of stupidity to knavery.

[10] R.M. Hare [7], ch. 3, 'The Archangel and the Prole'.

[11] This revision of the paper presented at Houston owes much to comments and criticisms made there, and to others made subsequently in discussions of it in Pasadena, Los Angeles, and at the University of Utah, Salt Lake City. Special debts are owed to Virgil Aldrich, Brian Barry, Margaret Battin, Dan Brock, Marshall Cohen, Randall Curren, Don Garrett, Catherine Hantzis, Will Jones, Stephen Munzer, Talbot Page, Tom Reed, Alan Strudler, and Jim Woodward.

BIBLIOGRAPHY

[1] Anscombe, G. E. M.: 1981, *The Collected Papers of G. E. M. Anscombe. Volume 3: Ethics, Religion, and Politics*, Basil Blackwell, Oxford.

[2] Burian, R.: 1986, 'The Internal Politics of Biology and the Justification of Biological Theories', in A. Donagan, A. N. Perovich, and M. Wedin (eds.), *Human Nature and Natural Knowledge*, D. Reidel Publ. Co., Dordrecht, Holland, pp. 23–45.

[3] Davis, N.: 1984, 'Using Persons and Common Sense', *Ethics* **94**, 387–406.

[4] Davidson, D.: 1980, *Essays on Actions and Events*, Clarendon Press, Oxford.
[5] Donagan, A.: 1977, 'Informed Consent in Therapy and Experimentation', *The Journal of Medicine and Philosophy* 2, 307–329.
[6] Donagan, A.: 1985, 'The Structure of Kant's Metaphysics of Morals', *Topoi* 4, 61–72.
[7] Hare, R. M.: 1981, *Moral Thinking*, Clarendon Press, Oxford.
[8] Harper, S.: 1985, *The Miracle of Deliverance*, Sidgwick and Johnson, London.
[9] Howard, M.: 1985, review of S. Harper, *The Miracle of Deliverance*, in *Times Literary Supplement*, Aug. 9, 869–870.
[10] Kant, I.: 1911–1914, *Gesammelte Schriften*, Bände 4, 5, 6, Königlich Preussische Akademie der Wissenschaften (ed.), Georg Reimer, Berlin.
[11] Kant, I.: 1923, *Gesammelte Schriften*, Band 8, Königlich Preussische Akademie der Wissenschaften (ed.), Walter de Gruyter, Berlin.
[12] Kant, I.: 1786, *Grundlegung der Metaphysik der Sitten*, Second Edition, J. F. Hartnock, Riga.
[13] Kant, I.: 1949, *Immanuel Kant: The Critique of Practical Reason and other Writings in Moral Philosophy*, L. W. Beck (tr.), University of Chicago, Chicago.
[14] Kant, I.: 1964, *Kant: The Metaphysical Elements of Justice*, J. Ladd (tr.), Bobbs-Merrill, Indianapolis.
[15] Kant, I.: 1965, *Kant: The Metaphysical Principles of Virtue*, J. Ellington (tr.), Bobbs-Merrill, Indianapolis.
[16] Kant, I.: 1788, *Kritik der praktischen Vernunft*, First Edition, J. F. Hartnock, Riga.
[17] Kant, I.: 1789, *Metaphysik der Sitten*, Second Edition, F. Nicolovius, Königsberg, 2 volumes.
[18] Kant, I.: 1983, *Perpetual Peace and Other Essays on Politics, History and Morals*, T. Humphrey (ed.), Hackett, Indianapolis.
[19] MacIntyre, A.: 1984, *After Virtue*, Second Edition, University of Notre Dame Press, Notre Dame.
[20] Marshall, S. L. A.: 1985, *World War I*, American Heritage, New York.
[21] McKenna, J. C.: 1960, 'Ethics and War: a Catholic View', *American Political Science Review* 54, 647–658.
[22] McKenna, J.C.: 1979, 'Ethics in War', in J. Rachels (ed.), *Moral Problems*, Third Edition, Harper and Row, New York, pp. 382–392.
[23] 'Rationality and Morality' (symposium): 1985, *Ethics* 96, 5–158.
[24] Scheffler, S.: 1985, 'Agent-Centred Restrictions, Rationality and the Virtues', *Mind* 94, 409–419.
[25] Scheffler, S.: 1982, *The Rejection of Consequentialism*, Clarendon Press, Oxford.
[26] Sidgwick, H.: *The Methods of Ethics*, Seventh Edition, MacMillan, London.
[27] Walzer, M.: 1977, *Just and Unjust Wars*, Basic Books, New York.

California Institute of Technology
Pasadena, California

JUSTIFICATION IN ETHICS

Normative ethics is believed by some to be on shaky ground, mainly because two aspects of ethical justification have seemed resistant to solution. One problem concerns how to reason validly from conflicting ethical principles to case resolution. It has been claimed that contemporary normative ethics offers no satisfactory basis for weighing such principles [17]. The other problem involves identifying the ultimate grounds of moral judgments. It has been asserted that the various time-honored theories of normative ethics are uniformly without foundation and that, consequently, we appear unable to arrive at a systematic knowledge of good and evil [21]. In this paper I hope to show that normative ethics – specifically, medical ethics – is indeed viable, that it has substance. I shall attempt to do this by suggesting a method of justification that seems to handle these two problems adequately.

Philosophers have been attempting to do applied ethics in hospitals for several years now. Some of us who have spent considerable time in the clinical setting have come to the view that traditional ethical theories, such as utilitarianism, Kantianism, natural law theory, and contractualism, are not suitable for resolving concrete dilemmas [1, 2, 15]. Indeed, these approaches often founder on the problem of reasoning from theory to case resolution in clinical situations. Consequently, other avenues are being explored for an adequate account of normative ethics in medicine. Several authors have discussed approaches that resemble a modern-day 'casuistry' [9, 15, 20]. In this essay I shall describe and defend one version of a casuistic approach. According to this method, the balancing of conflicting principles occurs in the context of individual cases. I do not claim that this method can resolve all conflicts between principles. However, it appears to give reasonable results sufficiently often that it can be a practical guide in contexts in which decisions must be made.

I. TRADITIONAL APPROACHES

Let me begin with the shortcomings of traditional theories in producing solutions in 'real life' clinical situations. Since a comprehensive discussion of

Baruch A. Brody (ed.), Moral Theory and Moral Judgments in Medical Ethics, 193–211.
© *1988 by Kluwer Academic Publishers.*

all major ethical theories would be rather lengthy, I shall focus on what I take to be the current leading contenders: utilitarianism in its various forms and contractualism. We might begin with rule utilitarianism, since it is a normative theory whose defense receives as much attention as any these days.[1]

Let us consider how rule utilitarianism might handle the problem of resolving conflicts between moral rules or principles. Presumably, rule utilitarians would have us adopt, as a policy for dealing with a type of conflict, that rule or set of rules the implementation of which would maximize utility. The ethically correct solution to an instance of that conflict type would be obtained by applying the utility-maximizing policy to the case in question. To implement this approach, presumably one should identify the possible policies for handling a type of conflict and evaluate them in terms of expected utilities. The difficulty, which becomes apparent once one attempts to undertake this approach in the clinical setting, is that usually there are a number of alternative policies and we cannot reasonably predict which one would maximize expected utility. Of course, utilitarians are accustomed to this type of objection, and there is a standard reply to it. Utilitarians acknowledge that often there is not as much information available as one would like for making predictions and that estimates of expected utilities will sometimes not be accurate. Utilitarianism only requires, it is pointed out, that one do the best one can, that one try to obtain the most reasonable estimates of expected utilities given the available data. We are assured by utilitarians that, even with limited data, common sense and thoughtful deliberation will enable us to arrive at defensible estimates of expected utilities.

Unfortunately, this reply seriously underestimates the difficulties in calculating expected utilities in the clinical setting. The problem is that the psychosocial dimensions of typical clinical dilemmas are sufficiently complex that we usually do not even have enough data to construct defensible 'best guesses' concerning which policy would maximize expected utility. Moreover, attempts to carry out studies to obtain information needed to construct defensible estimates would invariably encounter serious problems of scientific methodology and research ethics. Any type of clinical dilemma could be used to illustrate these difficulties. Consider, for example, refusal of treatment by Jehovah's Witnesses with dependent children. I recently encountered a case of this sort, described below.

Case 1

A 38-year-old woman was admitted to the hospital in labor with a full term fetus. She was having heavy vaginal bleeding, and fetal tachycardia (rapid heartbeat) was detected. A diagnosis of abruptio placenta (separation of the placenta from the uterus) was made and the situation was considered an emergency. An abruption would interfere with oxygen transport to the fetus and could cause fetal brain damage or death. The mother agreed to a cesarean section to protect the fetus but stated that she was a Jehovah's Witness and did not want blood transfusions. The abruption was confirmed at the time of cesarean section, and the infant was delivered free of complications. A normal amount of blood was lost by the woman due to the operation itself. Unfortunately, she suffered a complication of abruptio placenta, a coagulopathy in which her blood ceased to clot properly. This resulted in continued bleeding, soon creating an emergency need for transfusions. The patient continued to refuse whole blood as well as blood products such as packed red cells and fresh frozen plasma. Her husband, who was also a Jehovah's Witness, was present and agreed with her decision. He worked as a yardman at a private club, making a modest income, and was also receiving welfare assistance. There were six children in the family in addition to the newborn, of ages seventeen, sixteen, twelve, ten, eight, and four. When asked who would care for the children if the wife died, the husband said he would do it himself and that the patient's mother and the older children would help. He would continue to earn a living and receive welfare payments. The physicians and nurses attempted to persuade the patient to change her mind, but she was adamant. When asked how she would feel about blood being given without her consent, she said she was opposed to that.[2]

There are various policies that could be adopted concerning refusal of lifesaving procedures by adults with dependent children. One could administer the necessary treatment in all cases; one could always respect the patient's refusal; one could treat in selected cases, based on further factors to be identified. It might be argued that a policy of always treating would maximize happiness, since the probability of survival would be maximized, giving patients the greatest opportunity for future happiness while minimizing harm to the children.[3] However, there are a number of factors that make this prediction questionable. One would have to take into account the psychological effects which could occur to patients if their lives were saved and they subsequently regarded themselves as sinners, sentenced to eternal damnation. One would also need to consider the attitudes of family members, friends, and fellow Jehovah's Witnesses toward surviving patients. Such survivors may be regarded as 'tainted', in which case there might be a negative impact on their happiness as well as that of families and friends. Another consideration is the impact on Jehovah's Witness communities. There may be feelings of anger and heightened anxiety due to a threat to cherished values. The patient's children might even be harmed, such as by diminution of self esteem because their mother is tainted. The rule utilitarian who would advocate always treating assumes that the potential psychological harms to patients, families, friends, and Jehovah's Witness communities is less than the potential harms to the children in losing a parent. On the other hand, perhaps it would be argued that always respecting the patient's refusal would maximize expected utility. This argument, however, would assume that the psychological harms to patients, families, friends, and communities that would be prevented are greater than the potential harms to children. Furthermore, for each policy a rule utilitarian might defend, there would be a similar assumption concerning a balancing of harms. However, sociological data are not available to support these various assumptions. Since each option could therefore be criticized for its unsupported assumptions, there would be no rational basis for deciding among them without further data. In this context, appeals to common sense in support of a given policy might well be speculative, rather than defensible argumentation. The reason is that the assumptions in question involve rather complicated comparisons of the long-term emotional and psychological states of many individuals. These psychosocial dimensions of the problem of estimating expected utilities in the sort of case being considered are too complex to be easily resolved by common sense.

It might be objected that this problem is due to our current state of ignorance and that, if we wished, we could obtain the necessary data. Since rule utilitarianism is correct, it might be argued, this is precisely what we should try to do. In reply, this objection overlooks practical problems that would be involved in carrying out studies to obtain such data. Consider, for example, a scientific investigation that would implement the various policies, applying each to a different group of people and observing the results. Assuming we could devise ways of measuring happiness, the best policy would be the one corresponding to the experimental group in which overall happiness is greatest over the long run. Unfortunately, there would be a serious problem in scientific design. We would have no way of knowing whether the differences in happiness which might be detected between the various experimental groups are due to the different policies concerning refusal of medical treatment or are due to other factors. There are many variables which could potentially affect the happiness of individuals, and these could not be controlled. In addition, prospective studies of the sort being considered would involve serious ethical problems. Patients would presumably be assigned, perhaps by randomization, to experimental groups in which different policies are followed. This implies that some patients who refuse blood transfusions would be assigned to experimental groups in which treatment is mandatory. Thus, the right to informed consent of experimental subjects would be violated.

It might be suggested that we could gather pertinent data without having experimental groups. After all, it is possible to observe the long-term impact on affected individuals in cases in which treatment is instituted, as well as cases in which it is not, and then compare. This could be done retrospectively or prospectively. In response, the problem of uncontrolled variables would remain. In addition, this approach would not tell us about the effects of a policy of treating in certain situations and not treating in others, unless such a policy happened to be followed somewhere. Generally, we could not expect the various possible policies to be actually practiced. I suspect that these problems would be practical obstacles preventing investigators from conducting the sorts of studies being considered. In today's regulatory climate, no researcher would propose studies in which serious violations of informed consent would be necessary. Furthermore, no competent investigator is likely to undertake research involving such serious shortcomings in scientific design. I am not arguing that the data could not be obtained in principle, although the problems involving scientific design suggest that this might be so. I am arguing merely that it is doubtful that the data are forthcoming.

These problems concerning utilitarian calculations are a feature not only of the type of case example I have used, but occur in the attempted application of rule utilitarianism in clinical ethics generally. Granted, these are practical problems, as opposed to conceptual shortcomings of rule utilitarianism. Nevertheless, they are reason enough to turn elsewhere for guides to action in the clinical setting.

Act utilitarianism faces similar difficulties. Rather than focusing on policies, the act utilitarian would have us choose the option in each case which maximizes utility. However, the psychosocial dimensions of dilemmas in bioethics are sufficiently complex, as illustrated above, that our state of knowledge in most cases does not permit defensible predictions of the consequences of the various options with regard to the happiness of the relevant people. Perhaps it will be replied that if we had data on what usually happens to patients and families following the implementation of the various options, we could use that data to predict what would happen to the particular patient and family at hand. However, the same types of studies would be required to obtain this data as was discussed above, and the same problems with study design and research ethics would be encountered.

Let us turn to contractarian approaches. Some have suggested that the theory of John Rawls [22] could be applied to issues in practical ethics. Even if we put aside conceptual problems with Rawls's theory, however, we find that it is not very helpful in resolving issues in clinical ethics. In fairness to Rawls, it is doubtful that such a task was one of his objectives in writing *A Theory of Justice*. His theory aims, rather, at identifying and justifying general principles of justice upon which the structure of a society may be founded. The theory would have to be developed considerably in order to provide answers about bioethics in a broad range of cases. Whether this can be done remains to be seen.

I am aware of only one contractarian theory which attempts to provide a method for resolving individual cases, that of Robert Veatch [27]. He proposes a 'triple-contract theory' in which decisions are based on the results of three contract situations, with the specific aim of resolving ethical dilemmas in medicine. The first is a social contract establishing the most basic ethical principles for human interaction. The contractors would attempt to take the moral point of view, in that the welfare of other persons is considered on the same scale as one's own. The idea is that actual people are to come together. There is to be no selection of contractors, but rather the contract situation is open to all, so that in a sense the entire moral community would come together. Veatch claims that 'the real moral order' would be the one identified by a hypothetical group of contractors capable of perfect knowledge and of perfectly taking the moral point of view. According to Veatch, the real contractors should try to approximate the moral point of view as best as possible, as well as the qualities of the ideal observer, who is omniscient, sensitive, impartial, dispassionate, and consistent. Veatch believes that the main principles which would actually be chosen include beneficence, autonomy, truth telling, promise keeping, and avoiding killing. Thus, he thinks the contractors would select what are sometimes referred to as 'middle-level' principles.[4]

In the second contract situation the community of lay people negotiates with the medical profession. The purpose of the contract is to establish the role-specific duties of physicians. For example, it would set forth a principle for resolving conflicts between patient confidentiality and the well-being of other individuals. The role duties selected must be consistent with the basic principles agreed on in the first contract. Again, an actual meeting of people is envisioned, in which participants attempt to approximate as best they can the moral point of view and the ideal observer. The third contract is to be negotiated between the individual professional and patient. Its purpose is to reach agreement on moral dimensions of the professional-client relationship left as matters of choice by the first and second contracts. It could, for example, address the patient's wishes concerning access to information. Any agreement reached must be consistent with the first two contracts.

Veatch is correct in giving attention to middle-level principles, since these are principles one finds oneself working with in clinical ethics. In what follows, I shall focus on his discussion of reasoning from principles to case resolution, since this aspect of his theory is pertinent to the clinical usefulness of his contractarian approach. Veatch states that the problem of resolving specific cases calls for assigning priorities to conflicting middle-level principles. He argues for a lexical ordering according to which the non-consequentialist principles as a group take priority over beneficence, which he defines as the principle 'of producing good for one another' ([27], pp. 298–303, 328). The non-consequentialist principles are considered co-equal, and conflicts between them are to be handled by a 'balancing strategy': we should opt for the course of action producing the lesser violation of non-consequentialist principles, on balance. This balancing is to be carried out in the contract situation. Empirical studies would be relevant, to eliminate options which 'involve more than a necessary amount of infringement on the basic principles' ([27], p. 304). Taking into account such information, actual contractors would strive to assume the moral point of view and try to balance the conflicting principles.

Unfortunately, this approach is not very helpful in actual practice, in part because the concept of 'lesser violation of the non-consequentialist principles' is rather vague. As Veatch points out himself, this method 'is probably not a very satisfying one', in that it 'does not provide a precise measuring technique permitting the balancing of counterclaims' ([27], p. 304). Also, conflicts in medical ethics frequently are between non-consequentialist principles and the consequentialist principle that one should prevent harm to others, as in case 1. However, Veatch's theory is unclear concerning this large category of cases. He might intend such cases to be handled by his lexical ordering, but this would give implausible results, since it implies that the liberty of patients should never be circumscribed to prevent harm to others. What is usually referred to as the harm principle would thus be rejected. Perhaps he intends such conflicts to be resolved by choosing the 'lesser overall violation', but again this is too vague to be helpful. Ethical problems often arise precisely because, as in case 1, it is not clear which option would involve the lesser overall violation of the conflicting principles. Thus, Veatch's theory, in its current state of development at least, does not resolve the problem of balancing conflicting principles.

Another difficulty with Veatch's approach concerns how to conceive the problem of balancing conflicting principles. Can principles be properly weighed only in the context of a specific case, or is it possible to balance them with some greater degree of generality? The maximum degree of generality, for example, would be obtained in claiming that one principle always outweighs another. Veatch apparently recognizes that this degree of generality would reflect an inaccurate weighing, at least with regard to the non-consequentialist principles, which he states are lexically co-equal. If he were to hold that conflicting non-consequentialist principles can be properly balanced only in the context of a specific case, then his proposal would be highly impractical, since it would require that each case be resolved in a contract situation open to all. Thus, he apparently conceives the balancing as involving some higher degree of generality. I shall try to show below, however, that to conceive the problem in terms of higher generality is mistaken, that conflicting principles can be properly balanced only in the context of specific cases. If this is correct, then it is doubtful that Veatch's approach can succeed in balancing conflicting principles.

Yet another problem lies in Veatch's attempt to apply ideal observer theory. He seems to imply that the balancing which would be chosen by the contractors would be justified in virtue of the fact that it is actually chosen. The idea seems to be that the attempt to approximate the ideal observer constitutes a process which confers justification on the decision of the group. However, people may do better or worse at approximating the ideal observer. What is missing from his account is mention of a role for reasoned argument in arriving at a justifiable balancing of principles. Perhaps he means to imply that the contractors would consider arguments as to which balancing would be chosen by an ideal observer and would choose the balancing best supported by such arguments. Even on this interpretation, it is important to note a distinction between what would actually be decided by contractors and what ought to be decided on the basis of argument (whether it be an argument which appeals to what an ideal observer would choose, or some other argument). What is needed is an account of the arguments which would be suitable for the purpose of balancing conflicting principles. Furthermore, if such arguments were at hand, those arguments would themselves provide the justification, and an appeal to what Veatch's contractors would choose would be unnecessary. I shall try to show below that such arguments can be given and in what they might consist.

It seems, then, that no contractarian approach put forward to date is helpful in making decisions about clinical dilemmas. This does not mean that no contract theory could provide practical assistance. Nevertheless, to those who would defend contractualism on this point, I would reply that there are certain features which are typical of dilemmas in bioethics. Those characteristics have an important bearing, I suggest, on the method of justification which is appropriate. To be helpful in resolving cases, a contractarian theory would need to take into account those characteristics and would, I believe, have to incorporate something like the method of conflict resolution discussed below.

II. THE CASE COMPARISON METHOD

We have considered why the leading contenders among traditional theories are generally unhelpful in resolving clinical dilemmas. I do not mean to imply, of course, that the traditional theories lack utility in other respects or that they should be abandoned. However, their lack of helpfulness in this matter of great practical importance suggests that we should continue to look for an account of justification in medical ethics. In approaching this task, let me begin by identifying some common characteristics of clinical ethical dilemmas. I have already noted the psychosocial complexity of typical clinical situations. Another feature is uncertainty concerning the patient's prognosis, given treatment or non-treatment. For example, the degree to which an impaired newborn will be handicapped, the degree of recovery that will be attained by a stroke victim, and whether a comatose head trauma patient will regain consciousness are often matters of considerable uncertainty. Yet another characteristic is that dilemmas usually consist of conflict between so-called middle-level principles. Sometimes more specific statements of role-related obligations, usually themselves derivable from middle-level principles, are also involved. Examples might include the health professional's obligation to avoid abandoning a patient, as well as specific requirements of informed consent. In addition, for a given type of dilemma there usually are a number of morally relevant ways in which instances of it can vary from one another. In saying that they are morally relevant, I mean that the variations can make a difference in the decision that ought to be made. In case analysis considerable effort is often devoted to the identification of such morally relevant factors and to arguments concerning the influence they should have on one's decision. Also, given a type of dilemma, it is often possible to identify variations of it – sometimes actual, sometimes hypothetical – in which it is reasonably clear what course of action should be taken.

I believe that these characteristics are widely recognized by those who work in bioethics and that they influence the ways in which people reason about dilemmas. I shall attempt to describe a method of reasoning that takes these characteristics into account, which I shall refer to as the case comparison method. For the purpose of explaining the method of reasoning, I shall focus on the problem of resolving specific cases. However, the method has implications for public policy formation that will be considered as well. The method of reasoning can be formulated as consisting of several elements. When illustration would be helpful in describing the method, I shall refer to case 1. First, one should identify the middle-level principles and role-specific duties pertinent to the given situation. In case 1, for example, a central conflict was between respect for the obstetrical patient's autonomy and concern to prevent harm to her children. Then one should identify the alternative courses of action that could be taken. Sometimes an option can be rejected at the outset because other options take better account of the various ethical principles relevant to the situation. To illustrate, one of the options in case 1 is to try to persuade the patient to change her mind and, if unsuccessful, to seek a court order. Regardless of whether it is the best option, this course is preferable to seeking a court order without an attempt to persuade, since it gives greater weight to autonomy and at least as much weight to preventing harm. Thus, the latter option should be rejected. Options can also be rejected when it is reasonable to believe they would fail to achieve their aims or would be impractical or impossible to implement. In the case being considered, for example, the use of artificial substitutes for blood could be eliminated since, as it turned out, blood substitutes were not generally available. Rejecting the obviously inferior or impractical options will often leave one with more than one option remaining. In case 1 further attempts to persuade the patient were unsuccessful, and she rejected the idea of receiving blood without giving consent. At that point the choice involved two alternatives: withhold transfusions or seek a court order.

The third element is to identify the morally relevant ways in which cases of the type in question can differ from one another. Consideration of the middle-level principles previously identified in the reasoning process can help one ascertain these morally relevant factors. Comparing the case at hand with other cases of the same type also helps one identify these factors. With regard to cases involving the refusal of treatment for themselves by adults with dependent children, several factors are pertinent. One is the extent to which the patient's request reflects the informed, considered wishes of the patient. Another is the degree of physical harm expected to occur to the patient if treatment is withheld. That is, does the procedure aim to prevent death or some other, less serious harm? Yet another factor is the degree of emotional and psychological harm expected to occur to the patient if her wishes were overruled. This may vary depending on the attitudes of the family and patient toward the idea of her receiving treatment. Also, the degree and likelihood of harms which would occur to the children as a result of the parent's refusal would be varying factors.

Fourth, for each option remaining under consideration one should identify a case in which that option would be justifiable. We shall refer to these as *paradigm* cases. Paradigms can be actual or hypothetical cases. In addition, one should identify the middle-level principle which would provide that justification. For example, the following is a situation similar to case 1 in which a strong argument in support of treatment can be given.

Case 2

A 39-year-old man voluntarily admitted himself to a veteran's hospital for treatment of a bleeding ulcer. He had lost a large amount of blood, and his physicians believed that death was imminent without blood transfusions. The patient refused blood and his wife concurred, both being Jehovah's Witnesses. The couple had three children, ages seven, six, and three. The father earned a small salary working in a lumber yard. The mother was a 36-year-old housewife who had never worked for an income. The hospital applied for a court order to administer blood. Upon being contacted, the judge went to the hospital, where he spoke with the patient and his wife. The patient appeared to be coherent and rational, and let it be known that transfusions without his consent would be against his will. When asked who would take care of the children, the wife stated that the patient's mother lived nearby. Further discussion revealed, however, that the grandmother was a renal patient on dialysis, that she would not be able to provide much support, and that she in fact needed considerable assistance herself. Support from other family members seemed questionable, and the only foreseeable income was welfare checks. The judge signed an order allowing the hospital to administer transfusions necessary to save the patient's life.

The justification of the court order in this case rests on the principle of beneficence: in particular, the principle that one ought to prevent harm to others. The state is ethically justified in this case in preventing the patient from abandoning his children, since considerable harm would otherwise be expected to occur to them. Not only would there be the emotional harm associated with the loss of a parent, but there would be a significant financial harm in the loss of the family's breadwinner. Furthermore, this family appears to lack resources, whether financial or in the form of family members who can help out, which would alleviate those harms to the children. The expected harm is so great that the principle of beneficence is weightier in this case than the conflicting principle of autonomy.

On the other hand, treatment would not be justified in the following case:[5]

Case 3

A 34-year-old man was admitted to the hospital with internal injuries and bleeding caused when a tree fell on him. The need for blood soon became apparent, but the patient refused transfusions. The patient's wife, brother, and grandfather were present and supported the patient's decision. The patient and his wife had two young children. The hospital petitioned for a court order, and the judge came to the hospital and held a bedside hearing. Upon being questioned by the judge, the patient stated that he definitely did not want blood transfusions. The judge questioned the wife concerning the welfare of the two children. The wife stated that her husband had a business which he would turn over to her if he died. She also stated that her husband's brothers worked for him, and that they would continue to carry on the business if he died. They also had money saved, so they were financially secure. Their family was a large one and was prepared to care for the children if anything happened. Based on these considerations, the judge decided that there were not sufficient grounds in this case for a court order.

Since the family business would continue to provide for the material needs of the children, the degree of harm expected to occur to them was mitigated considerably. In addition, it appeared that a close-knit family would help promote the emotional well-being of the children. Therefore, the expected harm appears to be somewhat less than in case 2. The principle of autonomy provides the justification for the decision, since, in the context of *this* case, the degree of expected harm is not large enough for the principle of beneficence to override the principle of autonomy.

The fifth and final element is a comparison of the case at hand with the paradigm cases which can be identified. One should try to determine which of the paradigms it is 'closest to' in terms of the presence of the morally relevant factors. Selection and justification of an option are based on this comparison. When the case under consideration is closer to one paradigm than to the others, the course of action justifiable in that paradigm would also be justifiable in the case at hand. If the case being considered is in the 'gray zone' between paradigms – not seeming to be closest to any one of them – then more than one option may be ethically permissible.

Consider the application of this method to case 1. On reflection, case 1 appears to be more similar to case 2 than it is to case 3. While the three cases do not appear to differ with regard to the patients' autonomy, the degree of physical harm to the patients to be prevented by the treatment, or the degree of psychological harm to the patients in overriding their wishes, the same cannot be said concerning the expected harm to the children. Case 1 involves a low-income family with several young children and apparently few resources, as does case 2. Even though there are some mitigating factors in case 1, as mentioned, there is a serious question as to whether the families in cases 1 and 2 can provide the degree of emotional and economic support to young children, in the face of the death of a parent, which may be possible with an extended family which is relatively close-knit and financially sound, as in case 3. Comparing the three cases helps us to see that the expected harm to the children is relatively significant in case 1, and that a court order should be sought.

According to this process, one is not simply weighing the principle of autonomy 'in general' against the prevention of harm 'in general', but rather one is assessing the degree to which the morally relevant factors are present in the case at hand. Among cases of the type being considered, the argument in support of treatment becomes stronger as the degree of expected harm to the children increases, as the degree of physical harm to the patient prevented by treatment increases, as the amount of emotional harm due to overriding the patient's request decreases, and as the degree to which the patient's request reflects the considered wishes of the patient decreases. This method suggests, furthermore, that it is in the context of specific cases that the balancing of conflicting principles should take place, since the extent to which the various factors are present varies from case to case. This analysis may help explain the significance of the claim frequently emphasized by physicians – and often discounted by philosophers – that every case is unique.

It may be asked what justifies one's claim that a certain course of action should be followed in a paradigm case. The correct response, I believe, is that in such cases one can construct a reasonable argument concerning which middle-level principle should be considered weightiest. Such arguments are based on the degree to which the morally relevant factors are present, as illustrated above in the discussion of cases 2 and 3. Whenever such an argument could not be given, then the case in question would not serve well as a paradigm. Thus, what justifies a course of action in a paradigm case is the middle-level principle which is weightiest in that context, together with the argument that it is weightiest. Similarly, what justifies a course of action in a non-paradigm case is the appropriate middle-level principle, together with the argument that it is the weightiest, or at least among the weightiest, in that context. The argument that it is the weightiest, or among the weightiest, would in such cases be based on a comparison with paradigm cases.

Although I have focused on case resolution, the case comparison method has implications for public policy formation. By 'public policy' I have in mind governmental or institutional regulation of the manner in which types of dilemmas are handled. Of course, the judgment that an act is morally right (or wrong) does not necessarily imply that it should be permitted (or forbidden) as a matter of policy, since considerations may enter at the policy level that do not figure prominently in an individual case. For example, a policy might have symbolic value, as in the prohibition of withholding feedings and water from patients. Also, a permissive policy might give rise to abuses, a fear that has been expressed concerning active euthanasia, for example. Nevertheless, policies should reflect a cognizance of what is ethical in specific cases. In particular, policies should take into account the morally relevant ways in which cases of a given type can differ from one another. This suggests that there is a rebuttable presumption that policies should be flexible enough to permit different cases to be handled differently, depending on the factors present. Similarly, policies – when considered necessary – should be formulated in ways that explicitly recognize those morally pertinent factors, as well as relevant paradigms.

It might be asked why the case comparison method ought to be used rather than other normative approaches. In reply, the method is supported by several considerations. First, the traditional approaches are usually unhelpful in resolving dilemmas, as I have argued. Second, the case comparison method provides a way of resolving one of the major problems in practical ethics – how validly to reason from conflicting ethical principles to conclusions about what ought to be done in specific cases. Third, a method of justification in bioethics should reflect a cognizance of the actual nature of ethical dilemmas in clinical settings. The case comparison method is based on and attempts to take appropriate account of those features. In particular, dilemmas are appropriately conceptualized in terms of the middle-level principles and their conflict. It is reasonable to think, therefore, that when a choice of action is justifiable, its justification is based on the relevant middle-level principle, as suggested by the case comparison method. Similarly, cases of a given type can vary in ways that make a difference in the decision that ought to be made, as the above cases illustrate, and one's method of justification should take account of those variations, as the case comparison method does. Fourth, the case comparison method provides a comprehensive approach to resolution of clinical dilemmas. It is applicable to all types of ethical conflicts in medicine, not just those involving refusal of treatment by adults with dependent children. Fifth, the method yields conclusions in accord with our ordinary moral judgments concerning the resolution of cases. Sixth, it provides a basis for response to those who criticize practical ethics for its lack of an ultimate foundation. Let me now turn to this matter of foundations.

III. ABOUT ULTIMATE FOUNDATIONS

It might be thought that the case comparison method provides only a partial account of justification. In order for its conclusions to be justifiable, it might be argued, there would have to be a foundation for the middle-level principles themselves.

Several recent works have attempted to identify the ultimate grounds of moral judgments [11, 12, 13], but each has been shown to involve serious problems.[6] No doubt, the inquiry into such a foundation is a worthy philosophical task; in order to understand better the nature of morality, it is important to explore such questions. However, the case comparison method enables us to see, I believe, how it might be possible to justify normative statements without having such a foundation. I would like to suggest that the conclusions of the case comparison method, when reasonably drawn, are justified regardless of whether the so-called middle-level principles can be shown to be derivable from some higher-level theory. A couple of considerations support this view. First, there is no question that we have moral obligations to follow the commonly-used middle-level principles, such as autonomy, beneficence, and so on. Second, when a specific middle-level principle has been identified as the one supporting what seems to be the morally preferable way of resolving a case, it would be an error to claim that the resolution is unwarranted because that middle-level principle has not been ultimately justified. For example, it is a mistake to claim, with respect to case 1, that the decision to treat is unjustified because no ultimate justification of the principle of beneficence has been given. Perhaps treatment in a given instance is unjustified because it is not the solution best supported by the case comparison method, but that would be another matter. Similarly, it would be a mistake to claim that physicians are unjustified in providing patients information about risks and alternatives to proposed treatments on the grounds that the principle of autonomy has not been ultimately justified. The reason for this, I suggest, is that the middle-level principles are constitutive of morality. They constitute the core of our common, shared morality, which has its roots in the Judeo-Christian tradition, and which has been described by recent writers such as Gert ([12], pp. 60–127) and Donagan ([11], pp. 1–9, 26–29, 75–111). Thus, there is an important sense in which these principles are the bedrock of morality, in that they pose a constraint on any attempt to provide an ultimate justification of morality. Any higher-level theory of ethics which turned out to be inconsistent with the middle-level principles would, in virtue of that inconsistency, be reasonably considered inadequate. A similar view has been expressed by Gert, for example, in discussing act utilitarianism ([12], p. 8). As he points out, act utilitarianism yields conclusions inconsistent with common morality. While act utilitarians have been prone to think that their theory offers an alternative account of morality, Gert points out, correctly I believe, that it actually offers an alternative *to* morality. The fact that it does is the primary reason why act utilitarianism is incorrect.

Thus, the purpose of a search for a foundation for the middle-level principles would not be to determine whether it is a requirement of morality to accept those principles, but rather to try to illuminate further why it is reasonable and moral to act in ways that respect them. It remains an open question as to whether a defensible higher-order theory can be found from which the middle-level principles can be derived. However, one need not answer this question about ultimate foundations in order to arrive at justifiable conclusions about what ought to be done in specific cases.

This is not to say, however, that there is no sense in which there is a need for justification with respect to the middle-level principles. There may be unfinished work in identifying the principles which can be used with the case comparison method and stating them with precision. Views about such matters would stand in need of defense, at least when there is disagreement. In this sense my account is a partial one, since I shall not address here such questions of identification and wording. With regard to such issues, by the way, there may be a role for traditional theories such as Kantianism or contractualism, in that the precise wording of certain middle-level principles may be argued for by reference to such theories.[7]

In conclusion, the case comparison method appears to provide an acceptable way of justifying normative statements. Ethical disagreement may, of course, arise at various points in the case comparison method. There might, for example, be disagreement concerning what principles are pertinent to a particular case and how those principles are to be formulated. There can be disagreement as to whether the factors in a given case are sufficient to override a principle. Similarly, there may be disputes as to whether the case at hand is closer to one paradigm or to another. I would not claim that such disagreements are always resolvable. I do believe, however, that to some extent they are subject to rational adjudication. One can point out logical implications of views about what principles are pertinent. One can imaginatively identify paradigm cases. Sometimes the disagreements can be resolved, and when they cannot it can sometimes be concluded that more than one alternative is permissible. We do in fact have a reasonable and useful method for resolving conflicts between principles.

NOTES

[1] Rule utilitarianism is defended, e.g., by Richard Brandt [5, 6]. Other advocates of utilitarianism include R. M. Hare [14], Peter Singer [25], and J. J. C. Smart [26]. Discussion of the conceptual difficulties of utilitarianism can be found in [6, 18, 24].

[2] In selecting this case I have tried, for reasons which will later be apparent, to pick one for which the proper resolution is not immediately clear, for both the utilitarian and non-utilitarian. Although harm to the children is expected if the mother dies, several factors would allay such harm, such as the survival of the breadwinner and the ability of grandmother and older children to help care for the younger ones. Given these factors, the question for most non-utilitarians is whether the potential harm to the offspring is great enough to override the patient's autonomy.

[3] For purposes of this discussion, I shall interpret utility as happiness. However, my argument applies to the various interpretations of utility, as in hedonistic, ideal, and preference utilitarianism.

[4] One can distinguish overarching theoretical principles, middle-level principles, and rules. Examples of overarching principles, which have the greatest generality, include the principle of utility and the categorical imperative. Next in generality are middle-level principles. Finally,

rules state that certain specific types of action should or should not be performed. An example of a rule would be 'The informed consent of competent subjects should be obtained prior to participation in research'.

5 Case 2 is a composite, based on actual situations. Case 3 is an actual one, reported as *In Re Osborne*, 294 A.2d 372 (1972).

6 For critiques of *Reason and Morality* see [3, 4, 8, 16, 21, 23]. A critique of *The Theory of Morality* is found in [19]. Concerning *The Moral Rules*, see [7, 10].

7 Also, one would want to look to the traditional theories as possible sources of support for the middle-level principles. For example, Richard Brandt suggests that a set of rules similar to what I have called middle-level principles (but perhaps incorporating qualifications and exceptions) might be grounded by a utilitarian theory [5]. Alan Donagan attempts to ground a similar set of principles using a fundamental principle equivalent to Kant's second formulation of the categorical imperative [11].

BIBLIOGRAPHY

[1] Ackerman, Terrence F.: 1980, 'What Bioethics Should Be', *Journal of Medicine and Philosophy* 5, 260–75.

[2] Ackerman, Terrence G.: 1983, 'Experimentalism in Bioethics Research', *Journal of Medicine and Philosophy* 8, 169–80.

[3] Adams, E. M.: 1980, 'Gewirth on Reason and Morality', *Review of Metaphysics* 33, 579–92.

[4] Allen, P., III: 1982, 'A Critique of Gewirth's 'Is-Ought' Derivation', *Ethics* 92, 211–226.

[5] Brandt, R. B.: 1971, 'Toward a Credible Form of Utilitarianism', in B. Brody (ed.), *Moral Rules and Particular Circumstances*, Prentice-Hall, Englewood Cliffs, N. J., pp. 145–178.

[6] Brandt, R. B.: 1983, 'Problems of Contemporary Utilitarianism: Real and Alleged', in N. E. Bowie (ed.), *Ethical Theory in the Last Quarter of the Twentieth Century*, Hackett Publishing Co., Indianapolis, pp. 81–105.

[7] Bond, E. J.: 1973, Review of *The Moral Rules*, B. Gert, *Dialogue* 12, 486–501.

[8] Bond, E. J.: 1980, 'Gewirth on Reason and Morality', *Metaphilosophy* 11, 36–53.

[9] Camenisch, P.F.: 1976, 'Abortion, Analogies and the Emergence of Value', *Journal of Religious Ethics* 4, 131–158.

[10] Diggs, B. J.: 1974, Review of *The Moral Rules*, B. Gert, *Journal of Philosophy* 71, 88–90.

[11] Donagan, A.: 1977, *The Theory of Morality*, University of Chicago Press, Chicago.

[12] Gert, B.: 1970, *The Moral Rules*, Harper and Row, New York.

[13] Gewirth, A.: 1978, *Reason and Morality*, University of Chicago Press, Chicago.

[14] Hare, R. M.: 1976, 'Ethical Theory and Utilitarianism', in H. D. Lewis (ed.), *Contemporary British Philosophy*, Fourth Series, George Allen and Unwin, London, pp. 113–131.

[15] Jonsen, A. R.: 1987, 'On Being a Casuist', in T. Ackerman, G. Graber, C. Reynolds, and D. Thomasma (eds.), *Clinical Medical Ethics: Exploration and Assessment*, University Press of America, Lanham, Md. pp. 117–29.

[16] Lomasky, L. E.: 1981, 'Gewirth's Generation of Rights', *Philosophical Quarterly* 31, 248–52.

[17] MacIntyre, A.: 1979, 'Why is the Search for the Foundations of Ethics So Frustrating?', *Hastings Center Report* 9, 16–22.

[18] McCloskey, H. J.: 1979, 'Universalized Prescriptivism and Utilitarianism: Hare's

Attempted Forced Marriage', *Journal of Value Inquiry* 13, 63–76.

[19] McConnell, T. C.: 1981, 'Moral Absolutism and the Problem of Hard Cases', *Journal of Religious Ethics* 9, 286–97.

[20] McCormick, R. A.: 1981, 'Marriage, Morality, and Sex-Change Surgery: A Catholic Perspective', *Hastings Center Report* 11, 10–11.

[21] Nielson, K.: 1987, 'On Being Skeptical About Applied Ethics', in T. Ackerman, G. Graber, C. Reynolds, and D. Thomasma (eds.), *Clinical Medical Ethics: Exploration and Assessment*, University Press of America, Lanham, Md., pp. 95–115.

[22] Rawls, J.: 1971, *A Theory of Justice*, Harvard University Press, Cambridge, Massachusetts.

[23] Regis, E., Jr.: 1981, 'Gewirth on Rights', *Journal of Philosophy* 78, 786–95.

[24] Scanlon, T. M.: 1982, 'Contractualism and Utilitarianism', in A. Sen and B. Williams (eds.), *Utilitarianism and Beyond*, Cambridge University Press, Cambridge, pp. 103–128.

[25] Singer, P.: 1979, *Practical Ethics*, Cambridge University Press, Cambridge.

[26] Smart, J. J. C.: 1973, 'An Outline of a System of Utilitarian Ethics', in J. J. C. Smart and B. Williams, *Utilitarianism: For and Against*, Cambridge University Press, Cambridge, pp. 3–74.

[27] Veatch, R.M.: 1981, *A Theory of Medical Ethics*, Basic Books, New York.

University of Tennessee College of Medicine
Memphis, Tennessee

PHILIP E. DEVINE

THEORY AND PRACTICE IN ETHICS

This essay is concerned with the interrelationship between abstract moral principles, moral rules, and the description and evaluation of concrete situations, especially in the light of the open textured character of moral and other language. I draw four conclusions from my examination of the structure of moral reasoning. (1) Moral requirements are embedded in ways of life, to sustain which is part of their purpose. (2) Moral codes are constantly being tested by their being applied to concrete situations. (3) There is both a powerful case for, and a powerful case against, treating some moral rules as exceptionless and immune to revision. And (4) moral reasoning is dependent for its vitality on the continued existence of conditions outside the power of moralists to preserve.

I

Many courses in medical (or other applied) ethics have included paper topics or examination questions like the following: 'Different moral perspectives can give rise to different judgments about actions. Describe a medical situation in which different decisions might be made by a Kantian (or Rawlsian) on the one hand and a utilitarian on the other. Explain what the difference would be and how it would arise' ([3], p. 543). Such questions suggest a top-down (or state-and-apply) model of moral reasoning, in which one first adopts a certain ethical theory and then applies it to disputed issues.

Thus, for a utilitarian, the crucial issue in the abortion debate is when the fetus is capable of experiencing pain [8]. Voluntary euthanasia will be unproblematic, and there will be a powerful case for non-voluntary euthanasia in cases where the sufferer is incapable of asking for relief. But those non-human animals capable of experiencing pain will be protected against death or injury except under those circumstances in which such behavior toward a comparable human being would be permissible [6].

For a Kantian, by contrast, the first issue will be whether a given entity is a person. All moral agents, and at least some interest-bearers not now capable of moral agency, will fall into the class protected against treatment as means

Baruch A. Brody (ed.), Moral Theory and Moral Judgments in Medical Ethics, 213–223.
© *1988 by Kluwer Academic Publishers.*

merely.[1] Such persons may not be killed, injured, or subjected to medical experimentation, except perhaps with their own consent, to protect other persons against imminent danger of injury, or as punishment for crime. (For Kant himself, though not for most of his followers, a person is not entitled to consent to being injured, at least not lethally.) And both of these approaches may be usefully contrasted with a natural law ethics of a broadly Thomist sort, for which both abortion and euthanasia of all sorts are forbidden as infringements on an inviolable basic good of life and for which the rights of non-human animals are not an issue.

One deficiency in the top-down model of moral reasoning is that it neglects the fact that moral theories are to be checked against our considered moral judgments, as well as sometimes providing reasons for revising those judgments. No moral theory is so powerfully supported that it may not be revised or abandoned to preserve a deeply held moral conviction, at least in the absence of some independent reason for doubting the truth of that conviction. Thus, the present writer regards himself entitled to reject, on that ground alone, any moral theory that entails that parents are entitled to kill their children in order to escape the burdens of rearing them. If a critic points to cultures in which infanticide has been practiced as a method of family limitation (or in which some other practice reprobated in the West is approved), it is sufficient to reply that such an appeal to the practice of other cultures is self-defeating. For there have been many cultures in which it is considered impious to question the ways of the ancestors in any particular.

At least some of our concrete moral judgments are to be treated as data to be explained by a moral theory. To say this is not to imply that they are immune to revision, only that a stronger reason is required for revising them than that they fail to accord with some moral theory. The possibility that some of our moral judgments should be protected against revision of any sort will be considered below.

The argument so far does not enable us to be sanguine about the future of moral reasoning. For we live in a society in which virtually all inherited moral and intellectual standards have been questioned by someone, and in which sharply contrasting critical perspectives are advanced by those desiring to justify departures from received moral codes. The resulting chaos of conflicting intuitions is as evident in biomedical ethics as it is anywhere. In any case, the resolution of our disputes is not to be sought in an Archimedian point external to our moral tradition. We are sailors doomed to repair our ship on the open sea, without ever putting into drydock.

II

So far I have argued as if the logical relations between moral theories and concrete judgments were logically tight (or at any rate clear): as if we knew what various moral theories entailed in the realm of practice, and whether these entailments comported with received moral codes. But, in fact, both parties to this relationship are malleable, so that moral reasoning is not so much a matter of deduction or of hypothetico-deductive method, as of the mutual accommodation of standards.

The malleability of the elements of moral reasoning begins with the description of the cases to which rival approaches to morality are applied. It is not surprising that moral theorists of different schools focus their attention on different cases, and employ different language in describing similar cases. For any situation can be described in more than one way, each description emphasizing different aspects of the situation and suggesting different possible resolutions of it. And different moral theories lead us to ask different questions about situations, and illuminate different aspects of moral experience. Hence, they also invite not only different resolutions, but also different descriptions of cases.

A striking illustration is provided by the bizarre examples that have played such a large role in the abortion debate. These include violinists implanted with philosophers' kidneys [9] or kittens so injected as to produce supercats [10]. Such cases are designed to favor a conception of human nature for which, since the concept of the normal is irrelevant, there is no objective good for human beings; and, as L. W. Sumner has put it, 'the choice of a lifestyle becomes a matter of subjective preference' ([8], p. 169).

Nor is it possible to discuss controversial moral issues without taking sides, verbally at least. Lawyers have formulated a 'first substantive sentence rule', according to which a judge's statement of the case at once discloses both his [2] sympathies and his decision. And a writer's choice of language when discussing the abortion issue predisposes him to one view rather than another, not only on the status of the fetus but also on the nature of pregnancy and the responsibility of the pregnant woman for her situation. At minimum his choice of language will indicate what range of positions on the issue he is prepared to take seriously.

There is also room for manipulation in the formulation and application of received moral rules. A moral code forbidding murder requires interpretation on at least four fronts: (1) what entities count as human beings or persons 'within the meaning of the act'; (2) whether the killing of any human being (oneself included), or only the killing of another human being, constitutes homicide and thus possibly murder; (3) to what extent the fact that the victim's death is foreseen rather than intended makes the pertinent act not one of homicide; (4) what extenuating circumstances render homicide justifiable or excusable, and thus not murder (see [1]). Likewise, a moral rule forbidding adultery requires the specification, among other things, of what unions count as marriages, so that sexual behavior in breach of them will constitute adultery.[3] The ancient art of casuistry, concerned with the resolution of such issues, can be carried on in some independence of larger questions of moral theory. But it can also be used to narrow the gap between received morality and some preferred moral theory.

Moreover, moral theories are themselves manipulable, and can be used to support a wide range of concrete conclusions. The results suggested in the first section of this paper are not the only possible, nor even necessarily the correct, ones: they represent only those conclusions which many who have tried to apply moral theories to concrete cases have found most plausible.

Utilitarian moral reasoning depends to a large extent on unknown causal relations: virtually any repugnant conclusion can be avoided by postulating hidden costs of violating received moral rules. Moreover, utilitarian moralists need to be concerned, not just with the effects of acts taken in isolation, but also with the effect of changes in our institutions, a consideration that can easily lead a utilitarian to a far more deferential attitude toward received morality than he otherwise would adopt.[4] Indeed, a utilitarian could easily conclude that it would be of greatest utility for him to renounce utilitarianism in favor of Kantian or religious ethics. Utilitarians will appeal to the social sciences to resolve such issues, but there are deep reasons why the results reached in these sciences will always reflect, to some degree, the sympathies, hopes, and fears of the investigator.

The utilitarian conception of the good is also open to manipulation. What we want and what we like are not necessarily the same thing, and both of these may differ from that which we look back on with satisfaction rather than with regret. The most plausible broadly utilitarian conception of what is good for a person is that which he wants upon due consideration. But Plato himself could accept this definition, arguing that what we would desire upon due consideration is often radically different from what most people spontaneously desire. That tyrants do not desire the punishment that is good for them Plato could explain by the corruption of perception their wickedness has created, a corruption that it may take punishment to remove.

Finally, all moral questions involve a conflict between goods, each of which has some claim on us. Bentham attempts to resolve such conflicts by treating such goods as if they were simple physical pleasures. But even simple physical pleasures are more complex than Bentham's calculus allows: sexual pleasures, for example, have important imaginative and emotional dimensions. And once we are dealing with goods of any complexity, their commensuration will be largely or wholly a matter of getting the result we have already decided to reach. The evolution of the utilitarian tradition from the radicalism of a Bentham to the conservativism of a Moore should thus surprise no one.

If such is the case for a moral theory designed specifically to provide a fundamental moral principle capable of overruling, and resolving conflicts among, the principles of commonsense morality, the same will be true, a fortiori, of traditions in moral theory for which the capacity to derive precise practical results is less important. I here limit myself to one striking example with important bioethical ramifications.

The Kantian tradition stands in need of an empirical correlate to the moral self, which is entitled to be treated as an end in itself rather than a means merely. The traditional answer fixes on membership in the human species (cf. [2], esp. pp. 168–71). But Tom Regan has shown that if personhood is ascribed to some interest-bearers not presently capable of moral agency, it is possible to mount a plausible argument for extending personhood to many non-humans, an extension Kant avoids chiefly through his deference to traditional morality [5]. But Regan himself is unable effectively to block the extension of inherent worth to so many 'moral patients' that the concept becomes self-defeating. If sagebrush has inherent worth, moral sanity requires that the moral implications of inherent worth be weakened to the point where the Kantian tradition loses its distinctive shape.[5]

A great deal of moral reasoning, therefore, consists not in deduction or other easily representable forms of argument, but in the attempt to harmonize our perceptions of situations and their requirements, our moral rules, and abstract principles such as are found in our moral theories. The malleability that makes such reasoning possible has its source in the open texture of our language and the consequent possibility of ambiguities in, and conflicts about, even the clearest-seeming rule. According to the American Constitution, each State is entitled to two Senators. But if Minnesota were swept by a plague, so that only a handful of inhabitants remained, the inhabitants of the other States would be likely to argue that the depopulated territory between Wisconsin and North Dakota no longer constituted a State.[6]

The open texture of language cannot be evaded by appeal to essences, natural kinds, or objectively subsisting universals. Whether any of the possible ways of carving up the world is metaphysically or epistemologically privileged is a question of the greatest theoretical and practical interest. But any attempt to express conclusions about and to connect these conclusions with practical issues will have to use language. Hence the formulation and application of the metaphysical groundwork of ethics will be subject to the same ambiguity and conflict as are more mundane moral rules.

A glance at the history of ethics confirms this conclusion. Plato relied on the intuitions of privileged persons to reach the often striking conclusions he drew from his moral theory. And Aristotle's essentialism did not make it any less necessary for him to appeal to the judgment of the man of practical wisdom to determine what the virtues required in concrete cases.

III

From the open texture of ethics four conclusions follow. The first is that moral requirements are embedded in ways of life. Moral reasoning would be a hopeless endeavor if we did not agree on a large number of disputed moral issues. But given some agreement about concrete issues, the discussion of disputed questions can proceed with some hope of success. In medical ethics the framework for discussion is provided by a tradition of professional self-definition going back to the Hippocratic Oath, that requires physicians to regard themselves as servants of human life and health, rather than as functionaries charged with modifying the bodies of their patients in any way that the patient or his guardians may desire. And part of the purpose of moral rules is to sustain the way of life that makes moral argument possible: this good, like all of the goods of social life, needs to be taken into account in moral reasoning. A presumption in favor of tradition is for this reason inescapable in ethics.

A second consequence is that moral codes (like political and religious doctrines) are constantly being tested, as individuals and groups endeavor to maintain a way of life structured by a code, and in consequence apply their standards of conduct to novel situations. And it is always possible that a moral code will fail these tests, by the discovery of circumstances in which it is no longer possible rationally to observe the code or to sustain the way of life it is designed to protect.

The pragmatism of this conclusion needs to be qualified in at least three ways. First, there is pragmatic value in taking a non-pragmatic attitude toward at least some of our moral principles. The notion that our moral codes are at the mercy of those who have the power to shape the institutions of society to their liking, and to attach severe consequences to morally upright behavior, is subversive of any moral code whatever. And the notion of transcendent moral truth thus receives a pragmatic warrant. Second, the pragmatic test leaves open the question, under what conditions a given idea should be said to have succeeded or failed. Even the death of most of a group's members, and the dispersal of the rest, does not preclude the possibility that they are martyrs for principles that will later be vindicated. Third, the saying that a moral code is vindicated by its having worked invites the question, 'Worked for whom?' The question posed by the abortion and animal rights issues, whose interests are to be taken into account in ethics, and to what degree, thus reappears at the deepest theoretical level.

A third consequence concerns the ambiguous status of the entrenchment of moral rules. Such a rule can be entrenched in two logically independent ways: it can be protected against *exceptions*, so that any act acknowledged to be in breach of its requirements can be concluded without further ado to be wrong. Or it can be protected against *revision*, so that a valid argument purporting to show that acts in breach of that rule are legitimate will serve only to prompt an inquiry into which of its premises is to be rejected in order to preserve the entrenched rule. David Solomon has called the second of these forms of entrenchment 'moral fideism'.

A weaker form of moral fideism grounds crucial moral judgments in the teaching of an infallible (presumably religious) authority. This form of moral fideism is weaker than one resting on the inherent authority of the rule itself, since it makes possible an argument that the authority in question has been misinterpreted or has not on this occasion spoken infallibly.

One area in which the entrenchment of moral rules is attractive concerns the abuse of children by their parents. 'Child abuse' is a loose enough expression to allow, up to a point, for whatever flexibility might be thought advisable. The neglect or abuse of children, a cynic could conclude, consists in any form of parental behavior of which the majority (or the majority of family welfare professionals) disapproves.

But there are a number of ways parents can behave toward their children which can be specified in reasonably concrete terms, that nearly everyone would regard as abusive, and prohibitions against which should be entrenched if any prohibitions should. These include killing, sexual relations between parents and children, and consent by parents to medical experiments on their children entailing non-trivial risk of non-trivial injury. Rather than consider hard cases here, I shall observe only (1) that I do not think it necessary to consider cases for whose natural possibility there is no evidence (e.g., a world in which incest prevented cancer), and (2) that any non-consequentialist approach to ethics requires us sometimes to accept bad consequences rather than breach a rule (e.g., cases of duress).[7]

The case for entrenching rules against child abuse rests on two considerations. The first is the manifest utility of a rule protecting children against cruelty and sexual abuse; the second is the vulnerability of children, and in particular their inability to participate in the decision whether to modify existing codes. Together these considerations suggest that the rule forbidding child abuse (including the concrete forms of child abuse mentioned above) should be protected both against exceptions and against abandonment, and that we ought always to respond to a contrary argument by rejecting one or more of its premises.

On the issue of whether such an entrenchment is intellectually acceptable, the argument of this essay cuts both ways. On the one hand, the on-going, open-ended character of human nature and experience, as reflected in the open texture of moral and other language, and in the complexity of the moral problems faced by human beings at all times and places, precludes, at least in the minds of many, any defensible limitation of the sorts of resolution admissible in principle to moral questions. One way in which these features of our experience affects moral judgment is by way of the fact that even a typical specimen of a kind of action will, when scrutinized, disclose features that make stock moral categories not wholly adequate to it. For this reason, many Roman Catholic theologians exclude moral issues, so far as their resolution is based on reflection on human experience ('natural law'), from the domain where the Pope and the bishops are capable of teaching infallibly (see [7], pp. 148–152, and the authorities cited there). Such a conclusion must be carefully distinguished from the weaker claim that some particular teaching, e.g., that against contraception, is not infallible.

On the other hand, the open texture of morals can lend credence to the entrenchment of moral rules. For the line of thought just sketched, unless somehow constrained, leads to a thoroughgoing situationism, for which all moral decisions are made on their facts, without any appeal to some more abstract principle. Intuitively, and on the facts of human experience, it seems evident that moral reasoning requires more structure than that. The open texture of human moral experience has convinced many people that, if our morality does not contain at least some non-negotiable demands, we shall find ourselves at a loss whenever we attempt to reason about morality. That human beings are able to find loopholes even in the most stringent formularies may make us more rather than less inclined to plug as many loopholes as possible.

A fourth and final consequence is the fragility of moral discourse. That human beings reason about moral issues only within a context of shared moral judgments implies that pre-eminence in moral reasoning should be given concepts such as *murder, incest, cruelty,* and *fraud,* about whose application and moral evaluation there is more agreement than about abstract standards such as the principle of utility. Morals thus appears to be a matter of agreement.

But the conventionalism suggested by such an appeal to 'thick' moral concepts immediately runs into two decisive objections. The first objection is that our conventions reflect power relations, and that conventionalism therefore entails that might makes right – a conclusion repugnant to conventional opinion itself. Conventionalism is for this reason self-destructive.

The second objection is that the conventional morality of our day is deeply divided over precisely those issues that moral theorists struggle hardest to resolve. A non-conventional element is therefore necessary to the vitality of even conventional morality.

A characteristic crisis in the life of a philosopher, or indeed of any intellectual, takes place when he discovers that there is virtually no conclusion that cannot be defended from plausible premises using plausible modes of reasoning. And some real people will accept the repugnant conclusions their opponents draw from their positions. The complaint of the people of Athens against Socrates, taken at the deepest level, asks how, once the multitude of possible moralities has become public knowledge, the conflict among them is to be resolved, if not by power.

Moralists, like moral agents, act within a world whose workings they only imperfectly understand and over which they have only limited control. And one important limitation on their power is their inability to control the actions of the other persons who with them sustain, or fail to sustain, the way of life on which their moral code depends. Even moralists themselves are subject to passions and to circumstances that threaten to disrupt their adherence both to their chosen ways of life and to the moral codes that provide them with their structure. The remedy for the anxiety this situation produces, and the answer to the questions prompted by such anxiety, must be found, if at all, outside ethics proper, in a Power capable of sustaining both human beings and their world.

NOTES

[1] See [1], chs. 2–3, for a critical review of the criteria by which this question might be answered.

[2] Here and throughout 'he' is used in the sense of 'he or she' except where the context requires a male individual.

[3] Two men or two women are living together in a homosexual relationship, which they have promised never to end. One of them leaves the other for a member of the opposite sex. Is this adultery?

[4] A recent example is L. W. Sumner's discussion of the ethics of medical experimentation at the Baylor College of Medicine Conference on Moral Theory and Practice (November, 1985); for a classic bioethical example, see [4].

[5] Regan writes: '[My] argument ... does not logically preclude the possibility that there are humans and animals who fail to meet the subject-of-a-life criterion and nonetheless have inherent value .... This incompleteness does not infect the adequacy of the subject-of-a-life criterion, when this is understood as a sufficient condition ..., nor does it undermine the claim that normal mammalian animals, aged one or more, as well as humans like those animals in the relevant respects, can intelligibly and non-arbitrarily be viewed as having inherent value' ([5], pp. 246–47). Read restrictively, and contrary to Regan's intentions, the clause 'aged one or more' is a gross bit of special pleading on behalf of abortion and infanticide. But without some such restriction, Regan's position quickly becomes unmanageable.

[6] An exception illustrates the grounds and scope of the remarks in the text. Disputes about whether a chess player has been mated do not persist, in the way legal, moral, and political disputes do. The reason is that, since the number of possible chess positions is finite though very large, it would be possible if necessary to stipulate an answer to this question in each and every case.

[7] The application of the ethics of the parent-child relationship to abortion requires further exploration, but not here.

BIBLIOGRAPHY

[1]   Devine, P.: 1978, *The Ethics of Homicide*, Cornell University Press, Ithaca, New York.
[2]   Donagan, A.: 1977, *The Theory of Morality*, University of Chicago Press, Chicago.
[3]   Gorovitz, S. *et al.* (eds.): 1976, *Moral Problems in Medicine*, Prentice-Hall, Englewood Cliffs, New Jersey.
[4]   Kamisar, Y.: 1976, 'Euthanasia Legislation: Some Non-Religious Objections', in S. Gorovitz *et al.* (eds.), *Moral Problems in Medicine*, Prentice-Hall, Englewood Cliffs, New Jersey, pp. 402–414.
[5]   Regan, T.: 1983, *The Case for Animal Rights*, University of California Press, Berkeley.
[6]   Singer, P.: 1975, *Animal Liberation*, New York Review, New York.
[7]   Sullivan, F. A., S. J.: 1983, *Magisterium*, Paulist Press, New York.
[8]   Sumner, L. W.: 1981, *Abortion and Moral Theory*, Princeton University Press, Princeton, New Jersey.

[9] Thomson, J. J.: 1974, 'A Defense of Abortion', in M. Cohen, T. Nagel, and T. Scanlon (eds.), *The Rights and Wrongs of Abortion*, Princeton University Press, Princeton, New Jersey, pp. 3–22.
[10] Tooley, M.: 1972, 'Abortion and Infanticide', *Philosophy and Public Affairs* 1, 137–165.

Lesley College, Stonehill College
and Tufts University
Boston, Massachusetts

NOTES ON CONTRIBUTORS

Baruch A. Brody, Ph.D., is the Leon Jaworski Professor of Biomedical Ethics and the Director of the Center for Ethics, Medicine, and Public Issues, Baylor College of Medicine, Professor of Philosophy, Rice University and Adjunct Research Fellow, the Institute of Religion of the Texas Medical Center, Houston, Texas.

Allen Buchanan, Ph.D., is Professor of Philosophy, the University of Arizona, Tucson, Arizona.

Philip E. Devine, Ph.D., teaches philosophy at several Boston area colleges. Saint Cloud State University, Saint Cloud, Minnesota.

Alan Donagan, M. A., B.Phil. (Oxon.), is Professor of Philosophy, California Institute of Technology, Pasadena, California.

Bart K. Gruzalski, Ph.D., is Associate Professor of Philosophy, Northeastern University, Boston, Massachusetts.

Stanley Hauerwas, B.D., M.A., Ph.D., is Professor of Theological Ethics, the Divinity School of Duke University, Durham, North Carolina.

Michael P. Levine, Ph.D., is a Research Fellow in the Department of Philosophy, LaTrobe University, Melbourne, Australia.

Eric Mack, Ph.D., is Associate Professor of Philosophy, Tulane University, New Orleans, Louisiana.

Mary B. Mahowald, Ph.D., is Associate Professor of Medical Ethics, the School of Medicine, and Associate Professor of Philosophy, Western Reserve College, Case Western Reserve University, Cleveland, Ohio.

Jeffrey Reiman, Ph.D., is Professor in the School of Justice and Department of Philosophy and Religion, the American University, Washington, D.C.

William Ruddick, Ph.D., is Professor of Philosophy, New York University, and Director of the Philosophy and Medicine Program, the New York University School of Medicine, New York, New York.

Carson Strong, Ph.D., is Associate Professor in the Department of Human Values and Ethics, the College of Medicine, University of Tennessee, Memphis, Tennessee.

L. W. Sumner, Ph.D., is Professor of Philosophy and Law, the University of Toronto, Toronto, Ontario, Canada.

Laurence Thomas, Ph.D., is Professor of Philosophy, Oberlin College, Oberlin, Ohio.

INDEX

227

DATE DUE

Demco, Inc. 38-293